WAGING PEACE

Waging Peace

IN THE NUCLEAR AGE

Ideas for Action

EDITED BY
David Krieger and Frank K. Kelly

CAPRA PRESS
SANTA BARBARA

To the memory of Warren Wells.

To our children and grandchildren in a world without nuclear weapons.

To all those who Wage Peace.

Cover design by Francine Rudesill.
Design and production by Jim Cook/Book Design & Typography.

LIBRARY OF CONGRESS CATALOGING-IN-PUBLICATION DATA

Waging peace in the nuclear age.
  1. Nuclear disarmament. 2. Nuclear arms control.
I. Krieger, David.   II. Kelly, Frank K., 1914–
JX1974.7.W26   327.174   87-35513
ISBN 0-88496-285-7

Published by Capra Press, Post Office Box 2068, Santa Barbara, California 93120.

Acknowledgements

We wish to thank the extraordinary group of people who are the Nuclear Age Peace Foundation's directors, advisors, consultants, and members. In addition to the editors of this volume, the Foundation directors include Wallace T. Drew (Vice President of Development and Treasurer), Diana Hull, Ph.D. (Secretary of the Board), Charles W. Jamison, Eli Luria, Ann Minnerly, Walter L. Schaffer, and Ethel R. Wells. This book pulls together many aspects of the work of the Nuclear Age Peace Foundation, to which the directors have given generously of their time, energy, and ideas. It would be hard to find a more dedicated and creative group of directors.

The distinguished members of our Advisory Council have also given generously of their time and ideas. Several of them have contributed chapters which appear in this volume. The Advisory Council is composed of George Wald, Ted Turner, Jan Tinbergen, Niko Tinbergen, Senator Claiborne Pell, Rufus E. Miles, Jr., Karl Menninger, M.D., Alan McCoy O.F.M., Admiral Gene R. LaRocque, Johan Galtung, Adam Curle, Rt. Rev. Daniel Corrigan, President Rodrigo Carazo, Elisabeth Mann Borgese, and Robert C. Aldridge.

Our Consultants have often worked in an intimate way on Foundation projects, and contributed in immeasureable respects to the success of these projects, including this book. The Consultants are Dean Babst, Lawrence Badash, Ian Bernard, Eric H. Boehm, C.H. Hardin Branch, M.D., Henry B. Burnett, Jr., C. Edward Crowther, Keith Evans, Esq., Dietrich Fischer, Peter O. Haslund, Fred H. Knelman, Walter Kohn, Peter R. MacDougall, Farzeen Nasri, and Ronald Shlensky M.D.

This book would not have been possible without the generous participation of the authors of the Waging Peace series—whose articles compose the majority of this volume.

The Staff of the Foundation, Catherine Kelly and Laura Lynch, have also contributed in important ways to the work of publishing this volume, and to all aspects of the Foundation's work.

Finally, we are deeply grateful to Ethel R. Wells who has given extraordinary help to the Waging Peace series and to this volume.

Table of Contents

General Introduction

We offer in this book a wide range of ideas and constructive recommendations which have helped to change the world's atmosphere in the 1980s—from a cloud of despair and foreboding to a time of rising hope, when the world's leaders are slowly responding to the demands of the people for a just and lasting peace.

The statements in this volume were stimulated by the commitment of a group of Santa Barbara citizens to contribute some of their time, their thoughts, and their actions toward ending the nuclear arms race. These citizens created the Nuclear Age Peace Foundation—and invited people everywhere to participate in its work.

In 1982, when the Foundation was established, angry words were flying back and forth between the United States and the Soviet Union. The U.S. was accelerating a tremendous build-up of nuclear arms, and the Soviets were matching us bomb for bomb. The nuclear freeze movement was under way, but seemed to have little effect on governments. The National Peace Academy Campaign in the United States was apparently blocked by the opposition of a popular president.

We launched a series of *Waging Peace* publications. The first one dealt with the necessity for a change in thinking by leaders and citizens. Others offered new perspectives on the semantics of the nuclear debate, the role of the military, the necessity of preventing accidental nuclear war, ways of revitalizing the United Nations, creating a national institution to promote peace, the possibility of a nuclear age peace corps, and many other positive suggestions.

Meanwhile, the directors and staff of the Foundation took part in many kinds of actions. One of us participated in the establishment of a United States Institute of Peace. Another helped to draft a statement signed by Nobel Laureates throughout the world—and this statement was presented to Mikhail Gorbachev at the meeting in Moscow. Another was a participant in the fortieth observance of the nuclear bombing of Hiroshima and arranged for the distribution of Foundation pamphlets in Japan. In response to an invitation, one director spoke to seventy-nine Soviet officials on "The Role of the Public in Preventing Nuclear War."

We circulated petitions that were signed by thousands of parents and grandparents opposing the nuclear arms race—and sent petitions to leaders in Washington and Moscow. We conducted a peace essay contest for high school students—offering prizes made possible by gifts from Gladys Swackhamer, a ninety-four-year-old woman who cares deeply about peace. We published the prize-winning essays in pamphlets, and distributed them widely.

We addressed our publications and other activities primarily to the many people who did not fully recognize the unprecedented nature of the problems in a nuclear age—or felt apathetic or helpless in the face of overwhelming danger.

We made a series of awards to outstanding peacemakers—Senator Claiborne Pell, chairman of the Senate Foreign Relations Committee; former President Rodrigo Carazo of Costa Rica; Admiral Gene La Rocque, director of the Center for Defense Information; and Ted Turner, chairman of Turner Broadcasting System and a founder of the Better World Society.

We initiated and maintained an Accidental Nuclear War Prevention Newsletter, which reaches researchers and educators in the United States, Canada, Europe, and Asia. We have aided other organizations—such as the Center for

Defense Information—to become more active in this crucial field.

In 1987, we sponsored an International Peace Week for Scientists, endorsed by dozens of organizations in the United States and more than thirty other countries. In connection with this project, we offered a $50,000 prize for the best proposal to enable scientists to work on constructive projects rather than preparations for war.

We certainly do not claim an exaggerated share of the credit for the tremendous change which has occurred in the world in the last few years. But we do believe that our activities— exemplified in the book—have given some impetus to many of the accomplishments in this astonishing period of history. We think John Tirman, executive director of Winston Foundation for World Peace, was right in declaring recently in a newspaper article: "... the newly mobilized citizenry ... had changed the political dynamics of arms control forever."

We believe that the materials in this book can be useful in many ways to the millions of citizens who are in the process of removing the nuclear shadow from the life of humanity.

How one chooses to Wage Peace is a personal decision. Some people will write letters to editors and to elected leaders, some will organize meetings, some will write books or produce films, some will march, some will commit civil disobedience. There are many, many ways but they are all based upon the awareness that the nuclear age demands continuous effort and dedication.

The foundation of the future will be built upon what we do to build peace each day. The peace community is now worldwide and growing. The momentum of humanity is with us. We look to the future with hope and joy in the realization that together we *shall* create a safer and saner world.

—David Krieger and Frank Kelly
Santa Barbara, March 1988

I. NEW PERSPECTIVES

We are all citizens of a single beautiful planet which we know as Earth. We have come to recognize that all humans are entitled to certain basic rights, of which life is the most fundamental. Inherent in the right to life is safe drinking water, sufficient food, adequate shelter and a healthy environment. Other basic human rights include freedom from oppression and torture, and freedoms of speech, association, and religion.

Along with these rights come responsibilities. These include extending the hand of friendship to fellow humans, regardless of race or nationality; and working to preserve the planet and its varied life forms from destruction.

In the spirit of cooperation and concern for our unique island home in space, we have developed the following Earth Citizen Pledge, which we hope will provide a broad guideline for responsible living in the nuclear age.

Earth Citizen Pledge

Aware of the vastness of the universe and the uniqueness of life, I accept and affirm my responsibility as an Earth Citizen to nurture and care for our planet as a peaceful, harmonious home where life may flourish.

Believing that each of us can make a difference, I pledge to persevere in Waging Peace. With my spirit, intellect and energy I shall strive to:
- *Reverse the nuclear arms race, and end this omnicidal threat to the continuation of life;*
- *Redirect scientific and economic resources from the destructive pursuit of weapons technologies to the beneficial tasks of ending hunger, disease and poverty;*
- *Break down barriers between people and nations, and by acts of friendship reduce tensions and suspicions;*
- *Live gently on the earth, reclaiming and preserving the natural*

13

beauty and profound elegance of our land, mountains, oceans and sky; and

• *Teach others, by my words and deeds, to accept all members of the human family, and to love the Earth and live with dignity and justice upon it.*

CHARLES W. JAMISON

1. Can We Change Our Thinking?

The unleashed power of the atom has changed everything save our
modes of thinking, and we thus drift toward unparalleled catastrophes.
                                                        —Albert Einstein

The Nuclear Age Peace Foundation owes a great debt to Charles
Jamison. Not only was he one of the founding directors of the
Foundation, but it was in his law office that the five initial
directors met to discuss the dilemmas of current approaches to
national and international security, and to design the Foundation.
Charles Jamison was seventy-eight years old at the time. He had
served on Guadalcanal during World War II, and until shortly
before the Foundation was formed had always supported the U.S.
arms build-up. He provides an excellent example of one who has
changed his thinking, and thus is personally qualified to address
the subject.

An earlier version of this chapter was the first publication of the
Foundation, and the first booklet in the *Waging Peace* series. It has
been entirely rewritten and updated for inclusion in this book, but
it continues to take up the challenge laid down by Albert Einstein:
that we must change our thinking or face unparalleled
catastrophes.

Chieko Takano, a six-year-old, was at home alone
when she saw brilliant red flashes and felt the
swooshing impact of a gigantic blast. "Everywhere
fire. Red, red—and fire," she later described her horrifying
experience.

That morning, August 6, 1945, an atomic bomb called
"Little Boy" was dropped from the U.S. plane "Enola Gay."

15

The blast killed Chieko's mother, probably while walking to work. Her older sister was buried in the rubble of a nearby school. The city of Hiroshima was devastated—with 100,000 citizens killed in one quick blow. By November, 140,000 had died in that Japanese metropolis of 245,000 people.

Chieko was later to learn that her father, a Japanese infantryman, had met death in a suicide attack in the Philippines. Left alone and suffering from burns and nightmarish memories, Chieko devoted her life to the message of peace.

In August forty-two years later, with "Bike For Peace," a project sponsored by the Osaka YMCA, she bicycled from San Francisco to Los Angeles, to commemorate the 42nd anniversary of the bombing of Hiroshima and Nagasaki. On the night of August 4, 1987, Chieko retold her anguished story to a group in Santa Barbara, California.[1]

On that fateful morning, when Chieko was six years old, humankind had crossed a catastrophic divide, demonstrating the awesome power to annihilate all human life on earth.

Why are U.S. and Soviet leaders pressing so close to the line, toward making that result inevitable? Why do the two superpowers have some *50,000* warheads pointed at each other? Their combined firepower is the equivalent of *18 billion* tons of TNT—enough to kill every living person many times. This is more than *one million* times greater than the firepower of the bomb that struck Hiroshima.

Unable to grasp the magnitude of today's destructive potential, U.S. and Soviet leaders continue, in actual practice, under the obsolete delusion that national security still rests in the greatest number of nuclear warheads.

It is doubtful that either superpower would deliberately start a nuclear war. But the U.S. position has been stated numerous times: if a conventional war flared up in Europe and the NATO forces were losing, the U.S. would come to their aid by launching nuclear missiles.

In an atmosphere of intense hostility, it is easy to predict the Soviet response. Missiles would be fired in retaliation. The most logical sequence would then be an "all out" nuclear war.

Military and political leaders are not always rational. Napoleon marched his men 700 miles to take over Moscow. Later he attempted suicide. Adolph Hitler quickly conquered most of Europe. Later he committed suicide. Today the stakes are higher. With 18 billion tons of deadly missiles stockpiled, today's leaders could bring massive, international suicide.

Faulty Systems—Human Error

With 300 million people, worldwide, watching on TV, the Challenger shot skyward in a blaze of glory. Seventy-three seconds later, it suddenly exploded in mid-air. The seven passengers met instant death in the ocean below. The entire world mourned the loss of the gallant seven. But this did not reverse the results of defective equipment and human error in judgment.

A few months later an explosion occurred in a nuclear plant at Chernobyl, in the Ukraine. Thirty-one deaths resulted within a short time and 40 thousand residents were evacuated. Contaminated meat, milk and vegetables had to be destroyed throughout Europe. This was described as by far the worst nuclear power plant disaster the world has ever known. Cancer specialists predict that poisonous fallout may, in future years, cause 5,000 additional deaths.

"The ultimate lesson from Chernobyl," said Senator Edward Kennedy, "is that human and technological error can cause disaster, anytime, anywhere."[2]

An appalling statement occurred in a recent article in the *Defense Monitor,* published by the Center for Defense Information Center in Washington D.C. In the last ten years, nuclear warning systems have given over 20,000 false signals of nuclear attacks on the United States alone. On several occasions missile-carrying submarines and bombers were placed on alert.[3] Figures are not obtainable concerning false signals of weapons systems of other nations.

It is during a crisis, when emotions are at fever-pitch, that mistakes are inevitable. Six to eight minutes constitutes the travel time between launching and target for enemy submarines close to the shores of both superpowers. Hasty judgment could easily trigger a nuclear war.

Developing Constructive Approaches

"War is stupid, cruel and costly. Yet wars persist. In the name of self-defense, nations have paid the human price and, spurred on by fear and competition, have continued to accept the burdens of armaments, the size and cost of which grow ever more fantastic."[4]

This statement was made by a military leader, not a pacifist. The speaker was a West Point graduate and rated first in his class at the Command and General Staff School. He served as Chief of Staff under General George C. Marshall in World War I, was the Supreme Commander of Allied Forces in World War II and later served as Supreme Commander of NATO.

Only one person fits this description—Dwight D. Eisenhower. Even though he dealt with other urgent issues during his eight years as U.S. President, *WAGING PEACE* is the title he chose for his two-volume memoirs.[5]

Other top military leaders of World War II also reversed their thinking. General George C. Marshall initiated the Marshall plan for economic restoration of Europe, receiving the Nobel Peace Prize in 1953. General Douglas MacArthur, near the end of his life said, "Could I have but one line a century hence, crediting a contribution to the advance of peace, I would gladly yield every honor which has been accorded me in war."

And yet, arms production continues. An article in the *Defense Monitor* entitled "No Business Like Arms Business" states that production of weapons is one of the largest industries in the U.S.; annual sales are almost $185 billion. If it were a separate economy, the U.S. military would be the thirteenth largest economy in the world.

The Department of Defense awards contracts directly to 35,000 firms; these, in turn, subcontract to 135,000 additional firms. Some of the companies we would least expect are among the top ten arms suppliers, such as IBM, General Electric, Ford and General Motors.

As subsidies, the government provides $40 billion worth of materials, land and equipment to arms manufacturers at no cost to the suppliers. Lower investment adds to their profits—at the taxpayers expense.

Arms production companies bring heavy economic and political pressure to promote support for weapons programs.[7]

The practice of special favors to arms manufacturers is one of the most gigantic obstructions to updating thinking in the nuclear age. Candidates for Congress or president rarely make this a campaign issue. With TV advertising costing $250,000 a minute, campaigners must take care to avoid alienating large contributors.

Change can be attained only through a groundswell of awareness and action by the American public.

The U.S. Catholic Bishops pastoral letter, "The Challenge of Peace," was directed primarily to the 53 million Catholics in the U.S., but was also intended for government leaders and the general public. The bishops believe that nuclear deterrence is morally acceptable but only as a step toward total disarmament.

The General Assembly of the Presbyterian Church U.S.A. has advocated banning nuclear missiles since 1946 and began calling for a Comprehensive Test Ban Treaty in 1963. Recently, the General Assembly urged its subordinate groups to request the president and members of Congress to support negotiations for such a treaty and to oppose further developments in space.

Leaders of several other religious bodies have recently made official pronouncements on peace and war. The Council of Bishops of the United Methodist Church, a denomination with almost 10 million members, issued a pastoral letter stressing the need for arms reduction and opposing the Star Wars program.

The National Evangelical Association, an umbrella agency for 45,000 churches in seventy-eight denominations, representing 15 million Christians, issued a forty-seven page document, "Peace, Freedom and Security." Its aim is, "The discovery of processes by which competing views of justice may conduct and resolve their conflict without violence."[7]

In 1982 there were 3,500 peace organizations in the U.S. Today, there are 11,000—an increase of 300 percent. Equally significant, organizations are growing in strength. For instance, attendance at our last Nuclear Age Peace Foundation Awards Dinner was more than double that of the previous year.

Whatever your vocation or background may be, you will find a spot where you will feel at home. Special peace groups are now active for accountants, architects, artists, athletes, blacks, broadcasters, businessmen, businesswomen, educators, engineers, labor unions, lawyers, librarians, movie producers, newspaper editors, nurses, physical therapists, physicians, psychologists, students, veterans and women.

Find a group matching your vocation or interests and give it your support.

We must educate our people in foreign policy; we must teach it in our schools. An understanding of international issues is becoming needed by everyone. We are just beginning to recognize that events occurring in all parts of the world affect us at the local level.

To help educate future leaders in world problems, Congress in 1984 created the United States Institute of Peace. Forty-five thousand people took part in the development of this program. The institute makes grants to colleges and universities for special studies on arms control and non-violent conflict resolution.

Our colleges and universities are expanding their foreign affairs studies. Programs and degrees in peace studies have increased in U.S. institutions of higher learning from approximately seventy schools in 1983 to over 100 at present—an increase of over 50 percent.

Academic education on foreign affairs goes only part way. Direct interchanges are also necessary. Hundreds of international peace organizations take part in a wide variety of exchanges. The Institute of Soviet-American Relations, in 1983, published a handbook on organizations engaged in Soviet-American relations, listing 137 such organizations. A revised edition lists 230, an increase of 93 groups.[8]

These organizations include almost every field of endeavor. Samplings of such groups includes those in the arts, education, electronics, environment, firefighting, fishing, Gypsy Moths, health, housing, medicine, metallurgy, ocean, physics, space, trade and a broader spectrum of scientific specialties.[9]

The Fellowship of Reconciliation, established in 1914, is an ecumenical Christian group that arranges visits with Soviet churches each year. Although the USSR is often described as a atheistic nation, there are more than twice as many Christians in the Soviet Union as members of the Communist Party.

Nuclear Age Peace Foundation Senior Vice-President, Frank Kelly, visited Moscow in 1983 under the auspices of an international group, the Citizens' Exchange Council. This council sponsors the U.S.-USSR Citizens' Dialog; the subgroup arranges visits back and forth between citizens of the two nations.

During Kelly's visit in Moscow he met with both Soviet

21

private citizens and top level officials. He spoke to a group of 79 Soviet leaders, including members of the Central Committee and the Supreme Soviet Council, the equivalent of our Congress.

International Physicians for Prevention of Nuclear War (IPPNW) is another organization that has made great progress in changing thinking toward arms reduction. This organization started with five physicians. Dr. Evgueni Chazov served as the personal physician of General Secretaries Andropov and Chernenko. Dr. Bernard Lown, for many years, served as Professor of Cardiology at the Harvard School of Public Health. Working together in research across a span of 4,000 miles they became concerned over the severe inadequacy of medical care in the event of a nuclear war. Plans were discussed for opposing nuclear weapons.

At a Vienna meeting in 1980, Chazov and Lown, together with three colleagues—one from the U.S. and two from the USSR—founded the International Physicians for Prevention of Nuclear War (IPPNW). For the past seven years Dr. Chazov and Dr. Lown have served as co-presidents. Now worldwide, this federation has 175,000 members from fifty-eight nations. The Soviet Union has more members than any other country.

Dr. Chazov was appointed Minister of Health for the Soviet Union in 1987, resigning as IPPNW co-president. Another prominent Russian physician, Dr. Mikhail Kuzin, one of the founders of IPPNW, replaced Dr. Chazov as co-president.[10]

While key political leaders have shown distrust for each other, this cooperation in a mutual cause by physicians on a worldwide scale is indeed remarkable. The IPPNW stands as a model at the international level, for all those who are striving to eliminate the danger of a nuclear holocaust.

Changes Under Gorbachev

The Russian people have lived for centuries under authoritarian regimes. Tight controls have characterized the Soviets for seven decades. But three new watchwords have appeared under Mikhail Gorbachev. "Glasnost" or openness is a combination of less strictures and wider freedoms. "Perestroika" represents a restructuring in society, primarily for greater economic efficiency. "Democratization" consists of providing multiple choices in candidates for lower-level offices; candidates are selected by top-level officials.

After his election as General Secretary, Gorbachev began to move with bold, new strokes. Excerpts from his 84 page speech to the Plenum (general assembly) of the Central Committee in January 1987, signified the transformations he hoped to bring to the USSR. He stated: "Major changes are taking place in the life of Soviet society and positive tendencies are gaining momentum. As we talk about reorganization and associated processes of deep-going democratization we mean truly revolutionary and comprehensive transformations."

Proposed changes are to include economic reforms, creative endeavors of the masses, socialistic self-government, encouragement of initiative, greater openness and higher respect for the dignity of the individual. But Gorbachev emphasized that centralized government will be retained. He concedes that his contemplated changes will involve "a complex and painful process, requiring time and balance."[11]

The granting of freedom of expression to artists, musicians, authors, newspaper editors and particularly the arch dissident, Andrei Sakharov, will gradually open up many fresh ideas to the Soviet people. Respected Soviet economists are advocating greater flexibility in commercial management. Twenty-nine occupations have already been granted free enterprise status. The British Broadcasting Company

23

and Voice of America, no longer blocked, provide direct outside sources of world events.

Gorbachev is the first Soviet leader to publicly disclose the organic defects of the Soviet system. His readiness to discuss these problems and related issues with leaders of other nations will broaden the worldwide scope of interchange in ideas, leading to closer mutual understanding.

The sweeping offers for arms reduction by Gorbachev at the Iceland mini-summit in October 1986 paved the way for later progress in negotiations at Geneva. Rather than a quick show of vengeance toward Mathias Rust, the West-German pilot who landed his Cessna near the Kremlin, Gorbachev instead, replaced the minister of defense and the commander of the air force. Selecting leaders of Gorbachev's own choice brought better military support for his arms reduction proposals.

Some Kremlin watchers have doubted that Gorbachev could produce results in line with his radical goals for openness and economic restructuring. But the Communist Party's Central Committee in June 1987, unanimously adopted Gorbachev's plan. The New York Times News Service, quoted from a thirty-seven page document ordering an end to fixed prices, and de-centralizing control over thousands of enterprises. Also, three Gorbachev supporters were elected to full Politburo membership, giving him eight supporters of the fourteen full members and four of the six candidate members.

Gorbachev has often stated that he faces real opposition from entrenched leaders who seek to retain their power and privileges. But from the long range standpoint, an era in Soviet history has ended. Because of wide-spread existing problems and a new generation coming into leadership, a groundswell of change is taking place.

Basically, the change is internal. Gorbachev is willing to make concessions in armaments in order to improve conditions within the USSR. He has also made it clear that he realizes a nuclear war would be suicidal for the nations involved. But the underlying drive for military supremacy still continues in both the U.S. and the Soviet Union.

Understanding The Power Struggle

A Mexican vaquero can ride his mount full speed ahead, pull it back on its haunches, whirl around and go dashing in the opposite direction.

Not so with the world's superpowers. They must ride half a dozen stubborn elephants through tangled jungle trails. Each elephant lumbers along in its own deeply-rutted groove.

Many months dragged by after the Iceland mini-summit before progress began to appear. Proposals by each side were met with sparring tactics by the other. Finally, West-Germany's leaders broke the deadlock. Their willingness to dismantle seventy-two Pershing 1A missiles cleared the way for an accord between the superpowers. In December 1987, President Reagan and General Secretary Gorbachev held a summit in Washington D.C., signing a treaty for elimination of all medium and short range missiles in Europe—an entire class of nuclear weapons. This agreement, in itself, underlines a high point in world history, the first concerted action toward actually reversing the arms race.

To become effective, ratification is required by the U.S. Senate; ratification is expected. If ratified, this will mark the first destruction of nuclear missiles for arms reduction since the first atomic bomb struck Hiroshima over forty years ago. We are deeply grateful for this major first step. But concentrating on the types of missiles, their numbers and placement, rather than true changes in attitude, is still "war oriented." The reductions are calculated in terms of "war strategies."

What are the chief aspects of the power struggle between the United States and the Soviet Union?

Both nations fear attack by the other. Russia, throughout its thousand year history, has repeatedly been torn by war. A twelfth century poet laments, "And from all sides, victorious infidels invaded the land of Russia."

During that era, Tartar and Cossack horsemen from along the Chinese border swept across Russia, pillaging, burning and killing. Wars continued. David Shipley in his book, *Russia*, tells of a woman he met whose great great grandfather, great grandfather, grandfather and father were all killed in war. With the death of 20 million Soviet men in World War II, nearly every family knew the loss of a father, husband, son or brother.[12]

America was born in the War for Independence; she was held together by the war to free the slaves. The Pearl Harbor disaster will long be remembered. America fears war—she fears attack by the Soviets. Fear of attack generates preparation for war. The greater the preparation on one side, the greater the fear on the other. Both nations are driven into the upward swirl of the tornado.

George F. Kennan, former Ambassador to Russia and a specialist in U.S.-Soviet affairs since 1930, spells this out in his Foreword to Norman Cousins' book, *The Pathology of Power*. Fear in the U.S. of attack by the USSR has resulted in the emergence of a huge military-industrial complex beyond the scope of democratic control. Anchored in long-term contracts, it defies normal federal budgeting. Its tentacles reach to almost every congressional district, distorting the electoral process.

The cost of arms production is largely the cause of a $2 trillion national deficit, which weakens the U.S. economic structure. It weakens the economic features of our society by draining off the best scientific minds for arms production. It destroys the social fabric of our society by constant focus on the dark, barbaric side of life.[13]

In turn, the Soviet leaders, fearing U.S. attack, and determined to maintain huge armed forces, have limited the common people of the USSR to the bare necessities of life.

An equally insidious form of the power struggle between the U.S. and the USSR arises from the competition in seeking to influence or dominate smaller nations. Fears aroused by the Soviet invasion of Afghanistan in December 1979 and Soviet military involvement in Angola and Ethiopia earlier in the 1970s, are believed by many to have resulted in strong support for Ronald Reagan in the 1980 election.

Most Americans erroneously believe that communist conquest is on the increase. The *Defense Monitor* in September 1986 analyzed the situation in detail. They reported that Soviet domination peaked in the late 1950s, with significant influence in fifteen percent of the world's nations. Since then the number of nations in which the USSR has significant influence has dropped from thirty-five to eighteen.

Except for Afghanistan, Angola and Ethiopia, the Soviets have conducted little open expansion in the last fifteen years. They were unable to develop loyalty or cooperation from most of their attempted conquests. The Third World nations do not want interference, either by the Soviets or the U.S. They prefer to work out their own destinies in their own ways.

The most vicious type of power struggle is that of the secret agencies, the KGB in the USSR and the CIA in the U.S. Fear of the unknown is generated by secret activities. since neither the U.S. nor the Soviet Union knows what the other is doing in this kind of activity, the imagination is the gauge. To avoid being naive, the answer is simple—think the worst. As long as covert military operations, and particularly sale of military supplies, are conducted by either or both of the superpowers, permanent arms reduction agreements will remain extremely difficult.

Drastic differences in views on human rights raises one of the most severe obstructions to trust and cooperation. Soviet

27

leaders have been adamant in their position that human rights are internal issues. However, it was appropriate for Margaret Thatcher, in her visit to Moscow, to make clear that the harsh treatment given to some Soviet citizens is appalling to people in the democracies. President Reagan has also emphasized this issue.

The Soviet Republic was not founded by homogeneous groups, but through partial assimilation of diverse war-like tribes. Rigid control from the top was regarded as a necessity by the Czars and their successors.

Although Soviet human rights standards differ greatly from those of the democracies, too much freedom also has its flaws. We must admit that racial discrimination, high crime rates, unemployment, widespread homelessness and drug abuse exist in the U.S. In view of the wide differences within the two cultures, combining human rights issues with arms reduction negotiations would result in added delays.

In the human rights area, the best approach appears to be day-to-day constructive interchanges in a wide variety of ways. Internal human rights changes initiated by Gorbachev are gaining headway. Greater leniency toward Christians who have not registered with government officials was recently announced. Permits for Jewish emigration are now ten times greater than previous quotas. New freedoms enable more Soviet people to travel abroad. Changes in deeper respect for human rights are being felt within the Soviet Union and are improving relations between the USSR and many other nations.

Shaping Affirmative Courses

Norman Cousins, recipient of the United Nations Peace Medal and President of the World Federalist Association, ends the Postscript of his book, *The Pathology of Power*, with this statement:

"There is no defeat for the American people when they tie themselves to the great idea that human intelligence is equal to human needs. Beyond the clamor of clashing ideology and the preening and jostling of sovereign tribes, a safer and more responsible world is waiting to be created."[14]

Cousins stresses that the superpower leaders seem unaware of the obvious fact that a nuclear war would destroy all or most of life on earth. They need to recognize more clearly that the future of the entire world is at stake in the quarrels between the two nations. Moving to a global perspective would emphasize and coordinate the common interests of all nations.

The Pathology of Power advocates a double sovereignty. Each nation would have complete control of its internal affairs but in conflicts between nations world law would control. This is an extension of the United Nations principles. The U.N. Charter states that the nations of the world "must come to the abandonment of force." Today's society has truly become one world; it is often spoken of as "our global village."

How can we best work together for improving our global village?

Granting the World Court mandatory jurisdiction over disputes between nations is needed for real progress in settling disputes. Also, it is essential that the World Court and the United Nations be given the power to enforce their decisions.

Following the USS Stark disaster in the Persian Gulf, our administration insisted on placing more warships in the area. Near this same time the United Nations Security Council adopted a resolution requiring a cease-fire between Iran and Iraq. The Council had been working openly toward this goal for months.

Why did not the U.S. give strong support in securing enforcement of the U.N. Security Council resolution instead of rushing in with more warships? This move was hastily executed with little foresight as to real benefits and with great risk of additional bloodshed. By working vigorously to enforce the cease-fire resolution, the United States could have helped reduce the costly and dangerous hostilities between Iran and Iraq. This would also have led toward standards for settling conflicts between nations by non-violent means.

One more point. During this period, a United Nations Conference on Relations Between Disarmament and Development was held with 141 nations participating. The U.S. boycotted the conference, contending that economic development and military matters should not be intermixed. At the same moment the U.S. was defending the flow of economic goods with armaments.

The lack of power in the United Nations cannot pass unnoticed. But little funding has been provided for accomplishing its goals. According to a United Nations Association newsletter, the funding by all nations to the U.N. since its formation in 1945 only equals the amount expended by the Pentagon each three months.[15]

How can American citizens work more effectively to improve relations at the international level?

Soon after the Nuclear Age Peace Foundation was formed, I invited a prominent attorney to one of our luncheons. In graciously declining, he asked, "Do you really think that we know enough about arms control to go into that subject at all?"

If we fail to study and make evaluations in areas where we should be concerned, we lose by default to various special interests. No other nation in the world gives its citizens the opportunity to take part in shaping events to the extent of the United States. More and more, the privileges and responsibilities of average U.S. citizens are becoming global as well as local.

Government "of the people, by the people and for the people" is founded on the principle that individuals shall have the opportunity and the responsibility to participate in decisions that affect the nation as a whole. Having moved into an era where the action or non-action of the U.S. affects the entire world, individual citizens are placed squarely in the role where they can take part in international affairs. National and international issues often become blended.

We need a breath of fresh air; we are being suffocated by the concept that only military power can bring security. The opposite is true. Military power carried to the ultimate can mean only death and destruction.

People within the private sector must become more concerned with where we are heading. Many people, similar to my attorney friend, have abandoned the ship. Knowing little about international affairs they look no further. They simply ignore their opportunities and obligations as American citizens.

Working together in waging peace encompasses five levels:

1. individual effort
2. local groups
3. U.S. officials-private sector
4. U.S.-Soviet relations, and
5. global relations.

Through interlinking networks, the results obtained by one group can be passed on to others. By this method private groups can literally circle the globe. Regarding political matters of international significance, the 11,000 peace groups must work together like a diamond drill bit. Peace groups that are isolated and competing against each other, defeat the supreme purposes of all.

It is clear that we cannot always wait for our leaders to keep us updated with accurate information. In fact, they sometimes deliberately lead us astray. We need to insist on the abolishing of "nukespeak," the misleading jargon of politicians, unclear "experts," and negotiators. The intent is often to confuse the people and maintain control in distorted ways over the public discussion of what must be done.

A few well-known examples of "nukespeak" are: "peacekeeper" for the MX, the most deadly and destabilizing missile ever developed; "insurance policy" for Star Wars, the most speculative venture ever dreamed up by mankind; and "peace through strength," which through the present trend in missile production could mean the destruction of all life on earth.

If we are to create the waiting world of which Norman Cousins speaks, it must in important part be through an ever increasing grass roots movement of average American citizens. We have the freedom to search, to inquire and to speak out. We must also act.

As U.S. citizens we can take the lead in waging peace. The military-industrial establishment focuses on arms production. It is too soon to hope that the political leaders of the superpowers will forget about their power struggle and move toward large-scale efforts in creating goodwill. But there can be no doubt that both the leaders and the average citizens in most countries want to see an end to the arms race and better interrelations.

The policies of leaders are affected by the actions of individuals. It is necessary that, as individuals, we express our views on all crucial issues to our elected U.S. officials. Letters, telegrams and personal contacts with Congressmen and the President should be a regular pattern.

We must require greater depth of coverage of the issues in election campaigns. We must demand something more than pseudo-TV commercials, costing as much as $8 million for the campaign of one candidate. We must insure that presidential candidates are well-versed in foreign policy matters.

In order to express intelligent opinions as individuals, we must use greater effort in understanding the crucial issues. Some recommended sources for daily information include: the *Christian Science Monitor,* the *New York Times* and the *Los*

Angeles Times. For greater depth, *Surviving Together,* a journal of the Institute for Soviet-American Relations, *Foreign Affairs, The Defense Monitor,* booklets in the Nuclear Age Peace Foundation's *Waging Peace* series and the *Bulletin of the Atomic Scientists,* provide comprehensive coverage on issues of war and peace in today's complex world.

Beyond regular patterns in reading, attendance at seminars by outstanding authorities (when available), inquiry of specialists and group interchanges of views are essential. Above all, each of us needs to evaluate new ideas through exchanges with other individuals. We must wrestle with tough questions within our own minds, searching for objective solutions from the long range standpoint.

In closing, I am reminded of a statement by Justice Oliver Wendell Holmes, "Men of action control the present; the thinkers control the future."

Can we change our thinking? Yes! It is already occurring. Radical changes in thinking are taking place in the attitudes of people throughout the world, demanding arms reductions and peaceful settlement of conflicts.

ROGER WALSH, M.D., PH.D.

2. The Psychology of Waging Peace

Only on the basis of an understanding of our behavior can we hope to control it in such a way as to ensure the survival of the human race.
— J. William Fulbright

What can I do? This may be the most important question of our time.

The world—life itself—is threatened by nuclear holocaust, by nuclear "war" which could begin accidentally or by design. Today worldwide military expenditures have risen to some $1000 billion annually in a world in which 40,000 children die *daily* of starvation and preventable diseases.

These are well known facts. Yet, for most people they remain in the blur of background information rather than rising to a point of central focus. To understand why this is so it is important to gain the insights of psychology. The role of beliefs, perceptions, motivations and inhibitions in human behavior deserve thoughtful study. We need to learn what inner processes of the mind allow our dangerous world situation to be interpreted as acceptable, and which inner processes lead to asking the question, "What can I do?"

Asking the question is the first step toward accepting *personal responsibility* for changing the world and assuring the future. It is a step of enormous affirmation of life. The question is at once oriented toward action and grounded in spirituality. The question demonstrates reverence for the sacred gift of life and a desire to do one's part to preserve and enhance this sacred gift.

In this chapter, Dr. Roger Walsh, a psychiatrist and award winning author, explores the question of "What can I do?" in the context of delineating a psychology of Waging Peace.

Why is a book such as *Waging Peace in the Nuclear Age* necessary? Obviously because there are nuclear weapons. But why are there nuclear weapons? And why are there tens of thousands of them, enough to atomize, pulverize, and vaporize the waring nations (and perhaps the remainder of the planet) dozens of times over. Why are we spending over a trillion dollars worldwide on weapons each year? Why are we allowing 20 million of us to die of malnutrition when some $10 billion a year (about three days arms expenditure) could eradicate starvation from the face of the planet? Why do we allow such insanity to continue, indeed to increase, year after year? And why do so few people ponder or act on these, the most urgent questions of our time? These are surely questions which require and deserve the most probing psychological (and other kinds of) inquiries to determine the causes of our dilemma and their possible cures. Such is the purpose of this chapter.

The need for such psychological inquiry becomes all the more apparent when it is realized that for the first time in history all the major global threats to human survival—starvation, ecological disruption, war, and especially nuclear war—are human caused. All of them stem from human behavior and hence can be traced in large part to psychological origins. Our global "problems," in other words, actually represent "symptoms," symptoms of our individual and collective psychological condition.

At one level this may seem quite obvious, but it is tragic how little we appreciate or act on the basis of this understanding. Almost all discussion and action tend to be military, political, or economic. What this means is that we may be treating only the symptoms and not the underlying psychological causes within us and between us. Therefore, if we are to be truly effective and ensure human survival, we may need, not only to feed the starving and reduce nuclear stockpiles, but also to correct the psychological factors which led us to create them in the first place.

The question which therefore arises (and it may be one of the most important questions of our time) is this: how can we create and apply a psychology of human survival? How can we create a psychology which will help us understand the world's problems and our role in creating them, which will mobilize and empower us to correct them, and even to learn and mature both individually and collectively as we do so?[1]

We can begin by drawing open-mindedly from the best insights of all schools of psychology from both the East and the West. Each school offers a particular view of human nature, behavior, and pathology, and thereby of our current global problems.

Causes of Global Crises

For example, cognitive psychologies emphasize the importance of beliefs. Particularly important are those beliefs which limit our sense of power and effectiveness. "There's nothing I can do" and "I can't..." are the classic beliefs of self-imposed impotence. This impotence can then be rationalized with that all time favorite, "It's not my responsibility." People holding these beliefs tend to see themselves as helpless pawns, unable to influence the course of their lives or societies. The net result is a wonderful validation of the wisdom of the great American psychologist Henry Ford, who said that "those who believe they can do something and those who believe they can't are both right."

Behavior modifiers would point to the powerful role of reinforcers in creating and correcting our current crises. Clearly we reinforce our political and business leaders for decisions which favor immediate gratification for us, e.g.

copious oil and gasoline supplies, even at the risk of long-term shortages and disasters. Behavior modifiers would also point to the powerful role of our media in reinforcing consumptive, aggressive lifestyles and largely ignoring global issues.

Psychoanalysts emphasize the devastating role of fear and defenses. Clearly, many of our current difficulties are expressions of fear: fear of enemies, fear of losing raw materials or economic supplies, fear of being seen as less powerful than other people or countries. Unfortunately one of our responses to these fears has been to build the awesome weapons which now threaten our extinction. These weapons create more fear and so a vicious and potentially lethal cycle is set up.

To mask these fears we create a variety of psychological mechanisms with which to blind and distort our awareness. These defenses then present us with an illusory picture of the world and ourselves as we would like them to be rather than as they are. We therefore deny and repress our awareness of the extent of suffering in the world and the urgency of its problems, as well as our role in creating them.

Indeed, we go further by projecting onto others those motives and behaviors that we are unwilling to recognize in ourselves. We thereby maintain a convenient blame-free image of ourselves, a wholly negative image of "the enemy," and establish the conditions for a potentially lethal paranoia. Conflicts, competitions, and even wars are now entirely *their* fault, whether *they* be Russians or Americans, socialists or capitalists, blacks or whites. The current Soviet-American impasse is in part a powerful example of this. It is also a powerful example of the old idea that defenses create what they are designed to defend against.

The ancient psychologies of the East also offer insights into our dilemmas. Classic Buddhist psychology, for example, would trace our problems to three root causes of greed, hatred, and delusion. Clearly much of our resource deple-

37

tion and international competition can be traced to greed and hatred. "The world has enough for everyone's need," said Gandhi, "but not enough for everyone's greed." The idea of delusion suggests that our fears, defenses, greed, and hatred so color our awareness that we perceive only distorted images of the world and ourselves, yet assume these images to be correct. We live, in other words, in a cult(ure)-wide illusion, which the East calls "maya."

Eastern psychologies also describe the powerful and dangerous, yet usually unrecognized effects of excessively dualistic ways of thinking and seeing. We tend to see the world in terms of opposites: good and bad, us and them, in groups and out groups. Of course we need dualism; we need to be able to recognize opposites. The problem is that we tend to become fixated on this particular way of seeing and only see opposites, thereby ignoring the commonality and unity that underlie them. Then we see not one planet but only competing nations, not humankind but only communists and capitalists, or men and women, or blacks and whites; not us but me and them, not people with common human characteristics but only goodies and baddies. This fixation on dualistic seeing is the essence of conflict and a recipe for war.

It is obvious, therefore, that a psychology of human survival can clearly identify many of the psychological mechanisms creating our current crises. In doing so it points to errors in our ways of thinking and perceiving that must be corrected if we are to ensure our survival.

Effects of Global Crises

In addition to identifying their causes, psychology can also point to some of the effects that contemporary crises exert on us.[1] These effects can be both positive and negative. As the old saying goes, life will either grind you down or polish you up, and which it does is our responsibility. Tragically, it may be that we will choose to respond with yet more of the fear, defensiveness, and aggression that created our dilemma because the same psychological defenses, distortions, and inauthenticities that contribute to global crises may also result from them. For as stresses mount so also does the temptation to resort to defensiveness and deceit. Yet defenses are always purchased at the cost of awareness, authenticity, and effectiveness. When we deny reality we also deny our full potential and humanity. When we distort our image of the world we distort our image of ourselves. When we fear to look out at the world we fear to look in to ourselves. Therefore we remain unaware of the power and potential that lie within us and are us; the power and potential that are the major resources we have to offer to the world. In short, the costs of being unwilling to know the world truly are not knowing and underestimating ourselves.

Here then are the makings of another vicious cycle. For it is our sense of inadequacy and vulnerability that causes us to erect psychological defense mechanisms and behave unskillfully in the first place. Yet these defenses help create the global problems that in turn tempt us to greater defensiveness. As at the individual level, so also at the global: defenses create what they were designed to defend against.

In summary, as long as we are unwilling to look honestly at the world and ourselves then our responses to the world's problems may increase those very actions and defenses that created the problem in the first place.

On the other hand, these threats may also afford us great opportunities. Great threats can call forth great responses. Might our current global threats do likewise? Perhaps today's unprecedented threats may cause us to more thoughtful living and greater contribution. If we choose to let them, they might strip away our defenses and help us to confront both the condition of the world and our role in creating it. They might call us to examine our lives and values with new urgency and depth, and to open ourselves fully, perhaps for the first time, to the fundamental questions of our existence.

This opening, this willingness to question, to see the world and ourselves as we really are, may be vital to both our survival and to our psychological well-being. For to open ourselves fully to these fundamental issues of life is not only one of the hallmarks of psychological health, but also one of its causes. For when we are willing to recognize the enormity of preventable suffering in world, of the rampant inhumanity, greed, hatred, and defensiveness, and of the precarious existence of ourselves, our families, and our fellow humans, then we are moved to question and reflect. Then we are open to explore at new and deeper levels the meaning, purpose, and appropriateness of our lifestyles, values, and personal national goals. As has been pointed out by religious sages for centuries and more recently by psychologists, to the extent we confront these issues honestly and fully, to that extent will we mature and contribute. For such confrontations are likely to evoke the recognition of the fragility and preciousness of life, of our shared humanity, of the many ways in which we have been unconscious, unthinking, and insensitive, and of how, in the depths of our hearts, we really want to live with awareness and ethicality, compassion and contribution.

Such responses tend to flow automatically from a willingness to see things as they truly are. For to see the extent of needless suffering in the world is also to feel compassion; to see the cost of our defensiveness is to desire to let it go; to see what our lifestyles really do to the planet is to want to live with greater sensitivity. Awareness per se—by and of itself—can be curative. To see things and ourselves as we really are! This is a crucial means for psychological growth and well-being of individuals and for the well-being and survival of our planet. Perhaps then our crises may call forth from us, if we so choose, the very responses necessary to correct them and to accelerate our individual and collective maturation at the same time. For it may be that we will either live together as mature adults or die together as squabbling children.

Considerable research indicates that psychologically healthy people tend to be particularly concerned for the welfare of others. For as Albert Schweitzer said "The only ones among you who will be truly happy are those who have sought and found how to serve." It follows that if we do manage our current dilemma with maturing responses, then these responses may include greater compassion and contribution.

Obviously we need contributions of all kinds: letter writing, education, public speaking, media presentations, publishing, political lobbying, donations, and more. But inasmuch as the fundamental problem is psychological, then we especially need people who not only do these things, but who also do them with an understanding of the underlying psychological issues. We need, in other words, people who are both socially effective and psychologically mature.

Therefore, we need people who commit themselves to two types of service. The first is to the symptomatic relief of suffering in the world. The second is to psychological awareness, both their own and that of others, to relieve the mental causes of this suffering and to make themselves more effective. For as has been pointed out time and time again, "We have to start with changing ourselves." The most far reaching social and global transformations must all start in the same place: in us. For if we are serious about relieving the suffering of humankind, we must cultivate the only source of help we have—ourselves.

If we need this kind of two-pronged approach in the world and in ourselves then it would make sense to combine them. It would make sense to approach our work in such a way that we learn and grow from it. This approach has been used in many forms of service. In the West it is known as service-learning; in the East as karma yoga. This is the discipline of service and work in the world, in which that service and work are viewed as opportunities for learning and awakening. The aim is impeccable service that simultaneously relieves suffering and also awakens self and others. In doing so, it aims at inclusive treatment of both symptom and cause, self and other, psyche and world. An excellent and practical discussion of this type of service is available in the book *How Can I Help?*.[2]

People using this approach go into themselves in order to go more effectively out into the world and go out into the world in order to go deeper into themselves. The deeper this exploration and the greater their psychological understanding, the more they are able to appreciate that many of the psychological factors causing our crises stem from widely accepted cultural beliefs, values, and behaviors. Therefore in order to be most effective, these people work toward extracting themselves from limiting and distorting cultural biases. This is the process of "detribalization," by which a person matures from an ethnocentric to a global world view; from "my country right or wrong" to "our planet"; and from identification with one particular group or nation to identification with humankind.

Duane Elgin in his excellent book *Voluntary Simplicity*[3] has summarized the situation as follows: "In conclusion, hard material necessity and human evolutionary possibility now seem to converge to create a situation where, in the long run, we will be obliged to do no less than realize our greatest possibilities. We are engaged in a race between self-discovery and self-destruction. The forces that may converge to destroy us are the same forces that may foster societal and self-discovery."

What Can I Do? How Can I Help?

What all this leads to is simply the question "What can I do?" or "How can I help?"

But there is a still more important question we can ask.

This is not only, "What can I do?" but also, "What is the most strategic thing I can do?" Therefore, our first task is to look for ways in which our contributions can have optimal impact; the ways in which the talents and opportunities that are uniquely ours can be put to best use.

This is no small task. To find our optimal contribution (which includes both *what* we do and *how* we do it) requires a sensitive awareness of ourselves and our world. Yet most people assume that they should easily and immediately be able to know what they should do. This is not so. It may take weeks and months of careful thought, reflection, exploration and education before we find the particular contribution which feels right for us. Gandhi, for example, sometimes withdrew for months to think and pray before choosing his strategy. We, also, may require time.

The first step, then, is simply to reflect deeply and carefully on our life situation. We need to examine our desires and find the answer to, "What would I really like to do?" Here it is important to set aside the tyrannical self orders about what we should do, the limiting beliefs about what we cannot do, and first simply find what we would like to do. It is important to recognize that doing things out of guilt or "shoulds" is counterproductive. Such motivations spawns anger, tension, and righteousness which then infects other people. This is hardly helpful since emotions such as these are part of the problem and our task is to reduce them. That is why it is so important to learn a little-known secret about contribution and service: *it's okay to have a good time* while you're doing them. All too often we approach service with grim-faced determination and a hidden assumption that we are not really serious about it if we are not suffering.

From this education and reflection you will gradually become aware of the responses that feel right for you. These might usefully include any traditional approach such as organizing groups, lobbying and writing to those in power, educating others, donating or raising money, writing or public speaking, and more.

But the challenge for all of us is also to create new approaches that fit our particular talents and situations; approaches that reach new people and that have an impact in novel ways. What would Gandhi do if he lived at this time in your unique situation? How would he go about looking for the most strategic contribution he could make, and what would it be? Here is a challenge for creativity and a game worth playing.

There is another whole aspect to this game of strategic contribution, and that is its psychological side. We have been discussing what we can do, but equally important is how we do it. When we remember how crucial are the psychological causes of our difficulties then it becomes obvious that whatever we do should take this into consideration. The question now becomes this: "How do I approach whatever I do in a way that reduces the psychological causes of global problems and enhances psychological awareness and maturation in people, including myself?" In other words, "How do I practice and apply the psychological principles discussed in this chapter?"

The first step is a shift in attitude, a change in the way we approach our work, our world, and ourselves. It involves bringing to everything we do a desire to learn and grow. Every experience is viewed as a potential source of learning about the world, other people, and ourselves. We explore both the world outside us and the world within us, learning from our subjective experience, our hopes, fears, thoughts, and emotions, as much as from events outside us. To each thing we experience or do we bring as much careful attention and awareness as we can.

Once we have begun to adopt this attitude, then other people and all our experiences become a kind of feedback. If something we do works well, we explore it to learn why. If we make a mistake (which we will, repeatedly: it's part of being human), we explore it also. If we hold this perspective then there is no need for regrets and recriminations; these are sorry substitutes for learning. Our mistakes can ultimately prove as valuable as our triumphs, sometimes even more so.

As we slowly learn to bring greater sensitivity and awareness to all that we do, we become aware of the mistaken beliefs, perceptions, and actions that limit us and our ability to contribute. As we recognize them, then we learn from and relinquish them. If we find faulty limiting beliefs such as "I can't do that," or "I could never..." we recognize them as mistaken beliefs, and belittling ones at that, and go right ahead to do what we formerly thought was beyond us. If we notice ourselves condemning and attacking people, including ourselves, we learn from that, finding the causes of our anger, and noticing its costs.

If we become fearful and defensive ourselves, which being human we will, we have an opportunity to learn how these emotions affect our minds. We will also get a chance to understand the addiction and insecurities from which they spring. From this understanding can come empathy and compassion for those who are dominated by fear and defensiveness and who attack and destroy because of them. When we are tempted to be dishonest and unethical we can become aware of the costs of guilt and paranoia in ourselves and of the pain brought to others. However, it is important that this awareness is cultivated, not to condemn and punish ourselves, but to learn and grow.

As we cultivate awareness and make our contributions, we will soon see that we are addicted to having certain things happen. Perhaps we want praise and recognition or crave anonymity, perhaps we must have our ideas accepted, or perhaps we must always lead or always follow.

Almost all of us will find some addiction to having our contributions produce the results we want. This certainly seems a reasonable enough goal, which it is, but when we become addicted to it the result is sure to be trouble. For now we have said, "I must get my way," and we have set ourselves up to experience frustration and disappointment as well as anger at those who block us. Remember that many of the people creating our global crises are doing so because they are addicted to their particular solutions, whether those solutions be communism, capitalism, more resource usage, or nuclear weapons. That is why it is so important to remember that even our best intentions can be mistaken. It is also why it is crucial that we reduce our addictions, even those addictions to the successful outcomes of our contributions.

Once we have reached this stage we can use our suffering as feedback that we are addicted to things being a particular way. For psychological pain is like physical pain, a signal that something is wrong. If we respond only by trying to change the world then we maintain our addictions and suffer again the next time they are not gratified. But if we work to change the world *and* reduce our addictions then we are healing both psyche and world, self and other.

With increasing awareness and understanding we may begin to notice ways in which our lifestyles conflict both with what we truly want and with what would be ecologically appropriate. These discrepancies can take many forms. For example, perhaps we are buying, consuming, and discarding without regard for ecological impact. Perhaps we are using heat instead of insulation, a car even though good public transportation is available, or nonreusable goods rather than reusable ones. Perhaps we are working for or investing in an industry that is harming the environment, creating danger-ous products, or taking unfair advantage of underdeveloped countries. Perhaps we are buying from companies that sponsor particularly violent television programming or are not expressing our appreciation to sponsors and stations that show educational programs about global problems. Perhaps we could donate more of our time or money to the causes that inspire us. Perhaps as the excellent book *Volun-*

tary Simplicity[3] points out, we could have lives of greater peace and deeper satisfaction by consuming less. The list is endless since the stuff of social transformation is identical with the stuff from which our daily lives are made. The challenge for each of us is to examine our lives and find how we can live them with greater ecological and global sensitivity.

There is one further contribution we can make and that is to allow regular time for ourselves and our own learning. Given the urgency of our global situation, such a suggestion may seem paradoxical. Yet as we become more sensitive to the world and ourselves, the costs of our psychological foibles and the benefits of cultivating learning, awareness, and growth become increasingly obvious. As they do so we may feel a growing need to set aside time devoted specifically to our own healing, learning, and maturing. Such time is not selfish; it is vital both for our own well-being and for our ability to contribute.

Sadly enough, this fact is rarely appreciated even though many wise people have echoed it for many years. "Finding the center of strength within ourselves is in the long run the best contribution we can make to our fellow men," say psychologists thereby echoing the words of the Buddha, who argued that "to straighten the crooked, you must first do a harder thing—straighten yourself." For this reason the economist Schumacher[4] remarked that: "It is a grave error to accuse a man who pursues self-knowledge of "turning his back on society. The opposite would be more nearly true: that a man who fails to pursue self-knowledge is and remains a danger to society, for he will tend to misunderstand everything that other people say or do, and remain blissfully unaware of the significance of many of the things he does himself."

So crucial is this phase of inner exploration and work that it has been found in the lives of most of the truly great contributors to humankind. Such people tend to withdraw

47

periodically for days, weeks, or longer from the hustle and bustle of daily life in order to follow the perennial advice to "know yourself." In knowing themselves they seem also to better know how to help others.

The question that naturally arises then is what environment and situation would best help us to know ourselves. What environment and people will allow us to dip most deeply into our psychological resources and tap the strength and healing powers that lie there. Where is the best place for us to withdraw?

This is an individual question that each of us must ask and answer for ourselves. For some the answer might be that we need periods of solitude and quiet; for others it might be that we could benefit from spending more quality time with family or friends. Some of us may find greatest insight and inspiration in nature, others may find periods of time spent in quiet reflection, contemplation, prayer, or meditation to be particularly helpful. At times we may benefit from groups or workshops with people working on similar psychological and/or global issues. But whatever we feel will be most helpful to our learning and well-being, it is important that we give ourselves the time to do it. When we have done this and feel ready, we can go out into the world again.

As the cycle of withdrawal and return continues, the distinction between what benefits us and what benefits others becomes more and more transparent. Each contribution becomes a learning opportunity, each learning becomes an opportunity for greater contribution. As the boundary between what benefits us and what benefits others becomes thinner, then egocentric desires, fears, and comparisons diminish, and the boundary between us and others grows thinner. Gradually we look past the veils of separation and otherness and begin to recognize our shared humanity. And as we do, the words of an ancient Indian proverb begin to make sense: "When I do not know who I am I serve you. When I know who I am I am you." This, then is one form of service and contribution. It is a form recommended across centuries by both the great growth disciplines and the great religions and can be viewed either psychologically or religiously as one chooses. "Seek, above all, for a game worth playing," is the advice of certain psychologists. "Having found the game, play it with intensity—play as if your life and sanity depended on it. (They do depend on it.)" Conscious, choiceful contribution and learning is a game worth playing, and the fate of the earth may depend on the number of people who elect to play it. For we are called to a task greater than that demanded of any generation in human history: to preserve our planet and our species. In accepting this challenge we are also called to understand, develop, and redirect the awesome power of our minds. Never in the course of human history has the need been greater. There may, therefore, be no more urgent or rewarding task facing each and every one of us than to apply ourselves and our psychological understanding to human survival.

DIANA HULL, PH.D.

3. Informed Consent: From The Body to The Body-Politic

The voluntary consent of the human subject is absolutely essential.
This means that the person involved should have legal capacity to
consent: should be so situated as to be able to exercise free power of
choice, without the intervention of any element of force, fraud, deceit,
duress, overreaching or any other ulterior form of constraint or
coercion....
                    —Principal One of the Nuremberg Code.
                         United States v. Karl Brandt, 1984.

The root premise is the concept, fundamental in American jurispru-
dence, that every human being of adult years and sound mind has a
right to determine what shall be done with his own body.
                  —Canterbury v. Spence, Judge Spotswood Robinson,
                         quoting Schloendorff, 464 F2d at 780, 1972

There were about twenty men ... all in exactly the same nightmarish
state: their faces were wholly burned, their eye sockets were hollow, the
fluid from their melted eyes had run down their checks ... their
mouths were mere swollen pus covered wounds....
                                 —John Hersey, *Hiroshima*,
                                    Knopf, New York, 1946.

At twenty megatons we are trying to imagine 1400 Hiroshima bombs
detonated at the same moment at the same place.
                         —Howard H. Hiatt, in "The Last Epidemic,"
          Educational Foundation for Nuclear Science Inc., Chicago, 1981.

In 1985, a coalition of community and national groups challenged a
proposed MX deployment in Federal court in Lincoln, Nebraska (each

50

MX carries ten warheads). They argued that the deployment was illegal on the basis of international and constitutional law . . . and transfers from the congress to the president the constitutional power to declare war. The judge dismissed the claims, ruling that the questions raised were 'political questions' the courts could not decide.
　　　　　　　　　　　　　　—The Docket Report 1986-1987,
　　　　　　　　　　　　　　Center for Constitutional Rights,
　　　　　　　　　　　　　　Faculty Press, New York, August 1986.

Every human being has lost ultimate control over their own life and death. Who then is deciding the fate of everybody else?
　　　　　　　　　　　　　　—The Delhi Declaration, January 28, 1985.

In this chapter, Dr. Diana Hull suggests that the principle of informed consent is applicable to the relationship between government officials and citizens. She suggests that in the nuclear age citizens are entitled to a greater role in policy making than simply electing representatives. Citizens have a right to essential information and participation in security decisions which directly affect them. Government officials, like doctors, should be held to standards of full disclosure of relevant information, and face sanctions under law for failure to comply.

The nuclear age is not the time for half truths or disinformation. References to "missile gaps" which don't exist, for example, have led to decisions both costly and dangerous which have fueled the nuclear arms race.

By shifting the context of informed consent from medical issues to national security issues, Dr. Hull has taken a creative leap that has the potential for changing the way government and citizens go about solving their joint problems in a nuclear age.

The concept of informed consent was developed, and its practice made specific, by medical ethicists during the 1970s.[1] Until now its application has been limited to relationships, decisions, or procedures that take

51

place in health care or in the laboratory. But as a human rights construct with legal implications, and as a moral philosophy, it can be applied to any relationship where one party, on the basis of a claim to superior knowledge, authority, skills or judgment, makes decisions or follows a course of action that risks the health or life of others.

The Nuremberg trials established in its law the ascendence of ethical codes over the authority of governments. The obligation to refuse to commit reprehensible acts against others extends logically to the refusal to be a victim of reprehensible acts like nuclear war, or to permit such acts to be committed by the state as our agents.

Informed consent provides a way of dealing with danger to the physical body, but can be applied just as well to the body-politic. It is a singularly appropriate model for citizen-government relations in the nuclear age because never have those in positions of power exposed populations to such massive risks, and never has there been a greater duty to inform, or a greater obligation to obtain consent.

Medical Rights and Human Rights: Converging Paths

Respect for the autonomy of the individual, and the right to privacy are the moral and legal underpinnings of informed consent in medicine.[2] The notion of consent is also at the heart of democratic government, and precedes by two hundred years the recent examination of consent in the context of medical practice and research.[3]

The United States was the first modern nation that tried to make government a servant of the governed, and do away with the ideal of the "good monarch" who had the obligation to care for subjects. The beneficence model has also been a problem in medicine, and contemporary thinking identifies correctly the ways in which it can interfere with the patient as a free agent acting on the basis of good information in his or her own behalf.

Beneficence as a motivating force in public and private behavior has a poor record, and abuses in unequal relationships are more noteworthy than the success of voluntary altruism. Thus, the responsibility for the welfare of others is only appropriate when the cared for are very young or incompetent, and even a family relationship is no guarantee that those without power will have their interests safeguarded.

Although genuinely benevolent relationships have been more prevalent in medicine than in political life, it was the legal accountability of physicians that set the stage for a new ethic of patient's rights and the requirement of informed consent.

This concept has produced benefits that go beyond an increase in protection for both the giver and receiver of medical services. The requirement of informed consent, and participation in the protocols that make it work, have altered the passive stance of patients as they are required to evaluate alternative treatments, and take responsibility for the choices they make in health care. For doctors there are now guidelines that define full, truthful, and ethical behavior, and a body of probable risk data for almost every procedure that sets a standard for technical excellence.

The nuclear age is the time for all of us to insist on similar rights for ourselves as citizens, and on similar obligations from those who serve us in government.[4]

To do this we can advance the loose philosophical notion of the consent of the governed to a more specific informed consent, where the steps leading to citizen compliance ensure that it is voluntary and autonomous, and based on truthful and comprehensive information. In the coming era of the informed consent of the governed, politicians, like doctors or engineers, in exchange for their privileges, will be held accountable for their professional performance and its results.

Neither malignant nor beneficent power is relinquished

voluntarily, and the leverage that brings about shared control are personal penalties sufficient to discourage the making of decisions without the permission of those affected by them. Thus, the strict legal accountability of office holders will promote consent seeking.

Having or maintaining power is a motive in its own right, whether the ends are beneficent or not, and the special contribution of the American Constitution has been the attempt to see to it that the various branches of government, and the rights of states, check and balance each other. The most glaring exception to this division of power is the military authority of the federal government, which gives wide latitude to the executive branch and its various agencies. Once elected, the executive branch has been beyond the legal reach of the public in these matters, and there is no route through the courts at present that makes it possible for individuals to stop the government from taking risks in their behalf that they do not wish to take.

The Lawyers Committee on Nuclear Policy claims that nuclear weapons and official U.S. policies concerning their use, violate fundamental principles of the Constitution, and undermine the Bill of Rights, whose very existence recognizes that "reasons of freedom and personal security" should prevail over "reasons of state." The Lawyers Committee also agrees with the criticism of many legislators that the President's authority to order first use of nuclear weapons deprives Congress of its right and obligation to decide when and if the country should go to war.[5]

Until now it has been accepted that actions taken by the federal government for the alleged purpose of defense or national security cannot be legally challenged by citizens, and that the only way to force a change in policy is through the ballot at the next election. It has been assumed incorrectly that blanket consent is given at the polls for all governmental activities in these two areas, and that no further specific consent is required.

54

Representatives in the Congress, as well as citizens, can find their access to information, and the power to intervene limited in military and national security matters. Both groups now worry whether the president's right to conduct foreign policy covers equally the sending of marines to Grenada and the right to start a nuclear holocaust. This question focuses on the variation in the orders of magnitude of both risk and effects in the executive power to use our arsenal of weapons, and is the factor that has been ignored in the debate over appropriate congressional, executive, judicial, and citizen prerogatives. Without the direct consent of the people, all branches of government are overreaching when they are blind to the special circumstances of our time.

Because of nuclear weapons, new questions are being asked about the legality, as well as the morality of military activities that will violate the rights of civilians, nonparticipating countries, and future generations. Statements declaring an absence of intention[6] to use nuclear arms are neither binding nor reassuring, but the fact that they are made at all acknowledges that there are now limits to what governments can do in actual wars, and threaten to do in wars of intimidation. The annihilation of an adversary's population, and self annihilation are not a legitimate objective no matter what the provocation.

A few lawsuits that test the right of the government to put us in this kind of jeopardy have gone to trial. It is brand new ground, and so far the courts have cut off attempts by groups such as the Center for Constitutional Rights to introduce a measure of democratic decision making into the nuclear arms race.[7] But the issues can take years to shape, and lawyers have just begun to use their particular skills in the service of survival.

In this effort they will call upon a body of theory and international law that has a long history, establishing that "the means of injuring the enemy are not unlimited," and

55

especially prohibiting "unnecessary suffering." These principals were set forth in the 1868 Declaration of St. Petersburg, and in the Hague Conventions of 1907. The Geneva Convention of 1949 "imposed detailed obligations on all belligerents to ensure the health, safety, and sustenance of civilian populations."

The Nuremberg trial decisions directly confronted the individual's responsibility to respect human rights in the face of coercion from the state. The defendants facing the International Military Tribunal in 1946, were charged with conventional war crimes, and with two other new categories of crime: crimes against peace, and crimes against humanity.

The results of these proceedings were not only to punish German leaders, but to forge a legal code that held individuals accountable for the atrocities they committed, and do away with the excuse that they were just following orders.[8] These decisions enlarged the western democratic tradition by insisting on personal moral autonomy.

Informed consent breaks new ground in the pursuit of self determination, as we are faced with both the possibility of committing atrocities, and the danger of being a victim of atrocities, in the nuclear age. Medical practice and laboratory research are an example of how a different kind of fiduciary agent now insures that procedures and penalties are in place to promote informed choice. Because of this process there is also a shared responsibility for outcomes.

The judgment at Nuremberg was that neither national defense nor total war can excuse heinous acts, and that those who commit them, even under orders, are criminals. Forty years later, while we continue to search out and deport hidden Nazi's, we simultaneously permit our government to both threaten and prepare for making the whole world an instant Auschwitz.

Because we have knowledge that our government is preparing to use nuclear weapons, American citizens will be responsible for the catastrophes that will result from their use. We cannot evade this as many Germans tried to do by claiming that the gas chambers were hidden from their view. If we are responsible for the use of such weapons, we must also have the authority to prevent their use, and nobody, including our elected representative, can speak or act for us in those matters where we are individually accountable. Nobody has sought, nor have we given, our consent to use nuclear weapons.

The Government's Responsibility

The legislation and the court decisions that define informed consent in medicine and in the laboratory, require continuing participation in decisions by patients and research subjects. There are standards of truthfulness that must be met, including a comprehensive disclosure of hazards, and an acknowledgment in writing from the patient or subject that the agreement to participate is preceded by knowledge about the full extent of the injury or damage that might result.

Federal policies governing medical research also prevent the government from putting us at risk as part of scientific experiments or untried technologies. Nuclear weapons research is illegal under this standard since neither the Congress nor the executive branch have fulfilled any of the most rudimentary requirements for obtaining the informed consent of citizens as human subjects during all of the experimentation, development, and preparations for the use of nuclear weapons.

The political doctrine of "consent of the governed" is the progenitor of consent in medicine. Now the same kind of mandated, specific consent required for taking chances with the life or health of those in the medical system is a necessary restraint on government activities more danger-

57

ous to human welfare than anything ever done or imagined in laboratory or in the operating room.

The risks that the American military are now requiring citizens to take transcend individual welfare, and encompass threats to future generations, the gene pool, and nature in the broadest sense. It follows that government has more than the ordinary obligation of full disclosure, and of an unbiased presentation of alternatives. Most critical are the measures to insure that any agreement to consent is preceded by an impartial and absolutely candid presentation of the dangers, and the establishment of procedures to make sure that they are understood. Nothing less is acceptable.[9]

Instead, the task of alerting the public to the great danger, and pressing for information and understanding of what was at stake and what the alternatives might be, came from private groups and individuals. independent scientists and some ex-military. The government's initial response to this effort was a combination of lying, denial and moves to discredit the opponents of the nuclear arms race.

It is ironic that both the courts, and other agencies of the federal government itself, like the National Institutes of Health, and the Food and Drug Administration developed both the philosophical and operational foundations of informed consent, championing the right of the patient to know the harm that might conceivably result even from the most benign and low risk procedures. This occurred at the same time that other branches of the federal government were continuing their history of concealing the risks of nuclear weapons, and the intention to use them.

Consent in medicine is a stand-in, a preview, and proving ground for informed consent procedures in larger arenas of life. The evolution of the doctor-patient, and the research-investigator subject relationships are predictive of the changes that can be made when the insistence on complete information and self-determination is pursued.

A standard for disclosure by doctors, and participation in

decisions by patients, was never made specific prior to 1960, so the prevalence of consent practices in clinical medicine before that time can only be inferred from old treatises on medical conduct.

The earliest writings about professional behavior, the Hippocratic Oath(s), discuss truth telling, but the patient's right to know is not as compelling as the doctor's obligation to be beneficent and in control.[10]

The Hippocratic tradition was carried forward into the middle ages and beyond, and the historic literature supports the idea that benevolent dishonesty was proper professional behavior. A famous monastic physician is quoted by the medical historian Henry Sigirest as recommending, "if a canon is sick, tell him the bishop has just died. The hope of succeeding him will speed his recovery."[11]

The American physician Benjamin Rush, (1745-1813) broke with the past in advancing a more contemporary ethic, criticizing deception and emphasizing the education of patients and the importance of giving truthful and comprehensive information. But this was recommended to ensure compliance, and other of his writings indicate he was still in the authoritarian mold.[12]

Although Rush was a contemporary of Thomas Jefferson, he did not deal with the issue of consent, a concept he was surely very familiar with as one of signers of the Declaration of Independence. The idea of consent in medicine did not take its modern form until much later, in the second half of the twentieth century.

In tracing the history of informed consent, Faden and Beauchamp observe that obtaining the patient's confidence in order to ensure acquiescence, is very different from advocating consent or shared decision making. In their words, "It is a distant conceptual journey from confidence to consent—almost as distant as the beneficence model from the autonomy model."[13]

The barrier to patient autonomy had always been the

presumed duty of the physician to decide what constituted the patient's best interest, and what course of action prompted that end. Barriers to citizen autonomy, and direct involvement in matters of foreign policy and defense, are thwarted by the same insistence on the part of government that they alone are qualified to identify national security interests, and decide what actions are needed to protect them.

The struggle over secrecy and the suppression of information that is still so familiar in political life today, mirrors the situation in medicine well into the first decade of the twentieth century.[14]

Physicians of that period were often accused of blatant deception, especially in the prescription of drugs. It was an era of worthless patent medicines, flagrant quackery, and inadequate education and training. These excesses finally resulted in a major revolution in standards of care, and in the reorganization of both the professional and medical schools.

What happened then in medicine is exactly what is needed now in government: clear definitions of proper training and acceptable conduct, stiff penalties to ensure compliance and contain deception, and a floor under ethical and performance standards.

Secrecy in government as well as in medicine serves as a cover for exploitation and incompetence. The difference is that secrecy in government is still being justified, "because we live in a dangerous world,"[15] while secrecy in medicine and research has already been tagged as a far greater hindrance to exemplary performance than the information it is trying to conceal.

While secrecy withholds information, lying distorts it as the control of information puts the lied to at a disadvantage in making informed decisions. Both behaviors violate an implicit contract,loosening the glue of trust without which there can be no successful collaboration between doctors and patients, or citizens and their government.

The kinds of abuses we still tolerate in government, were challenged in the medical arena by a series of lawsuits, whose outcomes established the patient's right to the truth, and built slowly, over forty years, a body of decisions leading to the modern meaning of informed consent. The three most important cases were the Schloendorff Case, the Salgo Case, and Canterbury v. Spence.

In 1914, Mrs. Schloendorff sued the Society of New York Hospitals because the physician had removed a fibroid tumor after she had consented to an abdominal examination under anesthesia, but had specifically requested "no operation." The Schloendorff case established, in Justice Cardozo's words, that "every human being of adult years and sound mind has a right to determine what shall be done to his own body," and "a surgeon who performs an operation without the patient's consent commits an assault for which he is liable in damages."[16]

In 1957 Martin Salgo suffered permanent paralysis as a result of a translumbar aortography, and sued because the physician failed to warn him of the risk. The court agreed with the plaintiff, and established in its decision the physician's duty to disclose "any facts which are necessary to form the basis of an intelligent consent by the patient to proposed treatment."[17]

Canterbury v. Spence moved the law to a stricter meaning of the patient's right to self-determination, and an expanded view of disclosure. It established that consent required, "the informed exercise of choice; thus, the physician's disclosure should have provided the patient an opportunity to assess available options, and the attendant risks."

The language of the decision was that, "the patient's right of self decision shapes the boundaries of the duty to reveal. That right can be effectively exercised only if the patient possesses enough information to enable an intelligent choice."

Self-determination is further emphasized in the following passage, "The context in which the duty of risk disclosure arises is invariably the occasion for decision as to whether a particular treatment procedure is to be undertaken ... it is the prerogative of the patient, not the physician, to determine for himself in which direction his best interests lie ... to enable the patient to chart his course understandably, some familiarity with the therapeutic alternatives and their hazards becomes essential ... It is evident that it is normally impossible to obtain a consent worthy of the name unless the physician first elucidates the options and the perils for the patient's edification."[18]

Informed Consent in Research

While the executive branch of government, the Department of Defense, and the Department of Energy, conceal and legitimize the most unacceptable risk ever posed to living subjects, that "Final Epidemic"[19] which will follow the use of nuclear weapons, the courts have so far evaded all challenges to the legality of these activities.[20] At the present time, being entitled to truthful information and self determination depends on whether a person is in the role of a citizen, or in the role of patient or research subject.

Thus, the extent of the court's concern is determined by *who* is violating our right to be both informed and to give or withhold consent to be put at risk. Physicians and research investigators *cannot* violate those rights, but the Department of Defense *can*.

Meanwhile, other branches of the federal government continue to make protection of human and even animal subjects a paramount consideration. The National Institutes of Health, the Food and Drug Administration, and even Congress and the Army, as early as 1960, developed stringent regulations to protect the rights of subjects. So it seems that the division of powers, while providing for checks and balances, also creates a nation with multiple personalities.

During the period 1974-1983, The National Commission for the Protection of Human Subjects of Biomedical and Behavioral Research, and the President's Commission for the Study of Ethical Problems in Medicine, and in Biomedical and Behavioral Research, wrote seventeen reports and appendix volumes, finally analyzing informed consent into its components of information, comprehension and voluntariness.

So, although the early formulation of these protections was a result of lawsuits against doctors, it is in research, not clinical medicine, that informed consent has been mandated and monitored by federal controls and regulations, and through a system of prior review that has linked the funding of research to consent procedures.[21]

The exception to this is the research conducted by the Department of Defense.

Nuclear Weapons as an Illegal Scientific Enterprise

The development, testing and manufacture of new weapons is no different than other experimental projects that create new substances, new instruments, or new techniques. It is properly subject to similar kinds of evaluation and review, and judgment by standards similar to research supported by other federal agencies or private institutions.

The primary considerations for the sponsors of all other research is whether a project has scientific merit, makes a contribution to knowledge, and is an ethical undertaking. The only justification for exposing anyone to the possibility of serious harm, and for the outlay of time, talent, and money is the likelihood that the findings will lead eventually to an improved solution to a problem.

This kind of favorable outcome is the result of a good fit

between objectives and the techniques used to achieve them. Increasing the lethality of nuclear weapons defeats rather than promotes the objective of national security by introducing a hazard greater than any problem the project was designed to overcome. Thus, the design is flawed.

No other research sponsored by government would be permitted to justify itself for the reasons used to justify the continuation of nuclear weapons development: i.e., that nuclear arms themselves are responsible for the fact that a nuclear catastrophe has not happened yet. (The same inability to discriminate between cause and effect, and two associated events convinces the smoker of fifty years that since he does not yet have lung cancer, cigarettes have been a preventative.)

The bombing of Hiroshima and Nagasaki can be viewed as the pilot study, whose findings were that the ultimate weapon had been found. No continued development was indicated because no further practical or scientific purpose could be served. The proper conclusion at that time was that nuclear weapons should not be manufactured or used, and that the necessary follow-up was a concentration on containing proliferation. Indeed, this was the advice the military received from most distinguished scientists, and respected world leaders.[22]

The implicit hypothesis underlying the continuing effort to create larger and more destructive weapons is that threatening to eliminate life and it's support system is the best protection from a competing political philosophy. Because this hypothesis is not scientifically credible ,it was never stated clearly, and because military activities are shielded from intense scrutiny and peer review from those outside of the system, this absurd hypothesis and the reasoning that propelled it forward was not made explicit. Instead it started out, and remains today, hidden in the entangled and emotional language of enemies and ideology.

In violation of what is simply routine protocol in other

research, competing alternative hypotheses for solving a problem, in this case political conflict, have never been outlined objectively, nor the case made satisfactorily for the choice of nuclear weapons versus other possible choices.

The danger of nuclear weapons has never been described fully and responsibly to those put at risk, and the destruction that can take place because of technical and human error does not have acceptable safeguards. There is no evidence of full disclosure to subjects, or efforts to insure comprehension. Instead, the government is guilty of concealment, and other unethical practices that in another scientific setting would result in the immediate withdrawal of funds.

This research is lacking in justification, flawed in design, can yield no new information, and is illegal because there is no procedure for obtaining consent, and none has been given. The unacceptable risks to subjects alone disqualifies it, as much as the overall absence of scientific merit.

Thus, the exemption from standard research practices granted to weapons work has been a serious error, resulting in enormous expenditures and in the threat of incalculable harm to millions, perhaps billions, of uninformed and unconsenting human subjects.

Making decisions about nuclear weapons and nuclear energy is so awesome, it is a wonder that those who have the responsibility to safeguard others are not more chastened, more reluctant to sell us on a particular course of action, and more insistent that we take some responsibility ourselves. But instead of thoughtful exposition of alternatives, and appropriate restraint, the public has been subjected to the aggressive advocacy of nuclear technologies.

In a marketplace of competing merchandise, no one is confused about the motives of the sellers, but in dealing with our government as a vendor of ideas we lose our bearings and cannot appreciate the other choices that are withheld from view.

Governments in power are ultimately dependent upon

our willingness to accept the network of concepts that support the idea of the nuclear deterrent, a course carried forward from one administration to another that now has a financial and administrative life of its own.

In obtaining citizen compliance with these policies, there are few effective rules about full and fair disclosure or restraints on undue persuasion. When compared with the relationship of patients and research subjects to the medical community, government is ethically primitive in its failure to go beyond compliance, and insist on authorization for its dangerous activities. So, we have the paradox that small risks to a single individual require a higher standard of disclosure and accountability, and more care in obtaining consent than the risk to vast numbers and to the environment.

To transfer the concept of informed consent to the government-citizen relationship, elected officials, bureaucrats and even candidates for office will need to give up being salesmen who promote their personal or party version of reality. Instead, mature governance is based on scientific objectivity, and rewards skills in the impartial appraisal and communication of complex data. A critical issue like nuclear weapons deserves a meticulously unbiased and public evaluation.

Educating the citizen to make the autonomous and informed choices they have every right to make, and the refusal to proceed without these conditions being met, would bring a new depth of meaning to democratic process. The best traditions of science, and the new ethical imperatives of medicine and research can change a government now adrift in hubris in our dangerous time.

HANNES ALFVÉN

4. Honest Language: Semantics of the Nuclear Debate

Language plays an extremely important, but often unrecognized, role in determining what we think, believe and do. It is the screen through which our perceptions and understanding of the world are filtered, and communicated to others. Yet, despite its importance, it seems natural for us to take language for granted. We are so immersed in its use that we generally go about our lives without stopping to examine the critical role it plays in determining our viewpoints.

Language unobtrusively envelops our beliefs and behavior just as air surrounds us in a way so natural that we seldom stop to recognize its presence. When the quality of our air deteriorates sufficiently, however, we can generally recognize that our health and even survival are threatened, and therefore that steps must be taken to restore and maintain air quality. When our language deteriorates, the warning signs of danger are less clear.

In this chapter Nobel Laureate Hannes Alfvén of Sweden explains how our language has created blindspots in our thinking that keep us from recognizing both the perils we face and the moral implications of the nuclear arms race. The bottom line for Professor Alfvén is that a badly polluted language may ultimately be even more dangerous to our health and survival than is badly polluted air.

If we are to "change our thinking" as Einstein warned we must, we need to clarify our understanding of the perils and opportunities of the nuclear age. An excellent starting point is the careful examination of the camouflaged assumptions in our terminology which guide our thinking. In a world filled with nuclear weapons, we cannot afford to conceal, even inadvertently, offense within defense, insecurity within security, nor war within peace.

Clarifying our language may be the starting point for reassessing and reorienting the thinking which has fueled the nuclear arms race.

W hen Confucius was asked what was the first thing he would do if he became Emperor of China, he answered: "The most important thing would be 'the rectification of words.' "

In modern language this means that semantics is very important: we must use the correct words for everything we speak about.

This principle is applicable to the nuclear debate. Those who strive to stop the nuclear arms race risk losing every debate as long as they accept the euphemisms used by the leaders of the arms race in place of more appropriate terms. We shall try here to find translations for the terminology which the powerful scientific, industrial, military and political leaders of the nuclear arms race have succeeded in getting so generally accepted that what they really do is camouflaged. This is a difficult task, but it is of great importance.

Annihilators And Omnicide

An important euphemism is "nuclear arms." It gives the impression that these arms are similar to old-fashioned arms. In the back of their minds, people may associate nuclear arms with brave knights fighting in shining armor. But the criminal pressing the button which will annihilate millions if not billions of civilians, including women and children—or rather, torture them all to death—is doing nothing heroic. Annihilators would be a more precise term for such arms.

The American philosopher John Somerville has coined

the term "omnicide" (suicide-genocide-omnicide) as an adequate description of what the full use of annihilators would result in. This term omnicide is even more appropriate now, when it appears likely that a full-scale nuclear attack would result in a nuclear winter.

Science and Nuclear War

The nuclear threat of annihilation is a product of the so-called "progress of science." We should note that "science" has several meanings. It meant initially "natural philosophy" (reine Wissenschaft), the unbiased investigation of nature. But nowadays it is more frequently used for the application of science for technical purposes, with the result that large branches of science have turned into a threat to us all. It is inappropriate to use the term "progress" for an activity which is as opposed to life as anything could be.

Years ago some scientists discovered nuclear fission and later others enthusiastically worked at making nuclear fission increasingly more terrifying. At present more than half the scientists in the world are paid directly or indirectly by the military or political establishments. On the other hand, there are a great number of scientists who, since the Manhattan Project, have protested as strongly as possible against the development of annihilators.

Are scientists qualified to take part in the nuclear debate? By profession, scientists explore the world around us, the microcosm of atoms, the macrocosm of galaxies, and the biosphere with all its infinite complications. A particularly interesting part of the biosphere is human society, which is studied by such disciplines as sociology, psychology, criminology and political science. In each of these fields, scientists of different specializations try to find the truth in an unbiased way. One of the most important puzzles is why man, who normally lives in peace with others, sometimes kills another individual—homicide—and why he some-

69

times kills thousands or millions of other individuals—war or genocide. At present, a general madness appears to be sweeping the world, and humanity is girding its loins for omnicide, the killing of all of us.

What role can scientists play? It is our profession to clarify the truth to ourselves and to our colleagues. It is also our duty to tell everyone the truth and nothing but the truth: to educate people about the real state of the world.

It has been thought that this should be done by whispering advice into the ears of the world's political leaders. Decades of sad experience in the nuclear debate have taught us that this does not work. Politicians are under pressure from many groups more powerful than scientists and, according to the rules of the political game, politicians listen—they must—to those who can exert the most pressure. Of course they would be concerned if their actions led to world destruction, but clearly they are more concerned about winning the next election or, in dictatorial states, about retaining their power.

Hence, the only effective remedy for the nuclear threat would be that popular movements become strong enough to exert decisive pressure on the politicians. As I see it, this is the only way to save our culture, our society, and the scientific and technical knowledge on which our civilization is based. I find it very satisfying to see such grassroots movements now developing.

Is the situation really so dangerous? Yes! It is not necessary for me to repeat all the arguments—they are well known—but I believe that the more you study the present situation, the more terrifying it looks. There are an increasing number of scientists warning against the present buildup of nuclear arms. Still, it is surprising that more scientists do not speak out. Why do they not? One reason is that most scientists are specialists. To them the most important thing is their latest discovery or latest technical innovation. Whether this is to the benefit or the detriment of humankind is often of secondary interest. They are happy to pass that responsibility to the businessmen, the military men and the politicians, who pay their research grants and salaries. Since destructive results are usually rewarded more generously than others, scientists are often under pressure to accelerate the "race to oblivion."

But there is a second, deeper reason that scientists do not protest more strongly. Scientists are often—but not always—very "intelligent" people. However, in this context there seem to be two different types of intelligence. One kind is what we may call "nuclear intelligence." The people who possess this count their achievements by how many people their devices can kill: how large a figure they can enter in the "megadeath" column.[1] Their aim is to make this figure as large as possible for the "enemy" and as small as possible for their own masters. What "megadeath" means in human terms is something they either do not understand or refuse to think about. In particular, they never mention that killing people by nuclear means is not comparable to killing the same number of people by conventional weapons, because radioactive death is not a "heroic" death in the old sense; very often it is a slow torturing to death, as we know very well from Hiroshima.

The other kind of intelligence we may call a "humane intelligence." Those who possess it cannot avoid seeing the meaning of "megadeath" in human terms. Their intelligence is combined with empathy in such a way that they are compelled to identify themselves with those who would be killed. In their imagination they themselves constitute one millionth of what the people with nuclear intelligence call a "megadeath."

What I am referring to is best explained by a reference to the International Physicians for the Prevention of Nuclear War (IPPNW) or the Physicians for Social Responsibility who, inspired by Helen Caldicott and many others, have started a movement for saving humankind from "The Final

71

Epidemic." This movement is now the spearhead of a rapidly increasing popular movement. The Union of Concerned Scientists is another example of a group of scientists with humane intelligence.

There are a large number of other anti-nuclear movements. The most efficient one may be Greenpeace. It was attacked by the French Government during a fact-finding expedition to the region of Polynesia where the French were killing the population by their nuclear arms tests. This caused a worldwide reaction with the result that the Greenpeace membership increased dramatically.

How do you separate those who possess nuclear intelligence from those with humane intelligence? You need only listen to what they say for a few minutes. You can judge them by what they advocate: more nuclear arms—or less.

Political Slogans and Reality

Both superpowers contain fanatics who claim that for moral reasons the other superpower must be destroyed, because it represents all the evil in the world. This is, of course, a naive and highly distorted view. With the threat of annihilation as humanity's most pressing problem, the real boundary lies between those who advocate and produce more annihilators and those who wish to limit, reduce and eventually eliminate them.

So the real frontier in the world is not the frontier between "capitalists" and "communists." It is between the people with nuclear intelligence and those with humane intelligence.

The threat of omnicide derives from two factors, the annihilators themselves, including missiles and airplanes for their delivery, and the political slogans which justify them.

The construction of annihilators and delivery systems is extremely complicated and it is claimed, with reasonable justification, that only experts are competent to discuss these problems. However, this does not hold true for the second factor, the political slogans which are necessary in order to persuade the people of the world to accept the annihilators. These slogans are not at all sophisticated. They are primitive; indeed, stone age man also thought he could negotiate only from a position of physical strength.

Anyone who can read and think is competent to discuss and analyze the problems. In fact, the "experts" are perhaps rather less competent than ordinary people to discuss them because of their professional bias. And many experts possess more nuclear than humane intelligence. Decisive in these discussions is that honest language be used.

Annihilators are utterly aggressive. Their use will result in mass killing of innocent civilians (either by direct strike or by a following "Nuclear Winter"). Is it reasonable to call such an activity "defensive"? Only by a misuse of words can citizens be motivated to finance annihilators from the "Department of Defense." The development and construction of them should be financed—if at all!—from funds for the Mass Killing of the Civilian Population. In order to demonstrate that this has very little to do with defense, a new department should be organized: "Department for the Mass Killing of Civilian Population" or for "Mass Production of Hiroshimas and Chernobyls." We should look forward to the debates in Congress and in various Parliaments on how many billions of taxpayers' money should be allocated for this. We should try to find out when the Politbureaus of the Soviet Union and China introduce this honest terminology in their secret discussions about annihilators.

We cannot completely exclude the possibility that a partial defense against missiles (by laser beams, etc.) can be constructed in the future, and this is the basis for what is called SDI, which stands for "Strategic Defense Initiative," usually nicknamed "Star Wars." This project has been severely criticized by practically all who have studied it without being corrupted by the billions of dollars which are spent on buying scientists to work on the project. The debate has clarified the real character of the project. It aims at developing a new, utterly destructive technology. How can this be referred to as "defense"? By the same misuse of words which we have discussed. It is claimed that in principle an utterly destructive technology can be used even to destroy the destructive missiles before they reach their targets. This is possible if only one or a few missiles are launched, but it is unrealistic if thousands of them are launched simultaneously. The concept of a "strategic defense" is used only to camouflage the real character of the project which is to develop a superdestructive technology. What should we call the project if we want to use correct and honest terminology? We could very well call it SDI, but this abbreviation should rather stand for "Super Destructive Initiative."

Realistic Policy

The enormous escalation of the arms race is now producing a healthy reaction all around the world. With the physicians in the front, rapidly growing groups of scientists are joining the opposition against the "race to oblivion." However, the main burden of opposition is not carried by scientists but by several other professional groups and by people who are so far from science that they are completely free from "nuclear intelligence." The peace movement has already grown strong enough to produce some political results. It is high time to discuss what the strategic aims should be.

Many people believe that it is necessary to be what they call "realistic." This means that they want to accept the power structure of the world as it is today. In spite of all the rosy talk about democracy, the real power is possessed by leading politicians, the military establishments, the economic oligarchies, and the large bureaucratic organizations.

If we analyze these complicated networks we find that the poisonous spider in their centers is often a scientist with nuclear intelligence, sometimes a real destructive genius.

It is said that we have to respect these establishments and understand that nothing can be achieved which is contrary to their interests. What we can do is to try to persuade them to modify their actions, slow down the rate of increase in armaments or modify a formulation in an international treaty. It is further said that if those who have power are naive enough to believe that escalating the nuclear arms race is a "realistic" policy, we all have to try to accept this in order to please them.

This method has been tried now for decades, and for decades the result has been small steps forward at the same time that big steps have been taken towards catastrophe. The arms race is escalating, the nuclear situation gets increasingly unstable, and the threat of omnicide more horrifying.

It is essential that the anti-nuclear movement fights the production and deployment of annihilators but, under present conditions, not all arms. It appears at present unrealistic to be a pacifist in the sense of believing that it is possible to get rid of all arms now. Before it is possible to achieve a completely disarmed world, it is necessary to find a way of making such a world stable against aggressors. The victims of aggression cannot be saved by disarmament. Furthermore, in many cases the only hope of getting rid of ruthless dictators is by armed rebellion.

So we must state clearly that our fight against nuclear annihilators and the threat they pose to us all must take precedence over opposition to conventional arms, although we must oppose the production and use of biological, chemical, and similar weapons as well.

That there has been no nuclear war since Hiroshima-Nagasaki is credited to the balance of terror between the "superterrorists," the United States and the Soviet Union.

75

However, it is evident that the deterrence epoch is approaching its end. Modern annihilators are increasingly constructed for first strike attacks.

Against this background, it becomes increasingly evident that a strategy that says it is necessary to negotiate from a position of strength is either bluff or suicide (indeed omnicide), as has been stated by competent strategists. This also holds true for all kinds of threats, from any side, to use annihilators for political purposes. All these actions must be considered as crimes against humanity, indeed, crimes committed against ourselves.

The manufacturing of nuclear annihilators is a similar crime against humanity since once manufactured they will sooner or later be deployed. So is any research into increasing the efficiency of annihilators because it is hard, if not impossible, to prevent any new inventions of this kind from sooner or later being manufactured and deployed.

But logic takes us further. Mining uranium, constructing the reactors in which plutonium is produced, and developing easier methods of separating the uranium isotopes are obviously similar activities. If they are not stopped, commercial pressure, which exploits power-greedy politicians, will spread nuclear material and nuclear technology to an increasing number of states. We have already witnessed the beginning of this process, the acceleration of which will follow automatically. There was a hope that the International Atomic Energy Agency (IAEA) might be able to halt this spread. The way this organization has been run and is run, however, definitely destabilizes the nuclear situation by spreading nuclear technology and building up nuclear lobbies everywhere. It is probably necessary that there be an international organization like IAEA which controls the spread of nuclear technology. What is wrong with the IAEA is that it is run by the nuclear industry, by people with "nuclear intelligence." These must be fired and replaced by people who care for the future of humankind. A drastically new attitude is required. If the present leaders were replaced by people selected at the advice of Greenpeace, the IAEA could become a useful organization, serving peace.

An analysis of this kind shows that there is no possibility of accepting any nuclear activity.[2] The belief that we can accept some kind of nuclear activity and avoid the inherent risk of omnicide is mistaken. The mere existence of fissionable material coupled with the techniques which enable the manufacturing of nuclear annihilators being in the hands of ruthless political and commercial interests, constitutes a threat to us all.

Until someone demonstrates that it is possible to accept some nuclear technology and remain safe, there is only one conclusion: the sole means of avoiding the increasing threat of nuclear omnicide is to consider all nuclear activity as a crime against humanity.

Planet Earth cannot accommodate both life and nuclear technology. One of the two—life or nuclear technology—has to be buried forever. We have to choose.

Conclusion: The Only Realistic Policy

It is not "realistic" policy to limit our actions for saving ourselves from omnicide to those which are acceptable to the political, military, commercial and scientific establishments of today. We have all seen clearly enough that their actions lead to an escalating risk of omnicide. A policy which has such consequences cannot be called "realistic." If we believe that man has a brain to be used for saving the human race from extinction, we cannot allow the present establishments to eliminate the use of the human brain in promoting their short-sighted interests.

The only possible definition of a realistic policy is one which aims at rescuing us from the nuclear threat. Hence, the only realistic policy is to stop all nuclear activity as soon as possible.

Why do we not do so? The Physicians for Social Responsibility have shown that there is no cure for the consequences of a nuclear war. Those physicians who are psychiatrists have diagnosed the present state as a severe psychic disease of humankind. Humanity is threatened by a general madness of destruction, a most serious illness. It is contagious. If one leading politician has been infected, his counterparts in other countries run a risk of also being infected. It is a fatal disease, but unfortunately not fatal only to those who have been infected. It also threatens those who are not. The disease should be called the "Super Destructive Illness," or shortened to SDI. For everyone who wants to survive, who wants to save our children and grandchildren, who wants to preserve our culture and everything that man has achieved, the highest priority must be to cure mankind of SDI—the "Super Destructive Illness."

TED TURNER

5. The Nuclear Arms Race Is Bad Business

Ted Turner received the Nuclear Age Peace Foundation's 1987 Distinguished Peace Leadership Award, an award made annually for dedicated and courageous leadership in the cause of peace. He was selected to receive the award for two significant activities. First, he founded the Better World Society, an international, non-profit organization committed to using television to increase awareness around the world about the great global issues of our time. Second, Mr. Turner was honored for his role in conceiving and organizing the Goodwill Games which took place in Moscow in 1986.

This chapter is based upon Mr. Turner's speech upon receiving the award at a dinner in his honor. He discusses his view that the nuclear arms race is bad business, and that all nuclear weapons can and should be eliminated.

I would like to share with you the Better World Society's "Statement of Purpose" because it's so similar to the Nuclear Age Peace Foundation's, except we have a bit more of an expanded agenda. I had to put a parliamentary committee together to write this statement. We knew what we wanted to say, but see what you think of the way we said it, because the Society is one of the reasons I'm getting the award.

"The Better World Society is an international, non-profit, membership organization dedicated to fostering individual awareness of those global issues which bear directly on the sustainability of human and other life on earth. Beyond awareness, the Society seeks to instill in citizens of all nations a sense of common responsibility for the fate of life on earth, as well as an understanding of the constructive actions we can take, individually and in concert, to redirect our nations toward sustainable progress and world peace. From this perspective, the Society will focus chiefly on the issues of nuclear arms control and reduction, population stabilization, stewardship of the earth's environment, efficient use of its resources, and fulfillment of the basic human needs of the world's people.

"In pursuit of its educational and mobilizing goals, the Society intends to be an innovative and energetic global communicator. It will employ a broad range of communications tools to reach international citizenry. The Society believes that we cannot work toward a sustainable future that we cannot first imagine. As a communicator the Society will deliberately use television and other media to consciously explore and chart alternative paths to a sustainable future, and to urge individuals to make decisions, personal and public, that will put our societies on those paths. Principly, the Society will produce, commission, acquire, and distribute television programming that addresses its global issue concerns. This programming will be disseminated internationally by all feasible means. Television programming will be supplemented, when appropriate, by ancillary education materials, information kits, audio tapes, books, and other publications.

"Membership in the Better World Society is open to individuals, corporations, foundations, governments, government agencies, and non-profit organizations. The Society believes its goals can be achieved only by forging partnerships among these communities. Such partnerships are vital with respect to both the building of an alert, informed, and engaged constituency for global sustainability and the funding of the Society's television programming and other communications activities. Thus, the Society seeks financing and other support from all its varied constituents. In addition, within the parameters of a non-profit corporation, the Society generates revenues from activities customary in the television industry such as licensing and broadcasting rights, videocassette sales and rentals, and the sale of other ancillary rights and materials. And within the constraints of its tax-exempt status, the Society voices its concerns on global issues to policy makers, governments, and international bodies both directly and through its members."

That's what one sister organization is attempting to do. My vehicle here in this country to do that is primarily WTBS.

The other thing that we won this award for was the Goodwill Games. Six days from now, I'll be on my way to Moscow to where we will have our third board meeting of the Better World Society. This is our second full year since being organized, and this will be our first board meeting out of the United States. We have a Soviet on our board; his name is Georgi Arbatov, Director of the Institute of United States and Canada Studies. He is a very sane and sensible voice for peace within the Soviet Union. When I was at the Goodwill Games last summer, I met with Gorbachev because Georgi set it up.

Just a month ago, we received word—it took two years for the People's Republic of China to pick its delegate—that we now have a member of their Population Program who's going to attend our Moscow meeting. We decided we were going to have an international board. That's pretty ambitious, but the problems of the world today can't be solved by one country; they are global problems. But we do agree about one thing: *the number one problem is the arms race and the existence and the increasing number of nuclear weapons, and the increasing hair triggers and sophisticated launch systems and computer systems that are attached to the management of these nuclear armaments.* Everything that the Nuclear Age

81

Peace Foundation writes about the terrible dangers of accidental nuclear war is certainly true.

I go around and make lots of speeches. Last spring I made twelve just to colleges alone in a thirteen-week period. I'm really trying to sell this program, just like your organization is, but I'm a marketer. I'm in the marketing business with television programming. While I'm a wild-eyed do-gooder and proud of it, I think I've got a very practical background, too, because I've spent my whole life in marketing and advertising. *I'm absolutely positive that the arms race and nuclear weapons are very, very bad for business. I mean it's bad business.* I'll tell you why. We've been at it for forty years. When Kennedy was President, we were in a pretty dangerous situation. I don't think the Soviets were nearly as friendly or as tired of the arms race as they are now, but our military budget then was seventy billion a year. That's when we had the Cuban missile crisis. Now our military budget is over three hundred billion. It's four times as much. Where do we get out at the present rate? Every year it gets more expensive and more dangerous.

The only way out is certain death, because sooner or later, there will be a Chernobyl of nuclear weapons, like the Soviet nuclear Polaris-type submarine that had technical problems and sank off Bermuda not long ago, and our missile in Arkansas a few years ago that went a couple hundred yards and fortunately didn't explode when it took off accidentally. But with thirty thousand of them on each side, sooner or later an accidental war will be triggered.

Plus, look at the example we're setting. It's just an awful example. We were talking about terrorists up here at the table. Terrorists don't really bother me, because the most they could make is one bomb and just blow up New York. In fact, probably the best thing that could happen to us is for one bomb to go off somewhere accidentally and blow a city up. The sinking of the *Titanic* caused a whole new look at lifeboat safety and safety drills and so forth—and normally that's what the real terrible problem is in this world today. *We learn from disaster.* The big hotel and theater fires caused sprinklers to be installed, and the earthquakes in San Francisco caused the buildings to be built a little stronger.

If we want to live with some security, there shouldn't be any nuclear power plants. Georgi Arbatov, right after Chernobyl, said, "Ted, one thing that we've learned is we can't even fight a conventional war. We can't fight a nuclear war, of course; but we can't fight a conventional war." He said, "Your country and mine, each have a hundred nuclear power plants spread all over the countries. What if we just dropped conventional bombs on each other's nuclear power plants? They're nuclear weapons ready to go off. They don't explode with a mushroom cloud; they just spread out in a two-hundred mile circle and kill everything around. So we've already mined our nations. We can't even fight a conventional war because of those plants." Now think about that. This is a Russian who pointed this out. He said, "That was the first lesson that we learned from Chernobyl." This is while they were still cleaning the mess up.

So what does all this mean? On my first trip to the Soviet Union I met everybody in Soviet television, and those are the people we started the Goodwill Games with. Since I decided I really wanted to get to know the Soviets, it turns out that the head of Soviet television who has eighty thousand employees likes to hunt, so I said, "Hey, I like to hunt, too." So, he said, "Why don't you come hunting with me?" I said, "I'd love to do it." So I went back in the winter after the Goodwill Games had been organized.

On that hunting trip, they sent a guy along, named Vitaly. He said he was in the foreign service and he was along as an interpreter, but the guy who runs Soviet television speaks fluent English so we didn't need an interpreter. He was obviously there to get information. At dinner, we were sitting around the table the night before we went hunting. He was sitting next to me and asking a lot of questions. He was a very attractive young guy in his late thirties. I said, "Vitaly, obviously you want to ask me some questions and, hey, I'd love it." I said, "I'll be happy to answer them."

After dinner we went in and sat by the fire and had a brandy, and he said, "Ted, why are you trying so hard to be friends with us?" I said, "Vitaly, let me tell you. I've got five children back home. I've had a wonderful life. And I love my country and I love my fellow countrymen very, very much. And I've been studying this whole situation recently, and I'm very concerned."

And I said, "Vitaly, I learned we're never going to get rid of nuclear weapons, or I don't think we will, until we trust each other. That's the problem. And you can't really trust each other until you get to know each other. And it really helps to get to be friends. I mean, that's the first thing we need to do. . . ." So, I said, "Vitaly, I'm coming over here to try and get to be friends with you and get you to be friends with me."

I would encourage each of you to go over there and do whatever you can to get to be friends. It's just mind-boggling to be over there. Sure, they're different than we are. They don't have as much. They don't have democracy; they don't have capitalism; they don't have drunks on the street—well, they have drunks on the street, but they don't have bag ladies. Everybody's got a miserable little job and all that sort of thing. They've got a lot of disadvantages. On the other hand, if you take a dispassionate look—step back a few hundred miles and take a look at us—a lot of the things that we hold so near and dear could be criticized by someone else. I really think that the political problems in the world are similar to the racial and religious problems that we had in the last century and into this century.

When I was a boy in Georgia—I moved there from Ohio— I lived in a place where there was segregation. I saw the two restrooms, different parts of the bus and everything. Fortunately, during my lifetime, I watched that disappear. Only a hundred and thirty years ago, we had slavery; we got rid of that. A hundred years ago, women couldn't vote in this country. In the world, a hundred years ago, less than twenty percent of the women in this world were educated; today over eighty percent of the women in the world are educated. *Probably the greatest single thing that's happened in the last hundred years of this world is the global education of women.* Well, what does this mean? It means that those are three perfect examples where we did change, and we did it without war. We can change. Ultra right-wing conservatives who are distrustful and paranoid about how communism is going to destroy us if there is an accommodation—that's fear. First of all, we're all going to die anyway. Really, what's so bad about dying? The way I figure it, we're going to die, so why be so afraid of it? It's inevitable. There's nothing worse than living in fear of dying. Fear—what's worse that that? My God, I'm going to die. Look at life this way,the way I do: It's like a grade "B" movie—you don't want to get up and walk out in the middle, but you wouldn't want to sit through it again. I'm not trying to say life isn't precious and wonderful. It is. It is fantastic. Nobody has more fun than I do. Let me tell you, I've had more fun. I've had all kinds of fun. So, since we're all going to be dead anyway, it would be better to at least be like Nathan Hale who said that "I only regret that I have but one life to give for my country."

Why not carry that one step further. *I only have one life to give for my species.* We are all members of the same race, the human race.

You are citizens of Santa Barbara and proud of it, right? That doesn't make you less Californians because you love Santa Barbara. Because you're Californians,does that make you poor Americans because you love California or Santa Barbara? Of course not. Why not carry it the one last step and say we're all citizens of the world? We are citizens of the same world. Maybe you don't like Los Angeles, but you'd never start a war with Los Angeles, right? And California's not going to invade Nevada. So all we need to do is to expand that feeling to the rest of the world. Then you don't really want to fight anybody else because you won't want to kill your brother because we are all brothers.

Nuclear weapons were designed to kill other human beings; that's what they were designed for. The time has come to end war. It's asking a lot of humans who've been going thousands and thousands of years improving weapons to now get rid of the weapons. But what we've done is we've created weapons that destroy everything. They just don't make any sense. *Arbatov has told me the Soviets are ready, and what I think we should do is get rid of all nuclear weapons, at once. All nations.* At the United Nations, every nation signs a treaty that they will never build, deploy, use, or have anything to do with nuclear weapons. The Soviets have told me that they will do that right now. We could do it if we had the right administration in Washington, D.C.—which we have to work for next time. But for a good administration, we have to look very carefully at what the candidates say because the next election will be very, very important. We could get rid of all nuclear weapons in this world, I think, in a time period of five or six years. And I'm going to continue to try and work on that, and I am sure that the Nuclear Age Peace Foundation will too. There's nothing we can do that is more important.

RODRIGO CARAZO

6. Building a Culture of Peace

The Nuclear Age Peace Foundation's 1986 Distinguished Peace
Leadership Award was presented to a unique international states-
man, Dr. Rodrigo Carazo, a former president of Costa Rica (1978-
1982), and the founder of the United Nations University for Peace
in Escazu, Costa Rica. Dr. Carazo, who currently serves as President of the Council of the University for Peace, Has been tireless
in his global travels and efforts to promote peace education
throughout all academic disciplines and at all levels of study.

The genius which Dr. Carazo has displayed is in his clear vision
of education as a critical tool for building a peaceful world. The
University for Peace, under Dr. Carazo's leadership, is a noble
experiment in creating the educational and ethical foundations
for individual, societal and global peace. It is a university which
cooperates with educational institutions throughout the world in
developing and implementing innovative courses and research
programs aimed at teaching and achieving peace.

In accepting the Award, Dr. Carazo wrote that the award "truly
belongs to the people who work together with me at the University
for Peace, and who have steadfastly supported me in my endeavors
to pursue peace and stability in the world. It is indeed a source of
great pride to observe that these efforts have not gone unnoticed
in the eyes of the international community."

In his address at the Foundation's Annual Dinner, he said,
" . . . we must think enthusiastically that it will be possible to build
a Culture of Peace." For this great challenge the University for
Peace offers considerable promise for providing individual and
societal models. Costa Rica itself provides a model of a nation
which has existed without an army for more than a quarter
century in the midst of a strife-torn region.

Dr. Carazo's work helped to pave the way for the Central

American peace initiative by another Costa Rican president—
Oscar Arias—who was awarded the Nobel Peace Prize in 1987.

Contemporary technological developments and deep changes in human attitudes, morals and aspirations, have signaled in advance the beginning of the Third Millennium.

The world is quickly changing its economic center, projecting it to the West. As in past centuries, when the world's central axis moved from the Mediterranean to the Atlantic, today it is moving toward the Pacific through a very dynamic process. Meanwhile, the economic centers which governed world activity until the middle of this century, are today undergoing a process of political and economic decay. The Far East is each day less Orient and less Far, and is becoming more Central.

Technology is constantly changing human activities. Labor has ceased to be solely a human endeavor and has begun to be considered as something performed by machines, by robots. These have eased the need for use of mankind's physical effort in the production of goods and services, stressing now more than ever the importance of the creative capacity of human intelligence.

Progress has been such, and societies are being pushed so rapidly, that each day there is less time that is not dedicated to training in the practical applications of the daily developments of science and technology.

Prevailing political polarization has converted today's ideological confrontation into a dual-front monopoly. The two main centers try to direct their dominating actions, ever highlighted by military competitions, toward a pretended equilibrium between their offensive and defensive capabilities, in what can be best be considered a "balance of terror." The development of their destructive capacities has made evident that in an eventual war between the superpowers there would be neither winner nor loser. This fact escapes the logic of the Marxist concept of class struggle which presupposes the existence of a winner and a loser in all human confrontations. It also escapes the logic of the capitalist pursuit of material gains which presupposes the existence of a certain kind of domination by those who have over those who have not.

However, this two-headed monopoly of power is confronted by the relative incompetence of the Soviet Union to project its hegemony. The United States, through a more dynamic and powerful process, has increased its domination, whether direct or indirect, throughout the planet, based on the enormous projections of its technological development and the transformation of the financial processes of the world in order to bring them under its control.

Nevertheless, due to the existing paranoia, it may seem paradoxical to state that the destructive capacity generated by the prevailing arms race makes us conceive as illogical and, *omitting the possibility of error,* almost impossible, the occurrence of a direct war between the superpowers. But we cannot conceive of the destruction of the planet and of humankind as the mere total loss of material possessions. The environment is suffering today, as never before, destruction and abuse, and the integral development of culture has been postponed, together with the improvement of the heritage of generations, in the nurturing of spirituality, beauty, art and love.

Since the end of the Second World War, humanity has experienced more material changes than those which occurred since the beginnings of mankind. The human capacity for astonishment, long since exhausted due to so many technological achievements, has failed to give due attention to the formation of a culture which positively combines the values of the past with those generated daily in this ever-changing and materially progressing world.

More than a decade ago two bronze statues, reproductions of masculine figures, were found in the Mediterranean Sea to the south of Italy. I had the opportunity of seeing them recently. What an impact it is to realize that millennia ago, man could create—through art—such superb quality of masterpieces which today can be reproduced exactly using available technical methods but not, unfortunately, as marvelously *created*.

Setting the Stage for a New Culture

The past, both far and recent, is an accumulation of culture. The twenty-first century, the New Millennium, will be the stage for a new culture, created by a new human being with a constant desire to excel. In the face of the rational impossibility of total war, we must think enthusiastically that it will be possible to build a Culture of Peace.

Technological advancement projects our voices to the whole world, permitting us to see and hear whatever is happening at any given place on earth. It is possible to imagine that a Culture of Peace will compel humanity to make of interdependence (a fact that increases with time) a formula which may serve to model a society in which human aspirations will not be separated by arbitrary political boundaries. And which further may allow us to advance toward the practice of living in a planetary village, capable of generating happiness through the application of justice and freedom, as a result of respect by all for the rights of all.

Peace is a state of harmony, both of the inner self and in the behavior of people toward others.

Robots have given humanity more freedom, but in order to obtain advantage from this newly obtained benefit, it is necessary to intensify the use of spare time, by nurturing science, the arts, the intellect, and the development of health and the beauty of the human body through sports.

The New Millennium must be received with a positive

spirit, with full consciousness that it is necessary to be up-to-date in knowledge. Values produced in the past should not be taken only as a reference, since the history of humanity on this planet is a continuity. Thus arises the urgency of paying due attention to the Humanities and the Arts, as instruments of intellectual development and of cultural nourishment; in sum, as instruments of Education.

The future will be the result of the attitudes and efforts of the present. In facing the accelerated changes that we are experiencing, we must promote a crisis of conscience in order to transform all learning centers and universities into schools that combine the learning and training required by technology with the necessary education to form an entire human being: body, mind and spirit—capable of using robots, without running the risk of becoming one of them.

Education for Peace acquires primary importance when described as elements promoting the acquisition of ethical values which influence the behavior of a person toward his or her fellows (as much in interpersonal relations within society as through its connections to the world). An entire range of techniques and methods are being put into practice in different places of the world. Evaluation of the results has already begun.

Several institutions with a clear international educational orientation have been created within the United Nations, such as the United Nations University with headquarters in Tokyo and the University for Peace with headquarters in Costa Rica. These institutions promote concrete plans of action in the area of Education for Peace, and are the result of efforts supported by more and larger groups of people within and outside the United Nations System.

Turning Education and the Media
into Instruments of Peace

The choice between war and peace in coming years will depend on the continuance of the arms race, or on disarmament. But more than anything, it will depend on our decision to turn education and the mass communication media into instruments of peace. In terms of objective analysis, the foregoing takes for granted the fact that peace can be attained through education. In other words, peace can be taught. It requires inspiration and a pedagogical motive involving all plans and teaching programs from kindergarten to post-graduate studies.

Education for Peace must make humanity abandon the idea that a certain culture, ideology or way of thinking, is something which can be imposed on others through violence or by force.

Is it possible for man to learn to live in peace? It is unnecessary to go back to the days of Socrates or to the Dialogues of Plato in order to demonstrate that virtue is the object of all knowledge, and that through teaching the renewal of society is made possible.

We cannot love that which we do not know. Peace is not a spontaneous or free gift, but something to be won as are freedom and virtue. Its importance, efficiency and need must follow the same stages as occur in a human being's formation. The first stage of peace is tolerance, tolerating and respecting all other fellow human beings, even those who have offended us. Tolerance has to be applied, and the basis for a plurality of thought has to be found through respect for others and for their ideas.

Humans of today have a great responsibility to become active protagonists in the development of the type of education required for the New Millennium, conscious as they must be that the first university students of the twenty-first century are already walking on the face of the earth.

The routes for the attainment of international peace are already marked out. The first of these is general universal and controlled disarmament. The second consists of undertaking an enormous effort to organize fraternal collaboration among peoples. Peace, as well as human progress, of which it is the supreme goal, does not come about by itself; it entails a will for peace, a will that provides its own means of attainment.

The University for Peace proposes to form dynamic models of peaceful individuals and peaceful societies; and to work so that many men and women get to know these models, and contribute to shaping and completing them, propagating them in their own communities. This is a task to be achieved in dialogue and freedom. It is not a matter of creating a new ideology which must be imposed. We have learned too much from the painful experience of redeeming formulae imposed by force and watched over inquisitorially.

Peace—The Environment for Future Generations

The purpose of peace education is not to defeat anyone, but rather to convince many that peace—if it is really desired and if the people are educated to construct it—will stop being Utopia and will become the environment into which future generations will be born, will live, and will fulfill themselves. Peace, besides the many concrete actions it entails in the legal, political, ecological, psychological, economic, diplomatic and moral areas, should integrate all these areas in a new form of doctrine and action.

Creating models of peaceful individuals and societies is a problem and a challenge that could be an illusion and a falsehood like so many others. But it is not a matter of proposing a uniform model that suffocates the cultural peculiarities that shape the differences among people.

93

Instead, the idea is to maintain and encourage the legitimate differences among people, and to stimulate the development of every person and all people within a climate of peace. It is a project which, like any human project, should be subject to revision and improvement as it is carried out.

An intense effort must be made to develop attitudes and abilities in human beings that permit them to understand their fellow humans; face conflicts and difficulties in a rational and realistic way; and search for more imaginative solutions to the material problems that nurture tension, aggression and violence. The general principles that support the creation of the University for Peace by the General Assembly of the United Nations, away from any international political interference, included the following: "Peace is not merely the end of a conflict or an interlude between wars; it is a constantly renewed challenge. It must be our supreme objective and, as such, we must provide concrete means for affirming it, recalling that the present generation reserves its trust for words that are accompanied by deeds. In order to reach peace, we must put to use one of the greatest and most effective means of ennobling and transforming individuals: education. In this way we may forge in individuals the thoughts and habits of peace, bringing peace first to the spirits, minds and hearts of men and women, and then into the world."

Peace is made, not found. Peace is not rest. It is not another word for fear. It is the pulse of life. Peace is a way of life.

FRANK K. KELLY

7. Searching for a President In a Nuclear Age

The nuclear age demands leaders capable of maintaining peace; and moving beyond the current dangerous stalemate to a world constructed on more stable foundations. In moving the world away from the precipice of "mutual assured destruction," no world leader is in a more critical position than the President of the United States

We need a President who has the vision and the courage to foreclose the option of destroying our global civilization. We need a President who realizes that the great problems humanity faces today are global problems, requiring joint efforts by many leaders. And we need a process of selecting such a President which involves the citizenry in a full and vital debate over the necessary qualities of leadership in the nuclear age.

This chapter offers a proposal for revitalizing our democracy through an open and democratic process of seeking out skilled and gifted candidates with global vision to serve in the nation's highest office. Future presidents must be leaders for all of humanity as well as the people of the United States.

The recruitment and selection of Presidents of the United States in a nuclear age—an age in which a President has the power to wipe out whole nations and devastate the planet—should not be left simply to the rough grind of the political process which now exists.

The present system requires candidates to scrape up $30 million to $40 million to become serious contenders for a nomination from either the Republican or the Democratic

95

party. In a great democracy, the availability of a potential President should not depend upon an endless money-raising circus.

The current process forces candidates to spend two or three years in exhaustive tours of the country, appealing to special interests, making deals, devising television "spot messages" with distorted appeals, and engaging in frenzied maneuvers. Candidates who are willing to spend years in such a maelstrom must be completely dedicated public servants or have enormous egos. In any case, they tend to gather around them staff members with fanatical devotion to "the one and only leader" or technicians who are experts at "packaging people" in cellophane or Teflon.

Delegates at national conventions meet in an atmosphere which almost eliminates any possibility for calm and rational consideration of the qualifications of those who seek to be nominated. It makes a travesty of the whole idea of a nation choosing a future leader.

The conventions often do no more than ratify the results of the primaries in various states. These primaries are often focused on particular issues and are generally popularity contests, won by the candidates who can talk effectively with local groups and can spend lavishly on television advertisements—and have active local organizations to get out the voters on the primary day.

What the United States needs in the nuclear age is a national discussion of the kind of president we should have—and where we can find a considerable number of outstanding men and women who should be considered.

President Truman once told me that he knew there were many talented men and women who were never considered as possible candidates. "I don't think we should limit nominations to people who are dying to get the job," Truman said. "Anybody who wants it too much should be disqualified. We should find the best candidates and get them to run."

Truman did not seek the presidency himself. We went to the Chicago convention of the Democratic party in 1944 with a strong determination to nominate Senator Jimmy Byrnes for vice president as Franklin D. Roosevelt's running mate that year. Byrnes had convinced him that Roosevelt wanted Byrnes on the ticket. In Chicago, he learned that Roosevelt had decided to back him. He knew that Roosevelt was in poor health and might die in office. In that case, he would become President. He didn't think he was as qualified as others who might have been nominated. But he was persuaded by Roosevelt and other leaders that it was his duty to run—and he did it.

The enormous responsibilities of the presidency fell upon Truman when Roosevelt died in 1945, and it took him six months to cope with the demands of the White House. He was elected to continue his service by the voters in 1948, but he grew increasingly conscious of the burdens placed upon a Chief Executive. In 1952, he decided that he would not run again. Impressed by the record of Governor Adlai Stevenson in Illinois, he offered his support to Stevenson—who declined it. Truman then urged Averell Harriman to get into the race. Harriman asked me to be the Washington director of his campaign, and I accepted because I shared Truman's admiration for him.

The response to Harriman's campaign showed that many people recognized that he had the abilities and the background to become an effective president. He had never been elected to any public office, but he had an extraordinary range of experience. He had been chairman of the Union Pacific Railroad; he had been administrative officer of the National Recovery Administration under Roosevelt; he had been an officer of the Lend-Lease Program in World War II; he had been the United States Ambassador to the Soviet Union and to Britain; he had been Secretary of Commerce in Truman's cabinet. He was known and admired by people in many fields and in many countries.

97

At the Democratic convention in 1952, Stevenson finally decided that he would be the candidate. He was defeated, of course, in November of that year by General Dwight D. Eisenhower, who ran as the Republican nominee. Eisenhower was another candidate who had never held an elective office. He had been persuaded to run by other leaders who knew that he was extensively admired by the American people.

I cite these examples to show that the American nominating system can be opened up for unusual candidates—for leaders not regarded as professional politicians, for leaders without previous experience as campaigners for votes.

Bringing Forward New Candidates

In a nuclear age,I think we need to examine new proposals for finding potential Presidents.

I suggest that a nation-wide effort could be made by a Council of Citizens—formed by leaders of many national organizations representing Americans with a wide variety of views and hues—to conduct a systematic search for notable men and women who could serve the nation and the world in the coming years.

The Council might bring forward five or six persons with Republican backgrounds, five or six Democrats, and five or six Independents—whose lives and achievements could be presented in a series of widely distributed paperback books and national radio and television programs. With the cooperation of the mass media, relatively unknown leaders could become well known in a short time. The televised hearings on Judge Bork showed that a relatively unknown person can become known to most Americans within two weeks.

These candidates could be presented and discussed for a month. Then a national survey of their standings could be conducted on television and radio (and through the newspapers), and/or through the polling organizations, with the

98

results compared and analyzed by the staff of the Citizens' Council.

Then the top six candidates—perhaps two Republicans, two Democrats, and two Independents—could be presented to a Citizens' Assembly, to be convened by the Council in March or April of the presidential election year.

These candidates could be invited to make statements on the state of the nation and the state of the world—two each evening, with each one allocated an hour, for three consecutive evenings, on national TV networks in the presence of the 5,000 delegates of the Citizens' Assembly. One half of the delegates could be selected by the national political parties; the other half could be chosen by national civic organizations.

In the following three evenings, there could be three wide-ranging dialogues—each dialogue involving two of the candidates,with the two persons exchanging ideas and comments at first with one another and then commenting on questions from members of the Assembly. Each of these dialogues would last two hours, and would be broadcast nationally. After an intermission, the candidates would appear again for another two hours to discuss questions telephoned to them from radio and television audiences across the country.

After six days of intensive discussions of the merits of these candidates—and their views on the basic issues facing the people of the United States and the world—the delegates at the Citizens' Assembly would vote on the candidates, considering each as a possible President and each as a possible Vice President with the qualifications to become President. The balloting would be done openly on television and the results would be recorded.

During the balloting in the Assembly, members of the radio and television audiences would also be asked to give their preferences by telephone switchboards operated by the

Citizens' Council. These votes would be tabulated, and announced after the balloting in the Assembly.

These procedures are suggested because it seems essential to give the maximum number of people an opportunity to participate in the selection process. The Citizens' Assembly—although it may be composed of members of many national organizations and delegates named in party caucuses—might still be accused of being "elitist" or "not fully representative of ordinary Americans." The choices made by millions of radio listeners and television viewers would bring large numbers of people into the system.

The results of the Citizens' Assembly and the preferences expressed through other channels would be immediately available to the mass media, and would be called to the attention of the national committees of all political parties and other leaders in the parties.

In the months between the Assembly and the party conventions, polls would be taken to show the relative standings of the candidates endorsed by the Assembly (and those selected by the broadcasting audiences) in comparison with the standings of the regular Democratic, Republican and Independent candidates contending for presidential nominations through the primaries and other channels.

The candidates emerging from the search I have described would be asked whether they would be willing to have their names placed in nomination at the regular party conventions. If they indicated such a willingness, efforts would be made to find party delegates who would place their names for consideration by the conventions—thus making it possible for one or both of the major parties (and any independent party) to consider candidates presented with high credentials and substantial evidence of wide public support.

After the party conventions had chosen their candidates and adjourned, the Citizens' Assembly would be reconvened to review the records of the nominees. The Assembly would

100

be asked to vote on an endorsement of one set of candidates, to take no position, or to nominate other candidates as alternative possibilities for American voters to consider.

If these procedures were to be followed, the search for new candidates could have far-reaching effects on the choosing of presidential nominees in coming elections. The national parties might form Citizens' Committees of their own to widen the search.

Members of the old party organizations might resist the injection of new possibilities into the nominating process, but new candidates with demonstrated popular support could not be ignored for long. Wendell Wilkie in 1940 and George McGovern in 1972 showed that the "party regulars" could not always control the major parties.

Throughout the history of the United States, new movements have arisen to meet the needs of the times. In the nuclear age, the search for a President with the right qualities will demand a continuing program of information and discussion to engage the thoughts and activities of the people. In that process, the future of this nation and the world can be changed.

Questions for the Possible Candidates

In the hunt for new nominees, the Council of Citizens should develop a comprehensive list of questions to be used in evaluating all of the persons under consideration—including the avowed candidates striving for the nominations of the major parties.

The Council could employ researchers of the highest caliber to review the records of these persons, going deeply into their personal relationships, their attitudes, their knowledge, their philosophies of life. Each candidate might be the subject of a book-length study.

Here are some of the questions that could be considered in such studies:

101

1. Does the person have a global viewpoint—an understanding of the interdependence of nations, the connections between the United States and other countries, the necessity for international co-operation in tackling planetary problems?
2. Does the public and private life of the person show a consistent adherence to high moral and ethical standards?
3. Does the person have a comprehensive vision of the American constitutional system and what might be done to improve it?
4. How extensive are the sources of knowledge and advice available to the person?
5. Are the views of people in all areas and in all backgrounds—rich or poor, black or white or brown, young or old, male or female, radical or moderate or conservative—actively *invited* and *thoroughly examined* by the possible candidate?
6. What kinds of materials—pamphlets, fund-raising letters and telemarketing efforts, advertisements, public relations plans, television programs—have been used by this person in public activities?
7. What uses have been made of nonpartisan research projects and reports prepared by "think tanks" on issues and problems?
8. How does the person deal with critics and opponents? Does the value of criticism and opposition seem to be appreciated as a learning experience—or are all critics and opponents downgraded and/or attacked?
9. Does the person cling to slogans and platforms of the past—or show a growing awareness of the need for new measures to meet new times?
10. Has the person demonstrated a capacity to learn from mistakes—not to withdraw into defensive maneuvers or denials of errors?

11. Has the person shown calm strength in meeting emergencies and crises?
12. Has the person ever risked his career by being in a minority position and sticking to it—or resigning from a job rather than "going along" with what he or she considered to be wrong?

There are many other questions that can be explored. The twelve questions I have cited are simply examples of the kinds of inquiries that should be made.

The candidates' attitudes toward "the Presidency" as an institution should be laid bare. Does the person regard it as vital to enhance and strengthen "the Presidency" above all— or recognize the Jeffersonian concept of the Presidency as an ever-changing instrument, coordinated with the other branches of government, functioning in a framework of laws and clearly defined responsibilities?

Presidents of the future may have to be prepared to function in a network of international leadership, sensitive to the needs and demands of people all over the Earth.

Do the Candidates See the Possibilities of a New Society?

Political campaigners in the 1980's have become aware of the fact that many people do not respond to the old slogans and the old programs. People are looking for men and women who see the signs of a new kind of society developing through the currents of change—who realize that people in many countries are groping toward a new view of the future.

President Johnson, who lost sight of his other goals in his obsession with the Vietnam War, once painted a vision of what he called "a great society" in a speech at the University of Michigan: "It is a place where the city of man serves not only the needs of the body and the demands of commerce, but the desire for beauty and the hunger for community. . . .

It is a place which honors creation for its own sake and for what it adds to the understanding of the race ... It is a challenge constantly renewed, beckoning us toward a destiny where the meaning of our lives matches the marvelous products of our labor."

Acclaiming Johnson's vision, James MacGregor Burns declared in his book, *Presidential Government*: "The crux of the problem is whether a system of presidential government ... can redefine its purpose and shift its strategy in order to embrace new values with their implications for changes in means and instrumental goals."

Truman established the National Security Council and made the quest for "national security" the central element in national policy. Subsequent presidents carried the dedication to "national security" to extremes, pursuing "covert operations" that made a mockery of American constitutional principles—and led the United States to be regarded as an imperial power as dangerous as the Soviet Union in many parts of the world.

The men who carried out "national security" policies under Truman and his successors regarded themselves as "realists" who knew how to operate successfully in the "modern" world. The concepts of that world were built on quantitative measurements—on materialistic science and technology, on the assumption that the problems of the world could be understood and controlled by "objective" methods that produced measurable results.

Many scientists and thinkers in other fields now cite evidence that non-material factors—such as religious beliefs and mental states of consciousness—may be more significant than physics and chemistry. These thinkers and researchers believe that humanity is moving from the "modern" world-view to a "post-modern" holistic world-view which retains the benefits of science but opens up vast new possibilities for creative evolution.

A Nobel Laureate, Roger Sperry, has pointed out: "Beliefs

concerning the ultimate purpose and meaning of life and the accompanying world-view perspectives that mold beliefs of right and wrong are critically dependent, directly or by implication, on concepts regarding the conscious self and the mind-brain relation and the kinds of life goals and cosmic views which these allow. Directly or indirectly, social values depend on whether consciousness is believed to be moral, immortal, reincarnate, or cosmic—localized and brain-bound or essentially universal...." All presidential candidates should be asked to give their views on the "ultimate purpose and meaning of life."

Dr. Willis Harman, a regent of the University of California, has suggested that scientific knowledge may be considered on four levels—physical sciences, such as molecular biology; life sciences, dealing with natural selection, system functions and organ functions; human sciences, concerned with individual biological health and individual purposes; and spiritual sciences,concerned with wholeness and universal purposes, honoring "the deep subjective experience of untold mystics, prophets, artists, and poets, down through the ages...."

We have a right to inquire into the fundamental beliefs and spiritual knowledge of presidential candidates. Many Presidents have admitted that their decisions have been strongly affected by their religious education and experiences. President Truman told me that he based many of his actions on his readings of the Bible and the moral instructions he received from his mother. Abraham Lincoln was a poet and a prophet as well as a political leader.

Arthur S. Link of Princeton University, a noted scholar in American history, declared in an interview in the *Los Angeles Times:* "The imperial dimensions of the Presidency do not mean that the incumbent of that office has to yield to the seductive temptations the office holds out. The Presidency requires a man of very great moral strength—more so than any other office in the world because it does have such

105

power, such opportunities for the exercise of power. The Presidency does not have the restraints on it, for example, that the British cabinet does or that other major governments impose. . . ."

The current nominating system does not place much emphasis on "very great moral strength" or the wisdom of self-restraint or on the candidate's knowledge of what Dr. Harman calls "the spiritual sciences." Candidates now are expected to please or placate people with a variety of special interests—and to "come across" convincingly on television and radio.

If candidates suited for the future of humanity are to be found in this age of converging crises, the search may have to go beyond the ranks of professional politicians. Scientists, doctors, university presidents, diplomats with service in many areas, business leaders with international awareness, and others in many fields should be considered.

Since the consciousness of human beings in all parts of the Earth reflects a growing sense of humanity's shared problems and potentialities, each candidate should be asked to prepare a statement on what kind of world seems likely to emerge in the years ahead. This statement should be circulated to a group of consultants knowledgeable in all the sciences, and their comments should be transmitted as quickly as possible to the candidate. He or she would be given time to prepare replies to these comments, and then would be asked to meet with the consultants in a series of thorough discussions. At the end of this process, each consultant would be asked to give a confidential evaluation o the candidate in a report to be sent to all members of the Council of Citizens.

What Kind of People Must We Become— to Find and Support New Presidential Candidates?

The search for a president in a nuclear age must be conducted by citizens dedicated to the preservation of the whole Earth and to the full development of democratic participation in the process of self-government at every stage in the electoral system.

The connections between actions by people in many countries have appeared clearly in the outpouring of protests against the nuclear arms race.

John Tirman, Director of the Winston Foundation for World Peace, observed in an article in the *Los Angeles Times:* "It was the massive demonstrations in Europe in 1981 that first riveted attention on the new and perilous nuclear stand-off on the Continent. At the same time, a similar if less strident movement was spreading through the United States, coalescing in 6,000 local groups that forcefully articulated their concerns: speaking to neighbors, writing pamphlets, lobbying Congress. Nuclear-freeze resolutions were placed on city and state ballots, and were victorious in nearly every test. A citizens' diplomacy grew quickly as well, establishing sister cities with the Soviet Union, beaming televised space bridges around the world, sending delegations to Moscow. . . . The peace community is now a permanent fixture in the constellation of American politics, emitting its own light and exerting a powerful gravitational force."

If the millions of people now belonging to such groups—and to the peace fellowships of the churches, and to such organizations as the Nuclear Age Peace Foundation, the Beyond War group, the Institute for Noetic Sciences, the Union of Concerned Scientists, Common Cause, the Center for a Post-Modern World, and others—decided to participate actively in the search for presidential candidates that effort would certainly gather immense momentum.

A recent editorial in *Science* shows that many people are thinking along these lines. Daniel E. Koshland, Jr., editor of that periodical (published by the American Association for the Advancement of Science) offered some excellent ideas in this editorial: "The time has come to adopt a more scientific method for selecting presidents. The recent debate over the roles of character versus issues has highlighted the fact that issues actually get short shrift in any presidential campaign. Everyone says that we should discuss the issues, but practically no one does. The reason is that most pronouncements on issues are duller than daytime television. . . .

"To improve the selection process, a genuine objective test would require each candidate to devise a total federal budget. In that way, the candidate could no longer hide behind platitudes and would have to reveal his or her priorities . . . Advocates of increasing the budget in any category would have to name the new taxes they would levy or confess that the total deficit would be increased. Those who stated that they would reduce military or welfare budgets would have to indicate how, by how much, and where the money was to be shifted. . . .

"Those weak of heart would say that their candidates would refuse to follow this procedure, but in recent years candidates have learned that they must provide their income tax returns and financial statements, that they are expected to take part in public debates, and that their private lives are fair game. Persistent questions (mainly from reporters) demanding hard decisions instead of soporific cliches would lead some candidates to take forthright stands and shame others into following suit. . . ."

This suggestion by the editor of *Science* is certainly worth discussing. The annual federal budget has an enormous impact on every American and on people all over the Earth. President Truman used to spend many hours in going over his annual budgets with members of the press. He thought the people were entitled to a full and fair examination of his proposals and priorities. No other presidents have attempted to imitate him, but candidates in this age of crisis should be asked to present their proposed budgets.

The editor is right in saying that "the time has come" to adopt a better method for selecting presidents. It is doubtful that a completely "scientific" method can be found, but it seems obvious that new avenues must be explored.

An imaginative, open, and vigorous search for men and women who might be presidents—with many opportunities for many people to become aware of their abilities and their ideas—might break the lethargy which afflicts many Americans who have abstained from voting and withdrawn from the whole process of choosing candidates. Yet the choice of candidates through an open system is essential for the continued existence of a representative democracy.

If it did nothing else, such a search might make millions of people aware of their powers and responsibilities as citizens in a revived democracy. By participating in this effort, the people could prepare themselves to meet the tremendous ecological, economic, and social challenges which are converging upon all residents of this planet.

The challenges cannot be evaded. People in many countries are stirring and demanding the right to participate in shaping their future. Here in the United States—which has just celebrated 200 years of constitutional government—new avenues for participation must be opened.

II. STRATEGY IN THE NUCLEAR AGE

I believe that the successful negotiation of a Comprehensive Test Ban Treaty (CTB) is the simplest and quickest way of moving forward to lessen the constant threat of nuclear war. A CTB would halt that aspect of the arms race that is most threatening, the qualitative improvement of nuclear weapons. There is a critical need to take concrete steps to reverse the continuing build-up of nuclear weapons and it is important to focus on one step that everyone can understand. A CTB is so simple: we just stop testing. That's it. Testing is absolutely necessary to improve weapons; so, without testing, weapons would be frozen at their present state. They couldn't be improved and new kinds of weapons couldn't be developed. It's a first step, one upon which we could build our efforts to eliminate the threat of nuclear annihilation.

"A CTB is absolutely essential if the tenuous nonproliferation regime, which prevents the quantitative spread of nuclear weapons to nonnuclear states, now in effect is not to unravel. At the insistence of the nonnuclear weapon states, the superpowers pledged in both the Limited Test Ban Treaty (LTBT) of 1963 and the Non-Proliferation Treaty (NPT) of 1970 that they would move earnestly and quickly to end all nuclear testing; we have not followed through on this pledge. In my view, a CTB is the litmus test of whether a nuclear power is serious about arms limitations. If we had been able to negotiate a CTB with the USSR in 1963, when it was necessary to settle for a Limited Test Ban, we and the rest of the world would now be much more secure. We are negotiating today at a higher and more dangerous level. It would be to our great advantage to achieve a Comprehensive Test Ban now, before we proceed to an even higher and still more dangerous level.

—Glenn T. Seaborg
Nobel Laureate in Chemistry

ADMIRAL GENE R. LA ROCQUE

8. The Role of the Military

The central problem of our time—as I view it—is how to employ human intelligence for the salvation of mankind. It is a problem we have put upon ourselves. For we have defiled our intellect by the creation of such scientific instruments of destruction that we are now in desperate danger of destroying ourselves.

—General Omar N. Bradley, November 5, 1957

Now, electronics and other processes of science have raised the destructive potential to encompass millions. And with relentless hands we work feverishly in dark laboratories to find the means to destroy all at one blow.

But this very triumph of scientific annihilation—this very success of invention—has destroyed the possibility of war's being a medium for the practical settlement of international differences. The enormous destruction to both sides of closely matched opponents makes it impossible for even the winner to translate it into anything but his own disaster.

Global war has become a Frankenstein to destroy both sides. No longer is it a weapon of adventure—the shortcut to international power. If you lose, you are annihilated. If you win, you stand only to lose. No longer does it possess even the chance of the winner of a duel. It contains now only the germs of double suicide.

—General Douglas MacArthur, July 5, 1961

As a military man who has given half a century of active service I say in all sincerity that the nuclear arms race has no military purpose. Wars cannot be fought with nuclear weapons. Their existence only adds to our perils because of the illusions which they have generated.

There are powerful voices around the world who still give credence to the old Roman concept—if you desire peace, prepare for war. This is absolute nuclear nonsense and I repeat—it is a disastrous miscon-

113

ception to believe that by increasing the total uncertainty one increases one's own certainty.

—Lord Mountbatten, August 1979

Admiral Gene La Rocque was the 1985 recipient of the Nuclear Age Peace Foundation's Distinguished Peace Leadership Award. This chapter is based upon his speech in accepting the award. The admiral, as one connected with the military for nearly fifty years, in positions ranging from commander of a nuclear-armed ship to a Pentagon planner of nuclear and conventional warfare, is particularly well qualified to address the issue of "The Role of the Military in the Nuclear Age."

Admiral La Rocque is the founder and director of the Center for Defense Information in Washington, D.C. The Center is a non-profit educational organization headed by retired United States military officers. The organization, while supporting a strong defense, opposes excessive expenditures for weapons and policies that increase the danger of nuclear war. In applying a military perspective from outside of government to major strategic measures of the day, the Center for Defense Information has played a unique and important role in educating American citizens on the dangers of a continued nuclear arms race.

In this chapter Admiral La Rocque states bluntly that "fighting a nuclear war is utterly insane." He also tells us that fighting and winning a nuclear war is the task that the military thinks we have given them. If we want the situation to be otherwise, we—as citizens of a great democracy—must participate in redefining the role of the military in the nuclear age.

For nearly fifty years my profession has been one of war, not statesmanship. When I was seventeen years old, the army first put a rifle in my hands, and I've spent the rest of my life in military organizations. Next year that will be an even fifty years. I went from the infantry to the horse cavalry (yes, we had horses), to the army air corps, to the United States Navy and then chose Pearl Harbor to welcome the Japanese. My active duty spans three wars. My last active combat, actual combat, was Vietnam. So for fifty years I've dedicated my intellect and my energies to preparing for wars, fighting in wars and analyzing wars. I'm here to tell you tonight that war is a very dumb way to settle differences between nations. And nuclear war is utterly insane.

I'm supposed to talk tonight about the role of the military in the Nuclear Age. As always, the role of the military is the same—it is to fight and win wars. That's our job. That's what you have asked us to do. Our success depends on our professionalism, and a professional military force is one that kills and destroys efficiently. An unprofessional force kills inefficiently, ineffectively.

I want to tell you, we've got one of the most professional military forces in the world. Each branch of the service—the army, the navy, the air force and the marine corps—is striving always for greater professionalism. That professionalism leads us to try to acquire better and better weapons; that is, more destructive weapons, weapons that kill and destroy more efficiently. It is for that reason that we're building more and more nuclear weapons. You see, the urge to acquire better weapons leads us to the acquisition of nuclear weapons. Why? Because nuclear weapons are the best weapons man has ever invented.

Some of my colleagues tell me nuclear weapons can never be used, but nuclear weapons are desired by every branch of the military service because they are the most efficient way to kill and destroy. You may have forgotten—many of you may not—but in World War II we killed 50 million people. We civilized human beings killed 50 million people. so, you see, it's not a great big jump to be talking about killing hundreds of millions.

So pervasive have nuclear weapons become in or military today that they are now the conventional weapons. We've nuclearized our army divisions, our air wings, and 80 percent of U.S. Navy warships routinely carry nuclear weapons. When you see a warship off your coast, if it's a U.S. Navy warship, you've got an 80 percent chance that it is floating around with nuclear weapons.

When I had command of a guided missile cruiser, the Providence, in 1964, we used to ride up and down your coast with nuclear weapons. We were one of the first to get them on surface ships, and when I had command nobody told me I couldn't use them. Nobody said I had to get a message from anybody to use them. They were my main battery. They were, in fact, the only weapons that I had to shoot down a Soviet or any other enemy missile or aircraft that were any good. As a matter of fact, while I'm mentioning that, the only way that we could destroy a Soviet submarine today is with a nuclear weapon. The only way the Soviets can destroy one of our submarines today is with a nuclear weapon. The old fashioned depth charges are gone. We have nuclearized our military forces.

We've got them, you'll say, but we're never going to use them. Well, the United States and the Soviet Union are both planning, training, arming and practicing for nuclear war everyday.

We Are On A Collision Course

Okay, you say, but are we going to have nuclear war? Yes, we are. We are going to have a nuclear war if we stay on this course. We and the Soviet Union are on a collision course. They're trying to expand. We're trying to control them. We don't like their economic system. They're anti-God. We don't like their political system. We don't like anything about them, and we and the Soviets are on a collision course. It is a course which is going to lead to nuclear war if we stay on it.

Our Secretary of Defense has identified the Soviet Union as the enemy. Our President says the Soviet Union is an evil empire and ought to be relegated to the ash heap of history. Our Vice-President says we can fight and win a nuclear war. We're dramatically increasing the number of nuclear weapons we have. You and I are building five nuclear weapons a day. In a ten year period, we're building 17,000 new nuclear weapons. There's eight billion dollars this year in the Department of Energy budget for the sole purpose of building nuclear weapons. If you don't want them there, do something about it. If you don't want to build those nuclear weapons, then the control you have is not to spend the $8 billion to build them this year. We are also building many new vehicles to carry those nuclear weapons to the Soviet Union, as if we didn't already have more than enough.

Nuclear war can start by accident. We may very well work with the Nuclear Age Peace Foundation to try to find ways to prevent an accidental start of a nuclear war. Nuclear war can start by miscalculation, computer error, electronic malfunction, or it can start by design. Don't forget: Maggie Thatcher can start a nuclear war. So can Mitterand. So can the Chinese. So can the Russians. So can we. Give us another fifteen years to the end of this century, and there'll be a lot more countries that can start a nuclear war.

Everybody says that they don't want a nuclear war. But both sides are acting as if they did. If we stay on this course, we're going to have a nuclear war. But we don't have to, and that's where I think the Nuclear Age Peace Foundation and all of you come in. We don't have to stay on this course but you'd better do something. Can you win a nuclear war? No. No way to win it. But our Vice-President said we could. He thought we could. When our President, Mr. Reagan, submitted his budget to the Congress of the United States for fiscal year 1983, here is what the budget report said: "The military posture of the United States is to give us the capability to fight successfully a conventional and a nuclear war."

That's what we're arming for: to fight successfully a nuclear war. That's why we're building the MX, the Trident

117

II, the Pershing II, and yes, the Star Wars Strategic Defense Initiative. We are trying to find a way to fight and win a nuclear war, and we're building the weapons to do it. We're not satisfied with simply providing a retaliatory capability to deter an attack. We want to prevail in a nuclear war, which is what Mr. Weinberger says publicly often.

I was giving a talk at one of our major war colleges a couple of years ago to colonels, captains, generals and admirals, and I said, "Look, fellows, we're all professionals. You know, I know, there's no way to fight and win a nuclear war, right?" I finished my lecture, and a colonel gets up and says, "Admiral, you're right. We don't know how to fight and win a nuclear war. But it's our job to *find* a way to win a nuclear war!" That's what's driving the arms race. I said, "Colonel, I understand where you're coming from. Sure, you and I didn't join this outfit to fight a war to a draw. We didn't join this outfit to lose a war, but you ought to level with the American public. Tell them you don't know how to win a nuclear war, and stop trying to fool them by suggesting that if they'll give you thousands of more nuclear weapons and billions of more dollars that you can find a way to win a nuclear war." There isn't a way. That's the dangerous part of Mr. Reagan's Strategic Defense Initiative.

You hear a lot of people, even in the military, talk about controlling a nuclear war. "We're gonna use a few nukes, and they'll use a few nukes. We're gonna control it." That is just *crazy*. Once you start exploding nuclear weapons, the lid is off. You see, it takes only one country to start a nuclear war: The British, the French, the Chinese, the Russians, ourselves. But what does it take to stop a nuclear war once you've started one in Europe? It takes an agreement among four nations, the British, the French, the Russians, and ourselves to stop—otherwise somebody will keep exploding nuclear weapons.

If we have a nuclear war, we can't win it. Can we survive it? I don't know. Nobody knows. That's the tragedy of it—

nobody knows. Anybody that tells you that this many people are going to be killed and this many are going to survive doesn't know what he's talking about. I'll tell you why. We've only exploded one nuclear weapon at a time in the history of man. We know what happened in Nagasaki—it killed 100,000 people and destroyed a city with a little peanut of a bomb. But what we don't know is what is going to happen when thousands of nuclear weapons go off in the United States, the Soviet Union, Europe, and God knows where else. We simply don't know. There *may* be some survivors. The only question is, really, whether or not the plants and animals on this planet will survive. They may well not.

We're getting closer to a war we don't want, a war we can't control, a war in which we can't defend ourselves, a war we can't win, and a war we probably can't survive. So what do we do? Mr. Reagan's idea is to build a Strategic Defense Initiative, and try to defend ourselves. I don't think that's going to work. It's going to waste a lot of money. It's a theft from the American public because there is no way to defend a country against nuclear weapons. There are too many ways to get around the defense; too many ways to deliver nuclear weapons.

Is the United Nations going to solve our problems? No. A hundred and sixty countries there, and they're not going to solve them either. I wish they could, but when we ask can the U.N. do it, we're really saying: "Will somebody else solve our problems?" Nobody else is going to.

Einstein said that we had to have new ways of thinking. I think Einstein was right, but only half right. I think we must find new ways of acting, not just a new way of thinking! We must *act* as if there are nuclear weapons around. Yes, we may have to think differently, but we must find some new ways of acting in this world or we're going to blow ourselves up and end the whole thing.

We Have a Tremendous Responsibility

We have a tremendous responsibility. We're the most powerful country in the world. We started this whole thing! We invented the atomic bomb. We blew up Hiroshima and Nagasaki. We're three to five years ahead of the Soviets in the development in every strategic weapon system that has been built. We're still ahead of them, and we're determined to stay ahead of them. We have a certain arrogance that wants us to stay ahead when it has become meaningless. Once both sides can destroy each other, who is ahead has lost all significance. But we keep the arms race going. We keep building more sophisticated weapons that can arrive more quickly on target. That's not so bad, you say, that's just technology—but it puts a hair trigger on the response of both sides.

There is an inherent danger in this continual build-up of better and more destructive weapons. We may be the most powerful country in the world, but we're only 5 percent of the world's population. We're only one of 160 countries. We don't run the world anymore. We ran it for awhile, but we don't run it anymore. We're going to have to adjust to the fact that we're one of 160 countries and 5 percent of the world's population; and there are some wonderful things going on in other countries—as wonderful as ours is.

I've been to 86 countries in this business, and everywhere I go I find nice people like all of you. They want to make love, they want to listen to the radio, they want to play tennis, they want to do their own thing. They are not very much concerned about ideological, economic and political differences. They want to live their lives very quietly.

I think that you need to do something every day if you want to avert a nuclear war. You ought to be writing your Congressman. Oh, that's old stuff, you say. I've got a better idea that I want to suggest to you. There is one thing in this country that is different from other countries, and that is simply this: You can call the White House. You can't call the Kremlin; you can't call the Blue House in Korea; but you can call the White House. And I want to suggest that you do that on any weekday from nine to five. I call every week. When you call, they'll answer: "White House, Executive Office," and you say, "I'd like to speak to the Comment Section, please." Then say, "I want to tell Mr. Reagan to please not buy more nuclear weapons." And the lady will say, "yes, thank you, anything else?" Say that you'll call him next week about something else. I know about this because my wife, Lili, was a volunteer in the White House under Mr. Carter. They do keep records. Here's the telephone number, and you don't even have to write it down. Just call Washington, area code 202, then 4-5-6 (everybody can remember 4,5,6), and then the others are 76-39. You see, I'm 76, and Lili's 39. Now give the President a call; it's a very exciting and wonderful experience in participatory democracy because after you've called the White House a couple of times, you'll want to start calling everybody else, and that's good. The more people you call, the better off we're going to be.

I say do something every week. People often say to me, what should I do? What can I do? Well, I would say do whatever you feel comfortable doing. If you feel like a Daniel Berrigan or somebody else, go do that. If you feel like writing letters, do that. But you must do something. Join a group. If you don't belong to the Nuclear Age Peace Foundation, you ought to. One thing you have to do is give a little money to them. My mother sends us three dollars every year, and I promise her I'm going to spend it wisely. If you do not do anything, if *we* do not do anything, we're going to spend the rest of our years in perpetual fear and tension, draining the wealth of our nation, or we're going to have a nuclear war. And neither of those options is very nice to contemplate. Perpetual fear and tension, or nuclear war. So we must do something.

121

We have a great deal of pride in our country, and we should have. But it's *our* country, and I sometimes wonder when we talk about "our leaders" whether or not in fact we have any leaders in a democracy. I think it's a cop-out sometimes when we talk about "our leaders." We're the leaders! Mr. Reagan is on your payroll. He's on my payroll; I've hired him to go to Washington to work for four years, and renewed his contract for another four. He works for us; he works for you and he works for me. So I end on this note: the role of the military is very much the same in peacetime in preparation for the so-called non-nuclear war as it is in the preparation for nuclear war. The military is trying to fight and win a nuclear war. That's the job we've given them. That's the job they think you pay them to perform. But I would submit to you that war, as Clemenceau said, is much too important to be left to the generals, and survival is too important to be left to anyone but us.

Question: The military industrial complex seems to have a lot of power over Congress. Do you see any way to convert the complex in any meaningful way?

Admiral La Rocque: That's a very good question. When I came into the navy in 1940 the navy made everything itself. We made our own ships, our planes, our guns, our paint, our rope, our uniforms—we made it all! We did not make it for profit. Maybe we didn't make it very efficiently, I don't know, but we did not make it for profit and we didn't have a great deal of influence on the Congress. Now we don't make anything anymore in the military. We've given our arsenals and everything else over to civilian control for *profit.* It's all big business and, you're absolutely right, they have a tremendous influence on the Congress. A Congressman wants to get re-elected. So he listens to those people who come to him to build weapons, who make contributions to his campaign. It is a bit of a dilemma. After all, the Congressman is the representative. So we can't fault him or her too much either. He or she is representing their constituents, and their constituents have jobs in industries that want to make a profit. So that is a dilemma.

I will tell you what we have been suggesting. I've been testifying in the Congress that *we ought to take the profit out of preparing for war.* As long as you are making a profit, I think we'll keep building up. But there is no reason, in my view, for a little old man from upper state New York to be making a profit on General Electric stock when General Electric is making weapons designed to defend General Electric! There shouldn't be a profit motive there. Now, how do you do it? We can treat defense production like a public utility, and give it a 10 percent profit. You see you don't necessarily make a lot of money making weapons, but you can't lose if you are building weapons for the military. You are certain to not only break even, but to make a handsome profit if not a great big one.

Question: How do you feel about American foreign policy and our involvement with the Third World?

Admiral La Rocque: In 1947, this great nation of ours changed course. We did it consciously with a law in 1947, the National Security Act of 1947. We became a national security state. One of the things we did at that time was to provide for dividing up the *whole* world into military districts. We're the only country in the history of the world that has ever done it to this day. There is a Commander-in-Chief Pacific, a Commander-in-Chief Atlantic, a Commander-in-Chief Europe, a Commander-in-Chief South, a Commander-in-Chief Middle East, and so on. Now what happens when a problem occurs in a Third World country? The commander looks through his military binoculars and he sees a military problem, so he's got an immediate military solution. That generates a requirement for him to collect intelligence, have supplies, troops ready to fight, and something called a *Rapid Deployment Force.* That sounds almost benign, doesn't it? You know, quick start, dash off somewhere: Rapid Deployment Force. What that means is, we're going to send a lot of

123

soldiers, sailors, marines and airmen to go someplace to kill people, destroy their homes, blow up their bridges—very rapidly. I would submit that in terms of dealing with other countries as far as the military is concerned, we need a *Slow Deployment Force.* In other words, if we're going to kill a bunch of kids somewhere and destroy homes and factories, we ought to go very carefully, cautiously, deliberately, and know why we're doing it and say it's all worthwhile. Perhaps in that process we'll decide that it isn't necessary.

I think that we ought to let other countries decide what kind of political system they want and what kind of economic system they want. I don't think we ought to be supporting dictators anywhere.

I would like us to be interventionists everywhere in the world. I would like to intervene everywhere with whatever benefits we've had from living in this land—health care, education, housing. We also need to learn from those people, learn how their cultures have prospered in the past, learn from their mistakes and their successes. We ought to be actively involved everywhere in the world all the time, but not militarily.

DIETRICH FISCHER

9. No First Use of Nuclear Weapons

In this chapter Dietrich Fischer discusses the concept of no first use of nuclear weapons. The basic premise is that if all nuclear weapons powers agree not to use nuclear weapons first, then nuclear war will never be deliberately initiated. But, you may question, what if a leader of a nuclear weapons power lies, and only says he will not use nuclear weapons first with no intention of keeping his word? Fischer deals with this question by pointing out that a credible policy of no first use will entail a strategy of "transarmament," that is, a shift from offensive to defensive armaments. He makes a convincing argument that transarmament is a "unilateral step that increases common security." The ultimate reason that a no first use policy will be adhered to is that it provides a strong incentive to the other side not to use their weapons first.

Most Americans believe that the United States already has a policy of no first use of nuclear weapons, but we do not. We are still pursuing the development and enhancement of offensive weapons systems with a first strike potential. And we continue to rely for defense on nuclear as well as conventional forces. The threat of use of nuclear weapons is an extremely dangerous strategy which could lead to disaster. A policy of no first use based on self-interest and transarmament could provide a needed buffer while agreements are being achieved to reduce and eventually eliminate nuclear weapons.

According to a recent opinion poll,[1] 81 percent of the American people believe that the United States' policy is never to use nuclear weapons first (and 4 percent are unsure). The vast majority, 76 percent against 19 percent, strongly support a policy of no first use.[2] (A remarkably sizable minority, 33 against 62 percent, even advocate that the United States should *never* use nuclear weapons under any circumstances, not even in retaliation against a nuclear attack.)[3] However, it has long been official U.S. policy to resort to the first use of nuclear weapons, if deemed necessary, in case of a conventional attack in places such as Europe or Korea.

NATO commander General Bernard Rogers has written: "The basis of NATO's military planning is security through credible deterrence. There must be clearly perceived linkages among conventional, theater and strategic nuclear legs of NATO's triad of forces in order to maintain an incalculable risk for any aggressor. Should aggression occur, the Alliance would conduct a forward defense of NATO territory, responding as necessary with direct defense, deliberate escalation, and general nuclear release, to keep the level of violence consistent with maintaining the territorial integrity of all NATO members,"[4]

Some even advocate that nuclear weapons should be used early in a battle. For example, when a member of the U.S. State Department said at a conference in 1981 that if NATO were facing defeat in a conventional war in Europe, it might have to resort to the first use of nuclear weapons, he was criticized by an American officer assigned to NATO, who replied that this was not true—NATO would not wait until it was losing! Nuclear weapons formed an integral part of NATO's arsenal and in case of war they would be used right from the outset.

This brief essay critically examines some of the arguments that have been made against a policy of no first use of nuclear weapons.

The idea of no first use has a long history. In 1958, Carl Friedrich von Weizsaecker argued: If I have for my defense only a weapon that kills me at the same time as the attacker, it can deter someone who wants to kill me, since in that case

126

I might well use my weapon, if only to drag him to death along with me. But if someone intends to steal my briefcase, he will not be deterred, since no one is going to blow himself up for the sake of his briefcase.[5] In 1962, Helmut Schmidt, who later became Chancellor of the Federal Republic of Germany, wrote: "Successful defense [must be] possible without resort to nuclear weapons... unless the enemy launches his attack to the accompaniment of nuclear weapons."[6] In 1963, Robert C. Tucker and Richard A. Falk argued in favor of no first use.[7] Tucker pointed out that the United States maintained the same policy, for example, with regard to poison gas. In 1972, Richard H. Ullman stressed that a policy of no first use of nuclear weapons could be adopted unilaterally, since in case of a war it would automatically put pressure on an opponent to follow the same policy, regardless of what he might have declared.[8]

A policy of no first use began to be debated widely when four high ranking former U.S. government officials advocated it in a famous article in *Foreign Affairs* in Spring 1982.[9] They advocated a gradual strengthening of the conventional defense capabilities of NATO so that Western Europe could defend itself against a potential Soviet invasion without resort to first use of nuclear weapons. They were also concerned that internal disagreement about the policy of using nuclear weapons first could cause strains within NATO and weaken it.

In June 1982, the Soviet Union made a unilateral declaration before the United Nations Second Special Session on Disarmament that it would never be the first to use nuclear weapons, and it invited other nuclear armed nations to do the same. China has declared that it would never be the first to use nuclear weapons ever since it first tested a nuclear bomb in 1964.

If all nuclear powers were to adhere to a policy of no first use of nuclear weapons, *and* would also effectively prevent their accidental use, there would never be any nuclear war.

127

So far, the United States, Great Britain and France have refused to make any such pledge. Three reasons for this position have been advanced:

1. NATO is inferior to the Warsaw Pact in terms of conventional military strength and therefore must rely on the threat of using nuclear weapons first to deter a conventional Soviet attack on Western Europe; relying on a purely conventional defense against conventional aggression would be too expensive;

2. a no first-use pledge would be a meaningless propaganda exercise and an opponent would not rely on it in any case; and

3. even if the Soviet Union signed a mutual no first use agreement, we could not trust that it would respect it in case of war. These three reasons will be examined here in turn.

Strengthening Conventional Defense

There is little doubt that the threat to use nuclear weapons first, if it is believed, makes a deliberate conventional attack by a potential aggressor less likely. But if it fails to deter war, the result may be the total destruction of both sides. It is as if someone tried to deter burglary by packing his own house full of explosives and putting a trip wire around it that would automatically blow up the house in case an unauthorized intruder tried to approach it. This would kill the burglar, but of course also the people living in the house. There exist better methods to prevent burglary, such as having police patrols or good locks. Similarly, an adequate conventional defense is far preferable to prevent conventional aggression than a threat to commit nuclear suicide.

Former Defense Secretary Robert S. McNamara has criticized the strategy of "flexible response" which seeks to deter a conventional attack on NATO by threatening the first use of battlefield nuclear weapons. If the Soviet Union reciprocated, the United States would escalate to an exchange of strategic nuclear weapons. McNamara wrote: "The ultimate sanction, ... the launch of strategic nuclear weapons against the Soviet homeland ... would be an act of suicide ... One cannot build a credible deterrent on an incredible action ... Nuclear weapons serve no military purpose whatsoever. They are totally useless—except only to deter one's opponent from using them."[10]

Even the possession of a monopoly on nuclear weapons does not always deter conventional aggression. Stalin initiated the blockade of Berlin in 1948 when the United States was the only country in the world to possess any nuclear weapons. And the British nuclear submarines did not deter the Argentine military Junta from invading the Falkland Islands/Malvinas in 1982. A threat to use nuclear weapons first might be considered by an opponent to be merely a bluff. In that case, we face the dilemma of either capitulating or escalating to nuclear war.

Even more dangerous than an open threat to use nuclear weapons first is to adopt such a policy without publicly announcing it. This would be a scenario for Dr. Strangelove. In that film, the Soviet Union had secretly built a doomsday machine, which would automatically destroy the whole world if the Soviet Union suffered a nuclear attack. Since the Soviet government failed to announce this measure in time (it wanted to wait until the next party congress), the machine failed to deter an attack and the world was destroyed.

Far preferable to a threat of using nuclear weapons first is to deter conventional aggression with an adequate conventional defense. Such a deterrent is more credible, because it is not suicidal.

To deter aggression, it is not necessary to have military superiority over an opponent, nor to have numerical equivalence in all weapons categories. All that is necessary is to make aggression so costly *compared to the benefits an aggres-*

sor might expect to gain, that it does not appear worthwhile. The armies of Sweden and Switzerland were clearly inferior to the German army during the Second World War. Yet they were able to dissuade a German invasion, because their defense was sufficiently strong relative to the small advantage that Hitler might have hoped to gain from occupying them. They also deliberately sought to minimize the potential gains of an aggressor by preparing to paralyze their industries and refuse cooperation with a foreign occupation force.[11] Similarly, Yugoslavia was able to dissuade Stalin from a military intervention in 1948, when it broke with Moscow politically, because it was prepared to fight a long partisan war in case of a foreign occupation. McGeorge Bundy writes: "Those who think that either political will or less-than-nuclear strength is unimportant in such matters will find instruction in considering the record of Yugoslavia under Tito. If Tito could stave off the Soviet Union, must NATO fail?"[12]

Would it be too expensive for NATO to shift to a purely conventional defense against conventional aggression? Even if it was more expensive, a clear majority of the American public would be willing to pay more. Sixty-six percent against 25 percent said that they were willing to pay higher taxes if the United States and the Soviet Union sharply reduced their nuclear weapons, but replaced them with more expensive non-nuclear forces.[13]

Deliberate escalation to a nuclear war would be suicidal. Thus, if survival is at stake, cost considerations must become secondary. But in reality, a strong conventional defense is *not* more expensive than relying on nuclear weapons. The only two countries in Europe that stayed out of the Second World War were Sweden and Switzerland. They maintain a very strong conventional defense with mandatory military service for all adult males, and have *lower* military budgets than all of the nuclear armed nations. As a fraction of GNP, military expenditures in 1982 were 2.0

percent in Switzerland, 3.3 percent in Sweden, 4.2 percent for France, 5.1 percent for the United Kingdom, 6.4 percent for the United States, 7.1 percent for China, and 15 percent for the Soviet Union (according to U.S. government estimates).[14] This refutes a claim that a credible conventional defense is economically unattainable.

Transarmament

It is important to make a distinction between conventional offensive and defensive forces. Offensive forces can be used to carry out aggression, whereas purely defensive forces can only be used to prevent aggression. For example, tanks with long range mobility can be used to invade territory and are therefore offensive. Antitank weapons in fixed positions can only be used to stop an invasion and are therefore defensive. Only conventional *defensive* forces should be strengthened to help prevent war. Increasing offensive capabilities can on the contrary precipitate the outbreak of war, as will be illustrated.

NATO is currently debating the adoption of the strategic concept called "Air Land Battle 2000." It calls for counterattacks deep into Eastern Europe in case of a conventional attack on Western Europe. It calls for highly mechanized forces that can rapidly penetrate across a border, and for conventional rockets that can destroy follow-up forces and supply lines inside Eastern Europe. While a greater reliance on conventional rather than nuclear weapons is desirable, building more conventional *offensive* arms is the wrong answer. It could lead to the rapid escalation of a small border incident into a big war. Let us consider how this might happen.

The Soviet Union has announced a similar strategy. It has stated that since it has been invaded from the West three times in this century, if there was another war in Europe, it would make every effort to prevent the war being fought on

131

its own soil. In case of an invasion, it would bring rapid reinforcements to push the fighting back across the border. If both sides adopt such a "forward" defense with the aim to have any fighting take place on the other side of the border, the situation is highly explosive. A little spark, a mere accident, could start World War III.

Imagine, for example, that an American helicopter strays inadvertently into East Germany and is shot down. The crew survives and the United States demands their immediate release. The Soviet Union detains them and announces it will hold a public trial. The United States sends a rescue mission to free the crew. The rescue team encounters armed resistance. A tank column is sent into East Germany to assist the rescue team. Soviet tanks push the column back into West Germany and occupy some Western territory near the border. NATO sets into motion the Air Land Battle doctrine and attacks supply lines inside East Germany, while pushing the invasion force back into Eastern Europe. The Soviet Union and its allies stage a general mobilization, and World War III has begun.

This scenario may appear far-fetched and unrealistic. But as long as both sides maintain a strategy of *escalating* fighting once it has begun, there are numerous ways a war could start. If there is a war, both sides usually claim, and often believe, that the other side has started it. There is always *something* that the other side did first. For example, in the Mideast war of 1967, Israel maintains that Egypt started the war when it blocked Israeli vessels' access to the Bay of Aqaba. Egypt maintains that Israel started the war when it subsequently bombed Egyptian airfields. In order to stop a war rapidly if it should ever break out, it is important to adopt a policy that helps deëscalate the fighting.

One way to deëscalate war if it should ever start is to maintain a strong defense, while deliberately avoiding offensive capabilities. For example, in the scenario above, if NATO had plenty of antitank and antiaircraft weapons in fixed positions along the central front in Europe, the Soviet Union could not advance into NATO territory. New precision-guided munitions can offer an advantage to the defender. If NATO also deliberately limited its tank and bomber forces which might be able to carry out offensive operations, the Soviet Union would see no need to push across the border out of fear that otherwise it might be attacked. Therefore it is in NATO's own interest not to be misperceived as a threat to the security of the Warsaw Pact nations. (The same applies in reverse.) The best way to convince an opponent that we have purely defensive aims is not to build offensive capabilities in the first place. What we cannot do, we certainly will not do.

A shift from offensive to defensive arms is neither armament, nor disarmament, but can be called *transarmament*. (This term is sometimes also used to denote a shift from military to nonmilitary forms of defense.) Transarmament has the advantage that it can be undertaken unilaterally, without risk. Whereas unilateral disarmament would weaken our security and thus possibly invite aggression, transarmament reduces the danger of war and therefore increases the security of *both* sides, even if only one side makes a move. It is a unilateral step that increases common security. Unlike mutual disarmament, it need not wait for the successful outcome of lengthly negotiations. Kenneth Boulding once remarked that agreement is a scarce resource, and if we can improve the situation without depending on agreement, we should not wait.

Is the strategic defense initiative (SDI, or "star wars") a form of transarmament, a shift from offensive to defensive arms? It may appear so on the surface, but it is in fact the opposite. While a defense against nuclear missiles *alone* would threaten no one, a combination of offensive missiles with a defensive shield is even more threatening than nuclear missiles alone. If one side possesses nuclear missiles but is vulnerable to retaliation, it would be totally irrational

133

to use those missiles first and invite suicide. In that situation, the only sensible purpose of these missiles is to deter a potential opponent from using nuclear weapons. But if a country is protected against nuclear missiles (or merely believes, falsely, that it is protected), it can then threaten to use its nuclear weapons first, without fear of retaliation. This is why the United States is so afraid that the Soviet Union could gain an advantage with strategic defense. For the same reason, we must understand why the Soviet Union is so afraid of SDI. A combination of nuclear weapons with defense against retaliation is an extremely offensive system. Proceeding with SDI would therefore inevitably lead to a further spiral in the arms race.

Restructuring Nuclear Forces

The second argument that has been made against a no first use policy is that such a promise would be meaningless. James Schlesinger, defense secretary in the Ford Administration, when asked why the United States had not declared that it would never be the first to use nuclear weapons, replied that in case of a war, in the heat of battle, nobody would want to rely on any such promise made by an opponent. Therefore there was no use in making such a pledge.

It is, of course, true that a mere promise cannot be relied on. But this does not mean that a policy of no first use is therefore worthless. It only means that it must be made more convincing than through a mere pledge. The nuclear arsenals themselves must be restructured in such a way that a first use would never make any military sense, but that retaliation against a nuclear attack would remain possible, even after suffering a first strike.

A distinction is made between "first use" of one or a few nuclear weapons ("to show resolve") and a "first strike" which seeks to cripple the military potential of the opponent by destroying his nuclear weapons in a surprise attack. A limited first use would not necessarily remain limited, but could easily escalate to full-scale nuclear war. There is no guarantee that one side would capitulate as long as it still possessed nuclear weapons.

In order to deter a nuclear attack, two things must be made clear to a potential aggressor:

1. if he uses nuclear weapons, he faces retaliation, and
2. as long as he does not use them, he faces no danger of being attacked with nuclear weapons.

This has two implications for the design of missiles for nuclear deterrence:

1. a sufficient number must be able to survive an attack so that retaliation remains possible, and
2. we must deliberately avoid building nuclear missiles in such large numbers and of such accuracy that they pose a threat to the survival of the opponent's missiles.

There is widespread agreement on the first condition. But the second condition, which is equally important, often seems to be ignored by today's strategic planners, on both sides. The United States and the Soviet Union both have developed highly accurate missiles with multiple warheads (MIRVs, Multiple Independently-targetable Reentry Vehicles) that can destroy an opponent's nuclear missiles in their silos. But building such missiles makes sense only if they are intended for a first strike. Destroying an empty silo after its missile has been fired is militarily useless.

Building such missiles as the MX or the Soviet SS-18 which are vulnerable, in fixed positions, but at the same time pose an enormous threat to the other side, contribute nothing to deterrence. They undermine deterrence. Instead of signaling to an opponent "don't attack us with nuclear weapons or else you face the threat of retaliation" they give the reverse signal: "If you don't destroy these missiles you face a constant threat; if you destroy them, which is easy, you face a reduced threat." Giving such signals, even if unintended, is imprudent, to say the least.

Such a scenario has already precipitated a war, fortunately involving only conventional weapons. In 1967, both Israel and Egypt possessed vulnerable bomber fleets on open desert airfields. Each side knew that whoever struck first could destroy the opponent's fleet on the ground before it could take off. This was a highly volatile situation. When war appeared imminent, Israel did not want to take a chance and wait until the Egyptian air force might attack. It wiped out most of the Egyptian bombers on the ground in a surprise attack.

The most important step in a credible no first use policy is not to build first strike weapons. If our nuclear weapons are incapable of destroying an opponent's nuclear weapons, he will know that it would make no sense for us to use them first, and he will therefore not be tempted to seek to destroy our nuclear weapons out of fear of a surprise attack. If we also make our nuclear weapons survivable, the opponent will not dare to use his nuclear weapons first, regardless of whether he has officially announced such a policy or not.

Providing Incentives For Cooperation

The third argument that has been made against a policy of no first use is that we could not trust the Russians to adhere to their side of such a bargain. But it is not necessary to trust the Russians. A no first use policy is not something that we adopt as a favor for the Soviet Union, in return for a reciprocal favor. A no first use policy serves our own interests.

If we adhere to no first use, and make it credible, we provide a strong incentive for the Soviet Union not to use their nuclear weapons either. If they are afraid that during a war we might resort to the use of nuclear weapons at any moment, this would put them under strong temptation to seek to destroy our nuclear weapons in a sneak attack. They might do so not in the expectation of "gaining" anything (which would clearly be an illusion), but rather out of fear of suffering even greater losses if we attack first. If we make it clear that we would never attack first, that indeed it would make no sense for us to do so, then we provide no incentive for the Soviet Union to attack first during an acute international crisis.

An opponent will keep an agreement if it is in his or her interest to keep it. An American businessman who sells grain to the Soviet Union replied to the question whether he could trust the Russians to live up to contracts: "We do not trust their good will. When we write a contract, we write it in such a way that they would hurt their own interests if they broke it. We trust their self-interest."

Sometimes, we need not wait to negotiate any mutual agreement, but can take unilateral steps that reduce the danger of war, in our own interest. A NATO officer once proclaimed with deep conviction that it made sense to talk about confidence-building measures only if *both* sides were ready to adopt them. Clearly, it is preferable if both sides adopt such measures. But even if only one side instills greater confidence, it can improve its own security. For example, at the beginning of the Second World War, Switzerland unilaterally reaffirmed its policy of armed neutrality, that it would defend itself with all available means if attacked, but would not join the fighting unless it was attacked first. If it had waited for a reciprocal declaration of neutrality from Hitler's Germany, it would have waited in vain, to its own disadvantage.

A recent computer simulation study[15] has shown that the most effective strategies for eliciting cooperation from an opponent in a "prisoners' dilemma" game had the following four properties in common: (1) they never initiated hostility, (2) they did not accept hostile behavior passively but retaliated, (3) they did not retaliate excessively but were ready to cooperate again as soon as the other side did, and (4) they were simple and clear, so that an opponent knew what he was facing, and was not left guessing. These principles seem applicable to a far wider variety of situations.

Another application of these principles is a policy of "no first intervention."[16] We should announce to the Soviet Union that we will not intervene militarily in any third country as long as they will not. If we allow trouble spots all over the world to draw us into war, whether in allied countries or adversaries, we will constantly risk escalation to a larger war. Do we want to hand over the responsibility of whether our country is at war or peace to any small dictator? Allowing other countries to draw us into war is comparable to connecting a powderkeg to dozens of fuses, any one of which can go off at any moment. This is not a "security" policy but a national insecurity policy.

Initiating hostile behavior tends to backfire. To keep peace, it is not sufficient to make war disastrous for a potential opponent. It is equally important to make peace as attractive as possible. If we seek to make the present situation unbearable for an opponent, this reduces his incentive to keep such a peace. A secret U.S. defense guidance plan advocated fighting "an economic and technical war on the Soviet Union . . . as a peace time complement to military strategy."[17] Such a policy deters peace, not war.

During the big debate in 1969 on whether or not to build an antiballistic missile system, the argument was made that it was not technically feasible to build a defense against Soviet missiles, but this was not so important. The Soviet leadership was relatively reasonable and reliable. The great danger was the Chinese, they were so fanatic and unpredictable. Most important was to build a defense against Chinese nuclear missiles. Today we are hardly afraid of a Chinese nuclear attack, but not because of any antiballistic missile system. It is because we have normal relations with China.

There are over 13,000 Chinese students in the United States, and many Americans visit China. *Mutually beneficial relations are the best foundation of security.*

If we are perceived as a threat to the security of other countries, to the extent that they wish we would disappear from the face of the earth, and if they have the means to make us disappear, we are not very secure. On the contrary, to be secure, we should see to it that we are so useful to them, preferably even indispensable, that they would be very disappointed if we did disappear.

What We Can Do

Before a patient accepts a therapy, he must become aware that he is ill. But it is not enough to frighten him. He must also be offered hope. He must be shown that a therapy exists that works.

This implies a strategy for change: We must recognize the danger we face, and help others to recognize it, too. But we must not limit ourselves to criticizing existing policies. We must go beyond that and propose feasible, persuasive alternatives.

The vast majority, even among highly educated people, who believe that it is the United States' official policy never to use nuclear weapons first, must be made aware that this is not now our policy. Since there is already overwhelming support for such a policy, it should be possible to build a strong movement in favor of it. We must show that no first use of nuclear weapons is not a sacrifice on our part that we make in favor of the Soviet Union. It is an elementary measure for self-preservation.

We can write or call our elected officials to let them know of our concerns. Rather than writing an angry letter, it will be more effective to write a supportive letter when they have made a step in the right direction, asking them to go further. We can write to local newspapers, and talk to our friends and colleagues. We can join one of the many organizations working to create a safer world.[18]

We may sometimes hesitate for fear that we do not know enough technical details to participate in a discussion about defense policy. But the fundamental questions do not involve technical details about specific weapons systems, but rather an understanding of human nature, of how conflicts escalate and how they can be resolved without war. In that respect, all of us can equally contribute, whether we have access to classified information or not.

People who rise to positions of top leadership are not always representative of the average citizen. Those who have an unusually strong desire to exert influence over others and to dominate have a better than average chance to seek positions of leadership. But they are not always the best qualified to lead. (Of course, there exist many notable exceptions.) Some of our leaders are more interested in exerting power than the public at large is. If we leave it to such people alone to determine our foreign and defense policy, we may be led onto a dangerous course. If we, as citizens, do not take part in discussing these questions, certain people in leadership positions may be only too eager to decide for us, not necessarily the way we would have wished. It is our responsibility to speak up, or else we will never be heard.

We can point out that true security results from mutually beneficial cooperation in such areas as trade, scientific and cultural cooperation. We share many common problems with the Soviet Union which we can better resolve if we work together. We can search together for a cure to cancer and other diseases, can develop together new sources of energy, can jointly explore outer space. We need not put blind trust into anyone, but we can explore what gives other countries an incentive to cooperate with us. Intimidating others is not likely to lead them to cooperate.

Some people believe that if we sufficiently frighten the

Soviet leadership by building ever more nuclear weapons and threatening their first use, we can force them into making concessions. But the Soviet response may instead be a further buildup of their own nuclear arsenal, so that they could not be forced to give in. The situation resembles the game of "chicken" that is sometimes played by teenagers with automobiles. Two competitors drive toward one another at full speed. The one who swerves aside first to avoid a collision is the "chicken" who loses face among the gang. The one who is more daring and drives straight through is the winner. But if neither of them swerves in time, both are dead. Threatening the first use of nuclear weapons is comparable to playing a game of "nuclear chicken." But our leaders may tend to forget that they are not alone playing this game. And as Kenneth Boulding has remarked, "when you drive a schoolbus, you don't play chicken."

A policy of no first use of nuclear weapons is a relatively modest measure. But it is urgently needed. Initiating a nuclear war would be suicidal. Even the threat to escalate to nuclear war, without actually implementing it, could be suicidal, because it tends to invite a nuclear attack from an opponent in case of a conventional war or a serious international crisis.

A no first use policy is only a small, but essential first step toward a safer world. It is an immediately feasible measure that can give us some breathing space to implement more far-reaching changes in the world political system that have become necessary with the invention of nuclear weapons.

Continued reliance on nuclear deterrence is too risky. In John Kennedy's words, it is like Damocles' sword hanging constantly on a thin thread over all of our heads. The tragic explosion of the space shuttle Challenger with seven astronauts on board has vividly reminded us again that anything that can go wrong, ultimately will. Our fate resembles that of those astronauts, except that we are not volunteers.

141

Defense against nuclear weapons is impossible. Preparations to fight and "win" a nuclear war are insane. Even total nuclear disarmament, as difficult as it may appear, would not be sufficient, as long as nations continued to settle their disputes through war. Each side would be tempted to build nuclear weapons again in case of war, out of fear that the other side could do so first.

To guarantee human survival in the nuclear age, it has become necessary to eliminate war itself as an accepted human institution. Many say this is utopian. But to people living in earlier periods, the abolition of cannibalism, slavery, absolute monarchy, or colonialism appeared equally utopian. Yet those institutions have been changed. With determination and combined efforts, we can also eliminate war.

Seeing the enormous sums available to build weapons for war, and the modest resources available for peace efforts, we may be tempted to become gloomy. But we should not forget that during the last century the slave traders and slave owners made huge fortunes, while the people who fought for the abolition of slavery made personal sacrifices. Yet they prevailed in the end, because they were right. In the same way, the forces working for peace can ultimately prevail.

DAVID KRIEGER

10. Preventing Accidental Nuclear War

This chapter explores the question: *Could nuclear warfare begin accidentally?* In light of what we have learned from the occurrence of low-probability events such as the meltdown at Chernobyl and the Challenger tragedy, it is difficult to dismiss this question. Following the launch failure of the Challenger rocket and the death of its astronauts, Norman Cousins wrote: "What is to be learned from the space shuttle disaster is that the entire human race is in a spaceship and the decision-making time for correcting mistakes has been cut to seconds. The men at the controls have become so preoccupied with the momentum of the arms race that they are neglecting the painstaking joint attention required to keep the spaceship on course.

"The tragedy should remind the world that, despite the most systematic precautions, accidents are possible when dealing with high technology. No machines are impervious to accident or malfunction, whether bicycles or automobiles or computers or spaceships or intercontinental ballistic missiles or the firing devices on nuclear explosives."

From its beginning, the Nuclear Age Peace Foundation has played a leadership role in studying the dangers of accidental nuclear war, alerting the public to those dangers, and developing proposals for reducing those dangers. The Foundation publishes *Nuclear Alert,* the International Accidental Nuclear War Prevention Newsletter which is sent to researchers, educators, government leaders, and concerned citizens throughout the world. The Foundation also publishes a series of Technical Reports on key issues related to accidental or unintentional nuclear war.

Following this chapter is a three stage proposal to seriously reduce the risk of accidental nuclear war.

143

N uclear weapons are part of complex military systems which involve humans, machines and information. These systems stretch over large areas of the earth and oceans and into outer space. Despite the enormous cost and talent that goes into building these systems, they are subject to human error, technological malfunctions and communication failures.

One of the most significant questions confronting humankind today may well be: *Could nuclear warfare begin accidentally?*

It is a question to which no one may have a final answer. The interactions between the human psyche, earth and space based sensors, computers and weapons is so complex that it is beyond our capacity to predict if or when an accident might occur.

An accident is "an unintentional or unexpected happening that is undesirable or unfortunate, especially one resulting in injury, damage, harm or loss."[1] An accident could be the result of any of the following:

- a lack of understanding of the factors resulting in a given outcome (i.e., a lack of knowledge);
- a lack of care in using existing knowledge (i.e., faulty logic or reasoning);
- reasoning from false premises;
- lack of time to think clearly or act appropriately;
- inability to think clearly or act appropriately due to crisis-induced pressure;
- mechanical failure in equipment;
- faulty use of equipment; and
- incorrect information providing the basis for poor decisions.

These are only some of the many factors that may contribute to accidents. When combined with our knowl-

144

edge of human errors even under the most careful circumstances, they suggest that the possibility of an accidental nuclear war should not be dismissed lightly.

Author Schlesinger Jr., in an article in *Foreign Affairs,* wrote: "I continue to find it hard to suppose that either superpower would deliberately embark on nuclear war *ab initio,* but it is not hard to foresee a nuclear overreaction to the frustration or embarrassment of defeat in conventional warfare. It is still easier, with 50,000 warheads piling up in the hands of the superpowers and heaven knows how many scattered or hidden or incipient in other hands, to foresee nuclear war precipitated by terrorists, or by madness, or by accident, or by misreading the flashes on a radar screen."[2] All of these ways of initiating a nuclear war would fall within the broad definition of "accident" which we are using.

Self-styled "experts" who attempt to provide assurances that an accidental nuclear war will *not* occur can provide no sound basis for their optimism. The record, they argue, points toward safety since there has not been a nuclear war for nearly forty years. The assumption underlying their argument is that what has not happened in the past will not happen in the future. This resort to the record, however, appears increasingly unreliable as weapon systems have grown in sophistication and complexity, and as fear of a first-strike attack has increased.

With so much at stake, and with new and changed factors making the past pattern less reliable as a means of predicting the future, we should not be lulled into a false sense of optimism that inhibits actions and agreements capable of preventing accidental nuclear war in the future. Rather, we should ask whether or not the past does, in fact, provide an adequate basis for predicting the future of accidental nuclear war.

As a general rule we can say that the past will allow prediction of the future *only* if all relevant variables are identified and none of them have changed or can be expected to change over time. With an issue as complex as accidental nuclear war, or even warfare in general, it seems certain that it is beyond our human capacity to identify all of the increasing number of factors which could influence the outcome. Additionally, in the case of accidental nuclear war, certain important variables have changed in the direction of making such a war more likely. These changes include:

1. Nuclear weapons have become more numerous. With a greater number of weapons it can be assumed that the organizational difficulties of command and control increase as well, thereby decreasing centralized control over weapons use. More weapons also means more weapons handlers, some of whom are bound to be less reliable than others. Both psychological and drug-use problems have been found among handlers and guards.[3]

2. Delivery systems for nuclear weapons have become more accurate. The incredible accuracy of these delivery systems (to within a few hundred yards after an 8,000-mile trip) has led military planners to believe that so-called surgical strikes may be possible and even desirable. Increased accuracy has also led to targeting the opponent's weapons systems which raises fears of a potential disarming first-strike attempt.[4]

3. Warning time for a nuclear attack has drastically decreased. Whereas in the early days of nuclear weapons decision-makers may have had ten to twelve hours *warning time* of a nuclear attack, today this time has been cut to six to eight minutes in Europe and less than thirty minutes for an intercontinental attack. Due to the stationing of Soviet missile carrying submarines off the Atlantic coast of the United States, Washington, D.C. could have *less than* six to eight minutes of warning time. *This allows almost no time for reasonable decision-making.* The situation has led some theorists to suggest implementing a launch-on-warning policy which would turn

over the decision to fire nuclear weapons to computers. Brian Crissey, a computer expert, and Linn Sennot, a mathematician, have conducted a computer simulation of what would happen if the United States went to a launch-on-warning policy. They concluded that "accidental firing is virtually certain within one year of commencement of such a policy."[5]

4. The systems for warning against a nuclear attack have become increasingly complex and subject to error. False warnings have occurred frequently in recent times, some lasting for several minutes before being cleared. The United States has many redundancies built in to check on false alarms, but other nations may be less sophisticated in their warning systems.

5. The knowledge and materials for construction of nuclear weapons has spread to an increasing number of nations. More and more nations have the potential to develop nuclear weapons. In many cases nations which could easily develop nuclear weapons have exercised self-restraint and refused to do so. In other cases, though, nations continue to make concerted efforts to develop nuclear arsenals. These weapons in the hands of unstable leaders and governments will increase the likelihood of their use.[6]

When these factors are taken together, they suggest that the possibility of using nuclear weapons has increased over time, and will continue to increase. Since the devastation of such use, whether intentional or inadvertent, would be beyond the bounds of both reason and morality, it is essential that all possible steps be taken to prevent the use of nuclear weapons. While the emphasis in this essay is on steps to prevent accidental nuclear war, the same steps should substantially reduce the possibilities of intentional nuclear war as well.

What Factors Make Accidental
Nuclear War More Likely?

With nuclear weapons, we *know* that their use would result in enormous devastation of human life and possibly even the destruction of the planet. What we don't know is what unexpected event could trigger the use of nuclear weapons. We don't know what form of human or technological error could result in the use of nuclear weapons. We can theorize, however, based upon some of the methods currently used to prevent accidental firings. These methods include:

1. Responsibility for firing nuclear weapons is centralized. Weapons are engineered with "permissive action links" which require a special code to activate.
2. Nuclear weapons are guarded at all times by military personnel.
3. Early warning systems are designed to separate actual attack warnings from background noise (e.g., a flock of wild geese).
4. Weapons are engineered with safety devices to prevent their detonation even, for example, if one of them is involved in a plane crash.
5. Information on the development of nuclear weapons is classified so as not to be released to the public. (This is supposed to prevent the spread of such information.)
6. Safeguarding procedures are employed on special nuclear materials, which could be used to construct nuclear weapons, to prevent their falling into the wrong hands.

To summarize, the major concerns in preventing accidental nuclear war are that the existing weapons not be used in an unauthorized way by someone within the chain of command; that the weapons not be commandeered by persons outside the chain of command; that early warning systems are designed with sufficient independent verifications of attack; that an unexpected event such as a plane crash would not result in a nuclear detonation; and that information and materials for the construction of nuclear weapons do not proliferate.

How effectively these concerns have been addressed is arguable. Some would say very effectively since there have been no accidental nuclear firings. Others have pointed out serious problems with the control systems, particularly those for the prevention of nuclear proliferation. Critics have argued that the information and materials for nuclear weapons is so readily available that it is only a matter of time before other nations and even terrorist groups develop nuclear arsenals.[7]

Based upon this examination of current methods to prevent accidental nuclear warfare we can conclude that the following factors make accidental nuclear war more likely:

1. More decentralized command and control systems;
2. Poorly guarded nuclear arsenals;
3. Poorly designed nuclear warning systems which trigger false warnings of nuclear attack;
4. Nuclear weapons designed without "foolproof" safety devices or with poorly designed safety devices;
5. The dissemination of knowledge on how to construct nuclear weapons; and
6. The proliferation of special nuclear materials suitable for constructing nuclear weapons.

The nations which currently have nuclear weapons may be capable of reducing the probabilities of an accidental firing to a low level due to the sophistication of their technology. There is no guarantee, however, that less technologically sophisticated nations will be able, or even desire, to do the same.

Agreements Between the
United States and Soviet Union

The United States and Soviet Union have not been indifferent to the issue of accidental nuclear war. Neither side wishes to stumble into a nuclear war that could substantially destroy its population. As early as 1963 the two nations established the Direct Communications Link generally known as the "Hot Line."[8] The purpose of the system was to allow a continuously available communications link between heads of government to be used in time of crisis.

The original Hot Line called for a wire telegraph circuit with a back-up radio telegraph circuit. An updated agreement in 1971 established communication linkages between the two countries via satellite.[9]

Article 2 of the 1971 agreement states: "Each Party confirms its intention to take all possible measures to assure the continuous and reliable operation of the communications circuits and the system of terminals of the Direct Communications Link for which it is responsible in accordance with this Agreement and the Annex hereto, as well as to communicate to the head of its Government any messages received via the Direct Communications Link from the head of Government of the other Party."[10]

The method of communicating envisioned in this agreement is very primitive by today's standards. Messages are encoded and sent via teleprinter. They must then be decoded and translated before being answered. There is no provision for direct voice communication, nor for the transmission of maps, charts, graphs, or pictures. This system was criticized by the Reagan Administration as being inadequate to its important mission, and has since been upgraded to include facsimile capability to allow rapid transmission of text, maps and graphics.[11]

A second agreement was reached simultaneously with the Hot Line Modernization Agreement in 1971. This was the

"Agreement on Measures to Reduce the Risk of Outbreak of Nuclear War Between the United States of America and the Union of Soviet Socialist Republics."[12] It is also known as the "Accidents Measures" Agreement. In this agreement the U.S. and U.S.S.R. promised to maintain and improve their "organizational and technical arrangements to guard against the accidental or unauthorized use of nuclear weapons...."[13] The two parties also agreed to notify each other immediately in the event an accident or unauthorized use should occur, and to make every effort to render harmless or destroy a nuclear weapon which could create a risk of outbreak of nuclear war.

The parties further agreed to notify each other in the event of detecting unidentified objects on their missile warning systems, or in the event of signs of interference with these systems. If either party is launching a missile beyond its territory in the direction of the other, they agreed to notify the other party in advance. Should "prompt clarification" be necessary, the parties agreed to consult over the Hot Line.

This is a good agreement insofar as it goes. It would be interesting to know how often the two parties have had to consult over accidents to date. This information has not been made public, although U.S. presidents have said that the system was used during the 1967 and 1973 Arab-Israeli conflicts.[14]

The problem with the agreement is that it is reactive rather than proactive. It attempts to respond to a crisis rather than to take the necessary steps to avert a crisis from occurring. In a sense the agreement may be offering "too little, too late." Once a crisis is underway it may be too late to begin explaining.

Proposals by the United States

A decade and a half has passed since the "Accidents

Measures" Agreement was signed. In those years the nuclear arsenals of the superpowers have grown in size and complexity. During that period false alarms and near-misses have abounded.[15] It is time for new agreements.

In April 1983 Defense Secretary Weinberger presented four proposals to the Soviet Union to curb the risk of accidental nuclear war. These were:

1. Enhancing the existing "Hot Line" by giving it the capability of transmitting maps, charts, graphs, and pictures.
2. Creating a parallel communications linkage between the top military leaders of the two nations.
3. Installing new high speed communications linkages between Washington and its embassy in Moscow, and between Moscow and its embassy in Washington.
4. Developing contingency plans by a broader group of nations on procedures to follow if terrorists obtained nuclear weapons.[16]

Secretary Weinberger commented at the time of making the proposals, "These are very simple things. They're things that I believe would benefit everybody. I don't see why you couldn't get a quick agreement."[17]

A New Agreement

On July 17, 1984, it was announced that an agreement between the two countries had been reached on the first of the four proposals. They agreed to add facsimile transmission to the current teleprinter, thus making it possible to send maps and charts. The upgraded system will also reduce the time it takes to send a message on the Hot Line (for a two page document transmission time will be reduced from six minutes to two minutes). It is estimated that the agreement will take from eighteen to twenty-four months to implement.[18] (The new capability became operational in September 1986. —Ed.)

In announcing the new agreement President Reagan stated, "I see this agreement as both an appropriate technical improvement to the Hot Line, which has served both our governments well for over twenty years, and as a good example of how we can, working together, find approaches which can move us towards a reduction in the risks of war."[19]

While this agreement to improve the Hot Line is a welcome step it is aimed more at managing crises than preventing them. This is also true of the other U.S. proposals presented by Secretary Weinberger. One proposal which aims at crisis prevention as well as management is that for a United States-Soviet Union Joint Crisis Consultation Center.

A United States-Soviet Union
Joint Crisis Consultation Center

The late Senator Henry Jackson, a leading proponent of military strength, became a passionate advocate of the creation of a United States-Soviet Union Joint Crisis Consultation Center. Jackson, like other Senators, became concerned about the possibility of terrorists detonating a nuclear device, and one superpower thinking it was the responsibility of the other. He wanted to create a mechanism to prevent such an incident from resulting in nuclear warfare between the superpowers.

Senator Jackson described his vision of the Center in a speech at Washington State University shortly before his death.

"The Center," he said, "would be a permanent organization at a location agreeable to both sides. It would have areas where the Soviet and American representatives would meet and consult together, and also areas where they could work and confer in private. The American staff would be linked to Washington by secure American-controlled communication links, and the Soviets would be tied to Moscow by their own communications system. The Center would be open, fully staffed, every hour of the day and every day of the year.

"The two staffs should include technical advisers and military representatives knowledgeable about such matters as command, control and surveillance systems, force deployments, readiness testing procedures and the like. However, the Center's basic mission would be neither technical nor military. The decisive issues of nuclear war or peace are and always will be political and diplomatic, and the Center's staffing should reflect this fact.

"The Center would be instantly alerted when there were any war-threatening development. It would supplement, and work in tandem with, the modernized hotline. The superpower dialogue in time of crisis could thus become vastly more effective. The two sides at the Center would consult by actually talking with each other face-to-face across the width of a conference table, and each side would report its assessment as quickly as possible to the tops of their governments. As needed, Soviet and American experts on the kind of problem threatening the peace could meet with each other without any bureaucratic delays. The two teams would be *known* quantities to each other, and this could assist in understanding and in judging the credibility of their counterparts.

"The Center could work on crisis prevention as well as crisis resolution. It might draft proposed codes of nuclear conduct for the two superpowers. Each side might agree to refrain from doing things—undertaking certain types of force deployments or readiness exercises, for instance—that might appear threatening to the other side.

"The early establishment of a Joint Center would produce still further benefits. Popular fears over nuclear war are fueled in part by a concern that war might break out by accident just because Moscow and Washington were out of touch and not talking to each other. This permanent

154

Center—in business around the clock—could do much to lessen these apprehensions.

"Furthermore, agreement on the Center could help strengthen our relations with our friends and allies, and our European partners in particular. They have as big a stake as we do in preventing an accidental nuclear war. They would surely applaud an American initiative to create an institution making such a conflagration less likely.

"And, very importantly, I believe an early accord on creation of the Joint Center would increase the chances of success in the Geneva Arms Reduction Talks. The road we will have to travel to arrive at peace-serving weapons cuts will almost certainly be difficult and long. But the Center could so clearly serve the interests of both our sides that it should be possible to bring it into being at an early date. A negotiating success in this regard would be reassuring, and it could help build world confidence in the possibilities for stability and peace."[20]

Nunn-Warner Proposal

A proposal for U.S.-Soviet Nuclear Risk Reduction Centers is being pursued by Senators Nunn and Warner.[21] They proposed that initially there be two Centers rather than one— one in Washington and one in Moscow. In their version the two Centers would be in regular communication. "These Centers would maintain a twenty-four-hour watch on any events with the potential of leading to nuclear incidents."[21] On June 15, 1984 the Senate recommended this proposal by a vote of 82 to 0 as a non-binding amendment to the defense authorization bill.[23]

The Nunn-Warner Working Group suggested the following potential roles for the Risk Reduction Centers:
● To discuss and outline the procedures to be followed in the event of possible incidents involving the use of nuclear weapons;

- To maintain close contact during incidents precipitated by nuclear terrorists;
- To exchange information on a voluntary basis concerning events that might lead to nuclear proliferation or to the acquisition of nuclear weapons, or the materials and equipment necessary to build weapons, by subnational groups.
- To exchange information about military activities which might be misunderstood by the other party during periods of mounting tensions.
- To establish a dialogue about nuclear doctrines, forces and activities.[24]

(In September 1987, U.S. and Soviet leaders signed an agreement to establish Nuclear Risk Reduction Centers in their respective capitals. —Ed.)

An Accidental War Assessment Center

A proposal for an Accidental War Assessment Center was put forward in Congressional Hearings by Dean Babst and Alex Dely.[25] This Center would have the responsibility for evaluating weapons programs and policies for their impact upon accidental war. The theory behind their proposal is that someone should be examining existing and proposed weapons and doctrines to see if they add to defense as they are intended, or if they are in fact making accidental war more likely.

A New Way of Thinking

Our own imperfections as humans, including our inability to perfectly control complex systems, may prove to be our greatest enemy. Nuclear technologies have raised the stakes of error. In order to perpetually avoid mass annihilation by nuclear warfare we must aspire to perfection under not only conditions of hostility, but periodic times of crisis. This is too high a task for humans to achieve. We must find methods of cooperation and conciliation that allow us to reverse the costly and dangerous forward thrust of the nuclear arms race. The United States, along with the Soviet Union, must change its example to the world that now gives other nations reason to believe that nuclear weapons bestow both power and prestige upon their possessors. This signal is contrary to the best interests of both superpowers. While this process of reversal is taking place, new institutions for preventing as well as managing crises such as United States-Soviet Union Risk Reduction Centers are needed.

The United States Institute of Peace should study and assess the dangers of accidental nuclear war, report to the American people on those dangers, and offer proposals to the Congress on methods to reduce those dangers.

You Have a Role

It would be a mistake to overlook the danger of accidental nuclear war, or to hesitate to take all necessary steps to prevent such an occurrence. Even were the probability of the use of nuclear weapons to be very low (which is probably not the case), the gravity of the potential harm is so great that reason suggests every effort should be taken to reduce this risk. However, much that could be done has not been done. Many of the needed corrective measures which would not be difficult or dangerous to implement, will probably not be implemented unless citizens put pressure on their government to achieve the needed changes.

Reducing The Risk of Accidental Nuclear War: A Waging Peace Proposal

STAGE ONE—UNILATERAL STEPS (1988-1989)

1. Establish a Congressional Accidental Nuclear War

Assessment Center to evaluate all strategies, and all weapons systems and warning systems in light of their implications for accidental nuclear war. Make an annual report to the Congress and people of the United States on the level of the danger and the steps being taken to reduce the risk.

2. Pull back forward based missiles in order to give opponent increased decision time to evaluate a false warning. Establish a plan and time-table for removing all nuclear weapons from Europe.•

3. Strengthen command and control procedures to assure that no missile launch without authorization from the President will occur.

4. Develop decision procedures to reduce reliance on computer evaluation of attack warnings.

5. Do not develop or deploy highly accurate weapons which may be perceived as first-strike threats.

6. Initiate a moratorium on all the nuclear weapons testing in order to stop the technological and qualitative advances in nuclear weaponry and missile delivery systems. Invite the Soviets to reinstitute their moratorium.

7. Pledge a moratorium on all testing of missile "defense" systems (S.D.I.) in order to prevent the other side from increasing its offensive missile systems.

8. Make a pledge of No First Use of nuclear weapons.

9. Increase controls on nuclear power industry and nuclear materials and technology transfers in order to reduce risk of nuclear proliferation.

10. Establish tighter guidelines for psychiatric evaluation of all weapons handlers and all individuals in the chain of command who may authorize use of nuclear weapons.

STAGE TWO—U.S.-SOVIET BILATERAL STEPS (1888-1993)

*This process was begun in December 1987 with the signing of the INF Agreement by President Reagan and General Secretary Gorbachev to eliminate short and intermediate range missiles in Europe.

11. Establish U.S.-Soviet Risk Reduction Centers to work on crisis prevention and management.†

12. Establish a Joint Task Force on Accidental Nuclear War Assessment within the U.S.-Soviet Risk Reduction Center to jointly evaluate risks of accidental nuclear war and develop joint plans for reducing risks.

13. Establish a Joint Task Force on the Prevention of Nuclear Proliferation within the U.S.-Soviet Risk Reduction Center.

14. Agree to graduated reductions in nuclear arsenals under international supervision to achieve a "Guaranteed Nuclear Deterrent" (200 to 500 weapons) within a five year period. Begin the process of disarmament with the weapons having the greatest first-strike potential.

15. Agree in advance to a guaranteed 48 hour "Assessment" period in the event of a nuclear detonation.

STAGE THREE—MULTILATERAL STEPS (1990-2000)

16. Establish a Multinational Accidental Nuclear War Assessment Center to include all nuclear powers.

17. Agree to final reductions of all nuclear weapons on Earth over a seven year period.

18. Strengthen international verification and supervision procedures of the final stages of nuclear weapons abolition.

19. Implement strict international controls over the nuclear power industry to prevent diversion of nuclear materials for weapons.

20. Create an International Earth and Space Patrol to verify existing arms control agreements and provide information on military activities by all nations.

---

†An agreement to establish reciprocal U.S.-Soviet Nuclear Risk Reduction Centers was signed in Washington in September 1987.

DEAN BABST, ROBERT C. ALDRIDGE and
DAVID KRIEGER

11. Accidental Nuclear War Dangers of "Star Wars"

It is becoming increasingly understood that nuclear war may be more likely to occur by accident than intention. Despite this understanding the dangers of accidental nuclear war are not as yet being fully evaluated in relation to important security decisions such as the Strategic Defense Initiative ("Star Wars").

This chapter suggests that there would be serious accidental war dangers from the implementation of "Star Wars." The authors believe that "Star Wars" will increase the danger of accidental nuclear war. Without doubt, it will also increase the nuclear arms race, both in space and on the ground. The authors conclude that the Strategic Defense Initiative should be set aside and more promising approaches to achieving security in the nuclear age should be pursued.

The United States plans to spend $26 billion by 1989 on the "Star Wars" Strategic Defense Initiative (SDI). Most of that amount is slated for research leading to development of directed energy and kinetic energy weapons and sensors.[1] No money has been requested to assess how these various weapons might increase the danger of accidental nuclear war—a truly shortsighted omission.

Some types of assessment might be done fairly quickly and inexpensively. For example, the computerized mathematical model developed by Drs. Crissey, Sennott and Wallace demonstrates a reasonable approach.[2] Their simulation considers the number of false alarms, the time needed to clear them, and the time available during an international crisis. Other factors should also be introduced, such as the possibility of space debris colliding with critical satellites, and the nervousness of high military commanders when facing a knockout first strike capacity.

Satellite Interference

Since the SDI weapons being considered to destroy ballistic missiles in flight could also be used against satellites, what would happen if a crucial satellite went blind during a tense international crisis and there was little time to assess what happened? Would military leaders assume that the satellite was struck by space junk, or would they leap to the conclusion that they were under attack and start launching missiles?

Space is becoming an orbiting junk yard. There are currently some 5,000 known human-made orbiting objects and there could be tens of millions of undetectable fragments as well. Since these objects whip around the earth at six miles per second, even a tiny fragment colliding with a satellite could be devastating. In 1983, three spacecraft were hit. A window of the Soviet Salyut 7 space station was struck and cratered, and the shuttle Challenger suffered similar damage. An Indian communication satellite was struck by an eight-inch space object.[3] As the quantity of space junk increases we can look forward to more frequent and more severe collisions.

Another connection of Star Wars weapons with satellites is closely related to collisions. If the United States, in response to an alert, erroneously fired a laser beam at a Soviet military communications satellite, such an action could be perceived as the prelude to an attack.[4] Misinterpretation of such an accidental event involving SDI weapons could then escalate to use of nuclear weapons.

161

Computer Decisions

The potential for accidental nuclear war will be further aggravated by the need for a large, complex and extremely fast computer network to run the Star Wars System. Decision time for activating the first layer of the proposed SDI defense would be less than three minutes. Defense Secretary Casper Weinberger highlighted the problem in an interview with *Omni* magazine:[5]

WEINBERGER—The goal would be to try it against thousands of missiles, including missiles that carry ten independent warheads, and missiles whose warheads can change direction. It is, I am told, essentially a problem of very, very large and extraordinary rapid computer capability. We must develop that to the point where we can identify, track and destroy several thousand targets in a very, very short space of time.

OMNI—You are talking about a total battle time of as little as one hundred twenty or two hundred seconds?

WEINBERGER—It is very short. It is a very big task...

Since Star Wars will require decisions within seconds, completely autonomous computer control is a foregone conclusion. There will be no time for human beings to screen out false alarms. Congressional testimony has illustrated that destroying Soviet missiles while their rocket motors are still burning will require a decision so fast that it would have to be automated—there would be no time for White House approval.[6] These computers destined to activate "defensive" Star Wars weapons are likely to be the same systems which will alert strategic nuclear missiles to launching readiness.

Secretary Weinberger is proposing a far more sophisticated computer system when the Pentagon has not been able to make existing computers function reliably. The multi-billion dollar strategic missile warning computer network is the foundation on which SDI will be built. Consider the following examples of potential disasters and systems failures caused by unanticipated events:

—During an 18-month period in 1979-80 the U.S. had 147 false alarms in its strategic warning system. Two lasted three minutes, and one lasted a full six minutes[7]. In these cases, however, there were people in the loop to rectify the situation. With automated systems, and decreasing decision time, however, six minutes could be too much.

—During 1981, 1982 and 1983 there were 186, 218 and 255 false alarms, respectively, in the U.S. strategic warning system.[8] We can expect false alarms to continue increasing as weapons systems become more complex and automated. In addition, we need to ponder the danger of other nations launching to a false alarm.

—In 1984 the nations's backup warning system, outside of Washington D.C., failed during a routine test and it took officers 34 minutes to notify headquarters of the break-down.[9] This incident became publicly known because a CBS news team was doing a story on the system at the time.

There have been other major systems failures of which the Three Mile Island accident is one. Also note the major power blackouts in New York City, the Northeastern U.S. and Ontario—after experts had dismissed the possibility. During the Falklands war, the British Ship *Sheffield* was sunk by the Argentines with a French-made Exocet missile because the ship's computers were programmed to ignore an ally's missile.[10]

General Bennie Davis, U.S. Strategic Air Commander, believes that a completely automated decision-making process is very dangerous. He opposes a launch-on-warning policy (which an automated launch decision would be) and prefers to wait until some enemy warheads reach the U.S. before firing our missiles.[11] His concern is contrary to the direction in which we are headed, where a nervous twitch of

163

the finger, or an electron taking the wrong path on a chip, could launch us into World War III.

Computer Security

In the movie *War Games*, World War III was almost started by a teenage computer hacker breaking into the NORAD missile warning system. Becoming concerned, the Defense Department attempted a computer security study. But defense officials found they don't even know how many computers are used. They surveyed the 17,000 known computers and more than two-thirds of the cognizant officers, some in the most sensitive outposts, failed to return the survey form.[12]

Robert Brotzman, director of the Pentagon's Department of Computer Security, reluctantly concluded: "We don't have anything that isn't vulnerable to attack from a retarded sixteen-year-old."[13] While there is a security dilemma now, how will it be handled in a larger and far more complex Star Wars system? How secure are other nations' computers?

First Strike Nervousness

Defense against ballistic missiles, which is what Star Wars is all about, is an important element of a disarming first strike capability.[14] To be truly disarming, the initial assault would have to be followed-up by interception of surviving enemy missiles which are launched in retaliation. Star Wars actually appears more credible in this less demanding role than in the advertised task of protecting the entire country against a full scale Soviet assault. But supplying this important element of a first strike capability will put the nuclear standoff on a short fuse during an international crisis because the opponent would recognize a military advantage to using his missiles before they are destroyed.

As warning time shrinks and nations become more jittery,

decision-makers could misread the opponent's actions, or reactions, and move rapidly to the higher states of alert leading to nuclear war. Such an escalation could be triggered by a mistake similar to the accidental firing of a Soviet missile over Norway in December 1984.[15] During that incident the U.S. and USSR used the hotline. What will happen when there just isn't enough time to do even that?

Star Wars weapons, such as electromagnetic rail guns and killer lasers, are extremely sophisticated and their state of development after a $26 billion exercise will be uncertain. National leaders will be increasingly anxious about the other side having perfected this final element of a first strike advantage. Such uncertainty in crisis situations heightens the possibility of one side launching a preemptive strike because they believe the other side may be about to strike. In this manner, Star Wars weapons may increase the danger of an accidental nuclear war by making both sides anxious that nuclear weapons are apt to be fired.

Why Was Star Wars Proposed?

In light of the seriously increased danger of accidental nuclear war resulting from the Star Wars scheme, it is of interest to inquire why the proposal was put forth in the first place. The simple answer might be that concern with accidental nuclear was has not been perceived as a problem by the Reagan administration or by the public generally. There has been a tendency in government and public consideration of strategic issues to assume that the onset of a nuclear war would be by an intentional decision rather than by accident. No matter how mistaken this view may be, the fact that it exists has inhibited a serious examination of the risks of accidental nuclear war. This includes the risks inherent in development of Star Wars as well as other proposed strategic weapons and defense systems.

In addition to the generally low level of concern over the

dangers of accidental nuclear war, there is also a great desire on the part of the public to find an answer to the current dilemma of a nuclear armed world. Star Wars offers the promise of protection from the nightmare of nuclear war. It provides the illusion that we can achieve safety from the horror of nuclear attack. Star Wars allows the public (and perhaps Mr. Reagan personally) to believe what it would like to believe—that we can develop the technological capability to live under a shield safe from nuclear attack.

Star Wars, in short, provides hope for a future free of nuclear threat. No matter how unlikely it is to be successful, it provides that most important of ingredients for the human psyche in an age when total annihilation is possible—hope. Our desire to believe that there is a way out of this dilemma, however, should not blind us to careful analysis of the implication of any course of action, including, of course, that of the Star Wars proposal. That analysis must include the implications of Star Wars for initiating an accidental nuclear war.

Not to be overlooked in examining the reasons for the Star Wars proposal are the enormous profits which will flow to the defense industry. Already $26 billion is planned for research and development of Star Wars over the next few years, and that would be just the beginning should a decision ever be made to operationalize the system. With these enormous expenditures and the resulting anticipated profits to the defense industry, the system is sure to have industry support regardless of its strategic validity. The proposal thus speaks to the defense industry, informing them that the government intends to consider their welfare for many years to come. In the meantime, the national deficit, the budget deficit and the foreign trade deficit continue to mount, undermining the economic security of the country.

The Star Wars proposal was also put forward as a message to the Soviet Union. The message would say something to this effect: We are willing to keep the arms race alive and healthy, and run whatever risks are involved in increasing the threat to you of our developing a first strike capability. The Soviets have always responded to this sort of message by demonstrating that they are willing to keep pace with us and continue the nuclear arms race. They have responded specifically to the Star Wars proposal by stating that there can be no serious arms negotiations while we are pursuing such a system, and that they would develop new offensive weapons to counter it. In considering how the Star Wars proposal is viewed by the Soviet Union, we must understand that for them our development of an effective defense would put them at our mercy, and they are no more willing to accept that situation than we would be if the shoe were on the other foot.

Even though Mr.Reagan has offered to share Star Wars technology with the Soviet Union once it is completed, this cannot be very reassuring to the Soviets since they would then be vulnerable to us, and they have no guarantee that any successor to Mr. Reagan would uphold his offer. Looked at from a Soviet perspective, they would be foolish to allow their national security to rest upon the good will and generosity of some future American president. If we truly wanted to show good faith with the Soviet Union on sharing the benefits of Star Wars, we would offer to initiate a joint project with them on space-based missile defense systems so that they would be able to share in the information from the outset. This should relieve concern on their part about our having a first strike intention. Even more important, it would allow both sides to study jointly the accidental nuclear war implications of developing a Star Wars defense.

Thus, we may conclude that the Star Wars proposal offers hope to the American public, but it is a false hope that actually increases the danger of a nuclear war beginning accidentally; it offers profits which are very real to the defense industry, but at the expense of using these funds in

167

more productive ways to strengthen our national economy; and it offers the Soviets reason to believe that we are willing to commit to developing a means of making ourselves invulnerable to their threat and thus place them at our mercy.

Star Wars, Other Nations and Terrorists

The Star Wars proposal also sends a message to other nations and to terrorists. It informs them that the United States is committed to finding a defense against missile attack rather than to the reduction and elimination of nuclear arsenals. The message is read loud and clear in what we do and what we spend money on rather than in our statements. We can claim we want arms control and disarmament in public statements, but these statements do not ring true if we fail to show by our actions that we are capable of achieving serious arms control. In Article VI of the Nuclear Non-Proliferation Treaty (NPT), we solemnly promised, along with the Soviet Union, to pursue good faith negotiations toward achieving general and complete disarmament under international control.[16] That treaty was signed in 1968 and entered into force in 1970, and few nations today believe that either the United States or the Soviet Union has abided by its treaty commitment in Article VI. This has led to a lessening of the bonds of commitment of nations that agreed to forego the development of nuclear weapons in the NPT.

By their joint participation in the nuclear arms race, the latest upward leg of which promises to be triggered by the development of Star Wars, the superpowers have set the example for the rest of the world that nuclear weapons are prestigious and desirable. The cavalier attitude of both superpowers toward nuclear weapons development is apt to result in a breakdown of the NPT, and in an increased number of nuclear weapons states and perhaps even nuclear armed terrorists. By increasing the probability of more nuclear weapons powers in the future, the two superpowers are indirectly increasing the probability of nuclear war being initiated by one of the new nuclear weapons states or terrorists. Thus, any way that we find to ease the psychological discomfort with nuclear weapons and the nuclear arms race, short of negotiating deep reductions in nuclear arsenals, will only serve to increase the probability of a third power being an instigating force in an accidental or, for that matter, intentional nuclear war.

For a decade and a half the United States and the Soviet Union have treated their commitment under Article VI of the NPT very lightly. They do so at great peril of a much more complex and dangerous nuclear armed world, one that in the future could become uncontrollable.

Action

Rather than providing a defense against nuclear attack, Star Wars seriously increases the peril of accidental nuclear war. How long do you think this country, or the world, would last under a Star Wars defense, when decisions must be made spontaneously and exclusively by computers?

There is an urgent need for public pressure demanding careful evaluation of accidental nuclear war dangers while there is still time. Common sense tells us that, before spending $26 billion just to see if the concept will work, it would be far safer and much less expensive to assess the accidental nuclear war dangers through rigorous study and debate and the use of computer simulations with analytical models.

From an arms control perspective, it would be appropriate to involve the Soviets and other nations in the evaluation of the system at the earliest possible point in time. Multinational evaluation projects will help to assure that the implications of the Star Wars system for accidental nuclear war are widely discussed and understood. This should

169

contribute to a mood in all nations to move toward mutually verifiable arms reduction agreements and no more Star Wars schemes.

FRANK K. KELLY

12. Creating a National Institution for Peace

This chapter provides historic perspective on the sustained effort from the early days of the American Republic to create a national institution for peace.

As a result of the national effort to establish a Peace Academy, the Congress authorized the creation of a United States Institute of Peace in October 1984. After a series of struggles between Congress and the White House, President Reagan was finally persuaded to appoint eleven of the Institute's board of directors and permit it to function on a severely limited scale.

Dr. John Norton Moore, a professor at the University of Virginia Law School and a former counselor to the State Department, was selected as the first chairman of the Institute's board.

The first meeting of the Institute's board was held in February 1986. Chairman Moore and the other directors moved slowly and cautiously in 1986, explaining that the board was "charged with the creation of an extraordinarily important new institution of American leadership and innovation for a peaceful world," and "did not rush to give out grant awards, but instituted a process of outreach and review that would assure, from the outset, opportunity and encouragement to potential applicants and the application of the best standards from both government and private grantmaking systems."

In its fiscal year 1986, the board considered twenty-nine applications and awarded four grants totaling $231,604. It also designed the Jennings Randolph Program for International Peace, and in 1987 announced the appointment of eight scholars and leaders as the initial Fellows in the Raldolph Program. It began work on a National Peace Essay Contest, to be held in 1987-88, and authorized many other projects, including a television series on U.S.-U.S.S.R. relations and an annual State of the World Peace Report.

Despite its cautious approaches to the development of public support for the peaceful resolution of conflicts, the Institute has been sharply criticized by supporters of the original Peace Academy idea as well as by some members of Congress. As it continues to develop, the Institute should become an increasingly important educational institution in the field of peace.

Thomas Jefferson once wrote: "I am not an advocate for frequent changes in laws and constitutions, but laws and constitutions must go hand in hand with the progress of the human mind. As that becomes more developed, more enlightened, as new discoveries are made, new truths discovered and manners and opinions change, institutions must advance also to keep pace with the time. . . ."

Yet, Jefferson knew from his own experience—as all the founders of the American Republic learned—that the hardest task in American life was the creation of new institutions. The ringing statements he placed in the Declaration of Independence—that all men are created equal; that they are "endowed by their Creator with certain inalienable rights," and that governments are instituted "to secure these rights"—were not accepted by many Americans as self-evident. There were many thousands of Americans who resisted the American Revolution, and there were thousands who opposed the Constitution offered to the people in 1787.

On the day when the new Constitution was published in the press, the newspapers of New York printed a strong attack upon it by the chief executive of that state, Governor Clinton. Many of the most powerful leaders in New York and other states soon joined the opposition to the proposed new framework for the American government. The struggle over

172

the Constitution went on for years, and it was finally ratified by a narrow margin.

The issues involved in the debate over the Constitution are relevant to the debate over the establishment of a United States Peace Academy in the twentieth century. Then as now, leaders were divided over what the role of government should be. How much power should be allocated to the federal government—and how much to the states and to the people themselves? These are endlessly recurring questions in American life. They are fundamentally important questions, which call for thoughts and discussions of Americans in every generation.

The Constitution itself was designed to be an instrument for the peaceful resolution of conflicts—conflicts between the executive, the legislative, and the judicial branches of government; conflicts between the states and the federal authority; conflicts between the economic interests existing in different regions of the country. In its original form, it was a relatively brief document with only seven articles. Madison, Jefferson and others soon insisted that it did not contain enough protection for individual liberties, and they pushed through Congress ten amendments which became known as the Bill of Rights.

Dr. Benjamin Rush, one of the signers of the Declaration of Independence, tried to get the Congress to add another important provision. In an article he wrote in collaboration with Benjamin Banneker, a black mathematician, published in *Banneker's Almanack* for 1793, Dr. Rush called for a "Peace Office" for the United States on a governmental level equal to that of the recently established War Department. Dr. Rush and Mr. Banneker said: "Among the defects which have been pointed out in the Federal Constitution by its anti-federal enemies, it is much to be lamented that no person has taken notice of its total silence upon the subject of an office of the utmost importance to the welfare of the United States, that is, an office for promoting and preserving perpetual peace in our country."

The Constitution also did not attempt to deal with the problem of slavery, although Jefferson and other leaders knew that the bitter divisions over the slavery question might tear the new Republic apart. Nor did it deal adequately with the question of whether any state might secede from the federal union—another unresolved issue which led to the outbreak of the Civil War in the 1860s.

Could a Department of Peace, headed by an American with high stature and staffed by men and women skilled in the arts of negotiation have been able to prevent the Civil War? There were leaders in both the South and North who tried valiantly to prevent that catastrophe. Some scholars believe that it could have been prevented—and slavery could have been abolished by peaceful steps similar to those taken in other countries.

But there was no Office for the Promotion of Peace in the crucial decades preceding the Civil War. There was no Center for Conflict Resolution. There was no group of trained mediators and conciliators who could have gone through the states, opening paths for reconciliation. The two branches of Congress, swayed by the passions of people on both sides, were not able to devise an acceptable solution.

The bloodletting of the Civil War afflicted several generations of Americans with rage and resentment. The murder of Abraham Lincoln—who might have pacified the country after the shooting stopped-stirred new waves of violence. The atmosphere was poisoned for decades. The deep wounds of that tragedy—viewed by the South as a War Between the States—were slow to heal.

The Struggle For Existence—and the "Survival of the Fittest"

The armed conflict that raged in America from 1861 to 1865

was one of the bloodiest wars in the nineteenth century, but certainly not the only one. Tens of thousands of people were killed in the Napoleonic Wars in Europe. Many thousands died in the revolutionary struggles of the 1840s, and other thousands were slaughtered in the Franco-Prussian War.

It seemed to most men that the only effective way to settle basic differences was to use weapons. This grim belief was strongly reinforced by the findings of Charles Darwin, the British scientist who maintained that man shared a common ancestry with monkeys and observed that "the struggle for existence goes on everywhere." He contended that this struggle inevitably led through a process of evolution to the "survival of the fittest."

Darwin's theory produced a split between biology and religion. To many scientists, a wholly new description of the universe was required. The idea of a beneficent Creator, who had created man in his own image, was shattered. Ethics, economics, sociology—everything had to undergo an agonizing reappraisal.

The ferocity of the Civil War and the contentions of Darwin would not have shocked or surprised Alexander Hamilton, one of the framers of the Constitution, who died in a duel in 1804. In Number 6 of *The Federalist* papers, Hamilton asserted that the history of the human race revealed that "men are ambitious, vindictive, and rapacious," and he declared that "the causes of hostility between nations are innumerable."

Human behavior in the nineteenth century seemed to support Hamilton's and Darwin's picture of a world in which all creatures competed ruthlessly with one another. While some Americans gave some respect to the Quakers, the Amish, the Church of the Brethren, and other religious bodies dedicated to peace, many Americans supported the wars against Mexico and Spain—which added California, New Mexico and Arizona to the territories of the United States and planted the American flag in the Philippines.

175

While relationships between nations were chaotic—with wars likely to erupt at any time—this period in America was also a time of rough clashes between labor and management, with both sides convinced that disputes had to be settled by demonstrations of physical force or displays of political and economic power. People generally believed that there had to be "winners" and "losers" in these disputes. The idea that both sides could gain beneficial results through mediation or arbitration had not dawned upon many leaders.

In such an atmosphere, the idea of a Department of Peace or a Peace Office seemed utterly impractical. There were no objective studies to indicate that it might be possible to develop scientific ways of resolving conflicts peacefully. Although various publicists and other leaders offered suggestions for peace agencies—and the Quakers and others continued to offer good examples—their proposals were not taken up by large numbers of people or considered seriously by members of Congress or the state legislatures.

Yet there were poets and philosophers who had visions of peace—who foresaw that mankind would eventually see the futility and waste of violence. And these poets had effects upon the minds of several generations of Americans—and upon many political leaders, including Woodrow Wilson, Franklin Roosevelt, Harry Truman and Dwight Eisenhower, and many Representatives and Senators.

American Ideals and The Possibilities of Peace

President Wilson, a scholar with a deep knowledge of history, believed that individual citizens and nations could learn to settle their differences peacefully. He tried to keep the United States from being pulled into World War I. When this country finally entered the war, he voiced the hope that American ideals could provide a basis for a lasting peace. He believed that Americans had learned a great lesson from the bloody struggle which had torn the nation apart in the 1860s.

In an address to the Congress in 1918, Wilson outlined a fourteen-point program for a durable peace. He advocated "open covenants of peace, openly arrived at," the establishment of "an equality of trade conditions among all the nations consenting to the peace" and the formation of "a general association of nations . . . for the purpose of affording mutual guarantees of political independence and territorial integrity to great and small states alike."

"We entered this war because violations of right had occurred which touched us to the quick and made the life of our own people impossible unless they were corrected and the world secured once and for all against their recurrence," Wilson declared. "An evident principle runs through the whole program I have outlined. It is the principle of justice to all peoples and nationalities, and their right to live on equal terms of liberty and safety with one another, whether they be strong or weak . . . The moral climax of this, the culminating and final war for human liberty, has come. . . ."

The lofty idealism of Wilson soared far above the world of incessant conflict which Darwin and other scientists had observed. Wilson was a visionary man, who shared the high hopes expressed by Alfred Tennyson in *Locksley Hall,* a poem written in 1842. Tennyson foresaw aerial warfare and the bombing of cities—and then the emergence of a "parliament of man" into effective existence.

Wilson had a tremendous impact upon the people of several generations—including Franklin D. Roosevelt, Harry Truman, Dwight Eisenhower, and other presidents—but the League of Nations he helped to create after World War I was disrupted and eventually destroyed by conflicts between nations. Yet the ideals he had expressed in his eloquent speeches were never abandoned by many Americans.

President Warren G. Harding convened a Naval Disarmament Conference in Washington in 1922 which led to an agreement by the United States, Britain, Japan, France and Italy to limit the tonnage of their warships. This agreement did not prevent later expansions of naval power of all these nations.

A national movement to "outlaw war" arose in the United States in the 1920s and gained so much popular support that Secretary of State Frank Kellogg (with the cooperation of Aristide Briand, foreign minister of France) worked out a pact which was eventually signed by almost every country on earth. This pact, signed in Paris in 1928, called upon all nations to renounce war as an instrument of national policy. However, it contained no sanctions and left room for wars of "self-defense." It had relatively little effect on international relations.

The failure of the League of Nations to halt Mussolini's attack on Ethiopia in 1935 led to the League's collapse. The rise of Hitler to power in Germany signified a resurgence of German militarism and a rising threat to peace.

There were still American leaders who sought ways to develop peaceful settlement of disputes. Senator Matthew Neely introduced a bill in the United States Senate in 1935 to create a Department of Peace, and Representative Fred Bierman suggested a "Bureau of Peace and Friendship" to do research on peace and war.

The proposals of Neely and Bierman did not draw much support in the 1930s when Hitler began to rearm Germany on a vast scale and the Japanese militarists invaded China and threatened other countries. Hitler did not want peace— except on terms of submission—and neither did the Japanese leaders. The fury of another great war burst upon the world.

The carnage of World War II and the use of atomic bombs on Hiroshima and Nagasaki brought home to millions of people a growing awareness of the fact that a future war could destroy civilization and possibly the whole earth. The search for ways of maintaining peace resumed with higher intensity—and an increasing awareness that there could be no victory for any country in a war fought with nuclear weapons.

The man who had ordered the dropping of atomic bombs on two Japanese cities—President Truman—was determined to do everything he could to spare the world from a future war that might be fought with nuclear weapons. He took an active part in the founding of the United Nations. He had carried a copy of *Locksley Hall* in his wallet for many years, and he told a biographer: "Now Tennyson knew there were going to be airplanes, and he knew there was going to be bombing and all of it. And some day there would be a parliament of man. It stands to reason, and that's what I was doing when I went ahead with setting up the United Nations . . . The UN is the first step."

Leaders in the United States Congress realized that the creation of the United Nations was not the only step necessary for the advancement of peace. Senator Alexander Wiley of Wisconsin proposed in 1945 the formation of a Department of Peace, and recommended that the Secretary of Peace should represent the United States on the UN Security Council. In the same year, Representative Jennings Randolph (who later became a Senator) also introduced a bill to form a Department of Peace.

Randolph's bill was the first to incorporate the idea that an international exchange of people and ideas would be an effective means of promoting peace. He felt that the development of the atomic bomb had increased the urgency of taking action to prevent the outbreak of hostilities. In his speech in the House, he said: "It would be utter folly for us to believe that we can keep secret the atomic bomb and other devices of warfare." His ideas were not heeded at the time.

In 1945 and 1947, Representative Everett Dirksen (later a Senator, too) offered bills to establish a "Peace Division in the State Department." In 1947, Senator Karl Mundt of South

179

Dakota recommended a Department of Peace. These proposals, like those of Randolph and Wiley, received relatively little attention from the public and the press.

In the 1950s and 1960s, dozens of similar proposals appeared in the House and the Senate. Between 1955 and 1968, eighty-five bills advocated the creation of a cabinet-level Department of Peace. Some of these bills included provisions for an educational program to include research into methods for promoting peace.

The Peace Academy Idea Gathers Support

The movement gathered some momentum in the 1960s through the persistent efforts of Dan and Rose Lucey of Oakland, California, who persuaded members of the Christian Family Movement to work for the formation of a Peace Academy. Another energetic advocate of the idea was Thomas C. Westropp, president of a savings and loan association in Cleveland, who put a full-page advertisement in a newspaper there in 1969 outlining reasons for the creation of a Peace Academy.

In September, 1971, Senator Vance Hartke introduced what was known as a "Peace Act," calling for a Department of Peace with five major functions: developing and recommending to the President appropriate plans, policies and programs designed to foster peace; coordinating all activities of the United States government affecting the preservation or promotion of peace; coordinating research and planning for the peaceful resolution of international conflicts, in cooperation with other governments, and encouraging similar actions by private institutions; encouraging and assisting the interchange of ideas and persons between private institutions and groups in the United States and other countries; and fostering the work of private institutions and groups aimed at resolving international conflicts.

President Richard Nixon and many members of Congress

dismissed Senator Hartke's proposal, declaring the Departments of State and Defense were "peace departments." The idea was supported by some scholars, however, and David Krieger, a staff member of the Center for the Study of Democratic Institutions, declared in an article published in *The Center Magazine:* "Whereas in 1793 the lack of a Peace Department may not have been viewed as a defect in our federal Constitution, today the case may be put more strongly....It is crucial to the actual security of this nation that strategies such as peace through strength or through deterrence be challenged, be debated and thoroughly considered by the people of this country." This article reached the 100,000 members of the Center, but did not lead to any organized effort for a Peace Department or a Peace Academy.

In 1975, as plans for the celebration of the Bicentennial of American Independence were being developed, Senator Hartke and others in Congress decided to tie the idea to the name of the nation's first president, George Washington, who had sought to steer the United States into friendly relations with all nations during his service as Chief Executive.

Hartke and Senator Mark Hatfield prepared a bill to create a George Washington Peace Academy. Hartke enlisted the aid of Dr. Bryant Wedge, a Washington psychiatrist who taught courses at Tufts University and the Foreign Service Institute. Dr. Wedge, who had been speaking and writing about the possibilities of mediation and conciliation for many years, became a tireless advocate of the Peace Academy idea.

Dr. Wedge, Dr. Jerome Frank of Johns Hopkins University and Nachman Gerber, a Baltimore business man, persuaded a group of concerned citizens to join them in forming an Ad Hoc Committee for a National Peace Academy. This Committee launched the National Peace Academy Campaign, with the initial support of several hundred physicians and other professional people recruited by Dr. Wedge, Dr. Frank, Mr. Gerber and others.

The Education and Labor Committee of the Senate held hearings in 1976 on the Hartke-Hatfield bill, which had the patriotic number S.1976. Dr. Wedge and others in the campaign lined up impressive witnesses to testify in favor of the bill.

Senator Claiborne Pell, a leading member of the Senate Foreign Relations Committee, chaired the hearings on the bill. Pell had been successful in getting the National Endowment for the Arts and the National Endowment for the Humanities established by legislation. He was impressed by the testimony of the notable witnesses who supported the Peace Academy proposal, but he knew that S.1976 would not be passed by the Congress.

Realizing the importance of wide public interest in the idea and sensing that the time was ripe to attract the backing of many thousands of Americans, Pell suggested the formation of a federal commission to examine the possibilities of a Peace Academy at public meetings in all parts of the country. Advocates of the Academy immediately saw the value of Pell's suggestion.

Federal commissions had been effective on several occasions in the history of the United States. A commission appointed by President Hoover in 1929 to investigate law enforcement and law observance exposed the existence of graft and corruption in many places and paved the way for the repeal of the eighteenth amendment (the amendment prohibiting liquor) of the Constitution. A Commission on Reorganization of the Executive Branch of the Federal Government, established by Congress in 1947, led to the Reorganization of 1949 and many reforms in federal procedures.

The Campaign Grows—And A Federal Commission Is Established

When bills to create a federal commission were introduced in the House and Senate in 1977, support was evident from citizens who had joined the Peace Academy Campaign. Principal sponsors in the House were Representative Andrew Young of Georgia and Representative Helen Meyner of New Jersey, but representatives from other districts soon learned that some of their constituents were committed to the idea. In the Senate, the initial sponsors were Spark Matsunaga, Mark Hatfield, and Jennings Randolph, but other Senators soon joined them.

The atmosphere in the United States in 1977 was very different from what it had been in 1971, when President Nixon and others had scoffed at Senator Hartke's bill to set up a Department of Peace. Nixon, one of the architects of the "cold war" between the United States and communist countries, had flown to China and to Russia, seeking better relations with these giant nations. The war in Vietnam had proved to be immensely costly to both sides, and the people of the United States were eager to find better ways of dealing with conflicts.

Nixon, President Gerald Ford and President Jimmy Carter all realized that war in a nuclear age involved enormous risks—perhaps even the destruction of civilization. Nixon had declared in a State of the Union address: "We are moving . . . from an era of confrontation to an era of negotiation . . . I see an America at peace with all the nations of the world. . . ." President Ford had negotiated a Strategic Arms Limitation Treaty with the Soviet Union, and President Carter pushed forward toward another treaty in an effort to halt the arms race.

So the hearings on bills to create a federal commission to consider a Peace Academy occurred in an atmosphere of hope. Many notable witnesses again appeared to urge the Congress to establish the Commission as soon as possible.

The House took no action on the proposed legislation. In the Senate, however, an amendment providing for the commission was successfully attached to an Elementary and Secondary Education bill which had already been passed by the House. The commission then gained a real chance of winning approval.

The Senate amendment was accepted by a conference of House and Senate members on the education bill, and President Carter signed it in November, 1978. Appropriations for the commission were finally pushed through Congress in 1979. Appointments of the nine members were completed in December of that year.

Meanwhile, the number of supporters of the Peace Academy Campaign had leaped from 3,000 to 35,000. Much of this growth was due to the initiative of Dr. Wedge, who persuaded this writer and Henry Burnett, a direct-mail expert, to develop materials about the Peace Academy idea for mailing to several million citizens. The test mailings were done as a special project by the Anacapa Fund of Santa Barbara. The responses quickly showed that Americans from coast to coast were ready for the consideration of a Peace Academy.

Three of the nine Commissioners were chosen by the Speaker of the House, three by the President Pro Tempore of the Senate, and three by the President of the United States. All of them were outstanding in various fields. All of them proved to be diligent in their search for a wide range of ideas.

Senator Matsunaga, the chairman, had been a member of the Senate since 1976. Before that, he had served for fourteen years in the House of Representatives. He had served in combat in World War II and had been severely wounded. He was a graduate of the University of Hawaii and the Harvard University Law School.

The vice-chairman, James H. Laue, was director of the Center for Metropolitan Studies and associate professor of sociology at the University of Missouri in St. Louis. He had received his Ph.D. from Harvard, and was an authority in the field of racial and community conflict resolution.

Others members included Representative John M. Ashbrook of Ohio; John R. Dellenback, president of the Christian College Consortium, a former director of the Peace Corps and a former member of the House; Arthur H. Barnes, president of the New York Urban Coalition; Elise Boulding, chair of the sociology department, Dartmouth College; John P. Dunfey, president of the Dunfey Hotels Corporation; Representative Dan Glickman of Kansas, a member of the Congressional Clearinghouse on the Future; and William F. Lincoln, director of the Center for Collaborative Planning, a professional arbitrator, and lecturer at the Harvard University Graduate School of Design.

After a year of hearing testimony from hundreds of experts and thousands of Americans who felt that a new institution was needed to promote research and training and to give a strong impetus to the whole field of "peace learning," there was a firm agreement among eight of the nine commissioners that the time had come to recommend the establishment of a Peace Academy. Only one member, Representative John Ashbrook—who had been skeptical about the idea from the beginning—was vigorously opposed to it.

Commissioner William F. Lincoln,who had expressed some doubts about its value, was completely convinced that "a U.S. Academy of Peace is indeed necessary, appropriate, and feasible." He announced that he supported it "as a patriot, as a citizen of this nation and a brother to all peoples of the world, as an academician, as a professional practitioner of community dispute resolution, as an Independent, and perhaps most notably as a convert to the concept which the Commission recommends."

185

"It is meaningful and right—indeed mandatory—that this nation establish, operate, and maintain such an academy," Lincoln said. "No clearer signal could be sent to peoples everywhere that the United States is committed to the further development and implementation of international and intranational conflict resolution by peaceful means. . . ."

Lincoln said, however, that he wanted the new institution to be called a "United States Academy for Peace and Justice" rather than simply designated as a Peace Academy. He declared: "Peace and conflict resolution without the deliberate aims for equity and justice would be devoid of integrity, and too easily could camouflage covert and overt intentions of oppression, even exploitation. But peace and justice offers the promise of an ordered life in which creative freedom can take root and grow."

Referring to an internal conflict within the Commission over whether the proposed academy should deal with "intranational conflicts" as well as international issues, Lincoln noted that the Commission's report "clearly includes intranational conflict as a legitimate concern for the Academy."

"The rightful coupling of international and intranational concerns for conflict may help bridge the traditional schism between advocates of world peace and activists for civil and human rights," Lincoln said. "'That schism is usually along racial and/or ethnic lines."

Commissioner John Dellenback insisted that the Academy should devote most of its attention to international problems. He asserted: "The need to remove injustice and violence from America must not divert the Academy from its principal concentration on international concerns. The international and intranational are certainly intertwined, but except to the degree that there are international lessons to be learned therefrom, it would be a mistake to expect the Academy to concentrate on conflict problems within the nation as well as those among nations. The Academy could well founder on rocky disputes over crime,

186

education, migration, procreation, taxation, or federal-state relations. The immediacy and nearness of such issues as these could engulf and dilute the international peace mandate of the Academy. The forum to concentrate on study and discussion of those issues should be elsewhere."

In explaining his opposition to the recommendation of the other eight members of the Commission, Representative Ashbrook said: "Years ago, it became apparent to me that we should have some Freedom Academy, a place where Americans can be taught and courses on communism made available to teachers, scholars and other interested persons. I would favor that before we embark on the course cited in this report. . . ."

The Commission's Report And Its Impact On Congress And Two Presidents

The report of the Commission received relatively little attention in the press and the broadcasting media of the United States and other countries, but had a constructive impact in the Senate and the House of Representatives and it was well received by many religious and civic organizations, by the American Arbitration Association, the American Association for the Advancement of Science, the National Education Association, the American Veterans Committee, the Dwight D. Eisenhower Society, the American Federation of Teachers, the National Women's Political Caucus, and by other organizations with millions of members. It was endorsed by the state legislatures of California, New York, Hawaii, Illinois, Michigan, Wisconsin, Oregon, Washington, North Dakota and Nebraska.

The members of the National Peace Academy campaign were active in all fifty states, urging Representatives and Senators to introduce and support legislation to carry out the Commission's proposals. Bills were soon introduced in both the House and the Senate—and the number supporting the Peace Academy grew to 60 members of the Senate and more than 170 members of the House.

The Commission staff and members had done a thorough job of keeping leaders in the Senate and the House well informed about the Commission's progress. Senator Matsunaga, the chairman of the Commission, was widely and favorably known in the Senate. Representative Glickman, another Commissioner, gained many sponsors for a bill he introduced in the House.

Although the Commission report was not adequately summarized or analyzed by the principal news agencies, newspapers in various parts of the country—the Baltimore *Sun,* the Atlanta *Constitution,* the St. Louis *Post-Dispatch,* the Chicago *Sun-Times,* the Cleveland *Plain Dealer,* and others— had carried favorable articles and editorials, indicating that the time had come for congressional action.

In recommending creating of a new institution, the Commission had drawn upon the following findings:

• National and international peace and security face grave danger from violent escalation of political, economic, and cultural conflicts;

• International peace and national security require use of a range of effective options, in addition to military capacity, to leash international violence and to manage international conflict;

• Americans have extensive national experience in resolving conflicts without violence due to the peacemaking talents created from our constitutional, democratic, free enterprise, and immigrant heritage;

• Through the worldwide activities of government, private enterprise, and voluntary associations, Americans could expand their own and others' cross-cultural insights and abilities necessary to promote peace at all levels of society;

• During the past thiry years, peace theories, scholarship and education had developed into a rigorous interdisciplinary field of learning;

- Achieving community and national peace as well as international peace required an understanding of the relationships among conflicts at these three levels of society, especially conflicts over ethnic, religious, and justice issues;
- People could be trained in both simple and sophisticated peacemaking skills and techniques, including negotiation, conciliation, mediation, and arbitration; and
- Inadequate use of peace-related knowledge and experience had been costly to the nation and the world, and had limited the effectiveness of policy-making and policy implementation in international affairs, conflicts, and war.

President Carter, who had used the techniques of mediation with excellent results in the Camp David accords, expressed enthusiasm for the Commission's recommendations when a preliminary report was presented to him at the White House in 1980.

His successor, President Reagan, was given a copy of the Commission's final draft of its report in 1981. President Reagan took no immediate position on it, but members of his staff later indicated that he would not support it. His staff members apparently convinced him that there was no need for such a new educational institution on the federal level.

Yet the number of Americans actively working for the establishment of a Peace Academy continued to increase in the 1980s—and the negative attitudes of White House staff members did not daunt the Senators and Representatives who sponsored the legislation to create the Academy.

After nearly 200 years of thought and discussion, the "Peace Office" first recommended by Benjamin Banneker and Dr. Benjamin Rush had developed into a comprehensive proposal persistently supported by millions of citizens. Despite the attacks made on the proposal by critics in the White House and in Congress, many Americans continued to share the views expressed by Senator Mark Hatfield: "It does not make sense to limit the responsibility of our government in the field of peace-making solely to diplomacy and preparation for war. The untapped potential through other means is too great, and the cost of failure is too high ... It would be a tremendous perversion of our stated priorities if we were to declare ourselves unwilling to invest in this new opportunity for peace, while we continue to make investments in the more traditional search for peace through strength."

It was Senator Hatfield who brought into existence a United States Institute of Peace, based on the Peace Academy campaign. He attached a Peace Institute amendment to a defense appropriations bill, and the bill was passed by Congress in October 1984. President Reagan, who wanted the funds provided for arms in the bill, finally signed it—accepting the Peace Institute provision.

Enemies of the Peace Institute tried to end its short life in 1987, by trying to eliminate any money for it in an appropriation bill. But they did not succeed. The Institute received a small appropriation—and it held the support of many members of Congress.

At long last, an institution devoted to peace had become part of the American government's structure.

III. SHAPING THE FUTURE

A biomedical scientist cannot help but be aware of the enormous load of disease and starvation in the world. A biomedical scientist can also not help but be aware that enormous improvements could be made in the health of the people of the world by increased expenditures for public health measures, for food and nutritional supplements, and for research into better ways to prevent disease.

A citizen of the United States cannot help but be struck by the incredible disproportion in spending for arms and spending to improve the health of humankind. If our priorities were rearranged so that we spent more on improving the health of humankind and less on arms, we in the U.S. would be more secure. Such a change in our expenditures would dramatically indicate to the rest of the world that our concerns are with peace and not with war.

Since our adversaries have equal or greater problems with the health of their people and since most of the rest of the people in the world are much more concerned with health than with superpower conflicts, the entire political atmosphere of the world would change.

Although such measures would do nothing to prevent tribal, national, and religious animosities and other social conflicts leading to wars, war, although horrible, would remain local and not threaten the entire world population. In time, an increased concern with the health of the world's population might lead to the general realization that even small conventional wars are an equal threat to health as disease and malnutrition.

—Howard M. Temin
Nobel Laureate in Physiology/Medicine

FRANK K. KELLY

13. Needed: A Nuclear Age Peace Corps— An Alternative to Annihilation

The late President John F. Kennedy sparked the imaginations of idealistic young Americans with his concept of a Peace Corps. Kennedy provided a framework for the altruistic impulses of citizens of the wealthiest, most powerful nation on Earth. Through the Peace Corps in the last twenty-five years, Americans were able to go abroad and work to improve the lot of citizens in poorer countries throughout the world.

In this chapter, Frank Kelly suggests the formation of a new type of peace corps—a Nuclear Age Peace Corps. Kelly's concept would differ from Kennedy's in significant ways.

1. The primary function of Nuclear Age Peace Corps volunteers will be to educate others on the urgent need to reverse the nuclear arms race, using the results of recent reports issued by scientists.
2. The Nuclear Age Peace Corps will spread knowledge of the techniques of peaceful conflict resolution showing how violent conflicts can be averted.
3. The Nuclear Age Peace Corps will be composed primarily of young leaders (clergy, educators, civic leaders, etc.) who will return to their communities to teach others.
4. Training will be accomplished in a series of seminars, and the ordinary work of the Nuclear Age Peace Corps volunteers will go on in addition to their volunteer work.

The Nuclear Age Peace Corps will be built upon these propositions:

1. That the likelihood of climatic change and environmental destruction found in "Nuclear Winter" studies make the *destruction levels of a nuclear war unacceptably high;*

193

2. That the increasing likelihood of nuclear war occurring by accident or inadvertence make the *risk of nuclear war unacceptably high;*
3. That there are *feasible alternatives to the present course of action, including the expansion of trade, cultural and scientific exchanges between nations;* and
4. That citizens in a democracy have the *right and responsibility to create a better and safer world.*

This chapter provides a framework for combining education and action, information and compassion.

There are signs that millions of people are changing their ways of thinking—and that includes the leaders of the United States, the Soviet Union, and other nuclear powers.

The old ways of thinking are being battered and broken by a flood of new information on the biological and climatic effects of a nuclear war. While nuclear weapons continue to be built, the leaders and the people of the most heavily armed nations have been forced to realize that these weapons cannot be effectively used without suicidal results. The negotiations between the U.S. and the Soviets are now ostensibly aimed at the elimination of these monsters.

It has long been known that the use of nuclear weapons in a full-scale war would kill hundreds of millions of human beings and inflict terrible damage. The General Assembly of the United Nations declared in 1982 that the use of such weapons would be a crime against humanity. A recent scientific report entitled, *The Cold and the Dark: The World After Nuclear War*—based on a year's work by more than 200 scientists from many countries—shows conclusively that such a war would not only be a crime against humanity but a crime against life on earth.[1]

Dr. Carl Sagan, one of the contributors to this report, says that such a war "may carry in its wake a climatic catastrophe, which we call 'nuclear winter,' unprecedented during the tenure of humans on earth." Dr. Paul Ehrlich, a noted biologist who also participated in the project, said that such a war would produce "extreme and widespread damage to living systems."

Another participant—Dr. Donald Kennedy, president of Stanford University—asserted: "What our most thoughtful projections show is that a major nuclear exchange will produce, among its many plausible effects, the greatest biological and physical disruptions of this planet in its last 65 million years.... That assessment of prospective risk needs to form a background for everyone who bears responsibility for national security decisions, here and elsewhere."

Soviet scientists strongly endorsed the statements by Sagan, Ehrlich and Kennedy. Nikolai Bochkov, director of the Institute of Genetics of the U.S.S.R., declared: "In the aftermath of a nuclear war,the prospects for mankind must obviously be seen in the perspective of a world in which the ecosystems and ecological resources have been disturbed and destroyed. Thus, the biological and sociological conditions would not be such that human beings would be able to maintain themselves as a species."

A. Alexander Bayev, of the Soviet Academy of Sciences, said that nuclear war "raises the questions of whether the very survival of mankind is possible, or even whether continued life on earth in the forms that we know is possible." Dr. Nikita Moiseev, deputy director of the Computing Center of the Soviet Academy, disclosed that studies done in the Computing Center in Moscow confirmed the results indicated by Sagan and Ehrlich. Dr. Roald Sagdeyev, director of the Soviet's institute of Cosmic Studies, asserted: "The development of scenarios of the evolution of the biosphere and atmosphere after a nuclear war, which has been taking place over the past twenty years, has now finally given us a very serious model, the results of which have been reported by two independent groups, the group represented by Dr. Sagan and the group consisting of our scientists...."

Yevgeniy P. Velikov, vice president of the Soviet Academy of Sciences, concluded: "All kinds of policy positions on local or so-called 'limited war,' counterforce strikes, 'controlled' war, flexible reactions, or prolonged war are concepts that have become, in light of what we now know, totally baseless.... We see that no military or psychological arguments—and there are many of them—can refute these results. I think the only conclusion possible is that our nuclear devices are not and cannot be useful as weapons of war or tools of war; nor can they be a tool of politics. They are simply tools of suicide."

Dr. Walter Orr Roberts, a physicist who is a past president of the American Association for the Advancement of Science, said: "It is imperative, in the name of humanity, to accelerate the search for world security in the policy domain... We must indeed invent and enact policies that covenant a stable future for the planet...."

Dr. Lewis Thomas, chancellor of the Memorial Sloan-Kettering Cancer Center, said that the two studies in climatology and biology "change everything or ought to change everything in the world about the prospect of thermonuclear warfare." Dr. Thomas added: "It is no longer a political matter, to be left to the wisdom and foresight of a few statesmen and a few military authorities.... It is a global dilemma, involving all of humankind."

Donald Kennedy urged that leaders in all countries give more consideration to the resolution adopted by the American National Academy of Sciences, which stated that "science offers no prospect of effective defense against nuclear war" and called upon the leaders of the United States and the Soviet Union to "take all practical actions that could reduce the risk of nuclear war by accident or miscalculation" and to intensify their efforts to achieve verifiable agreements leading to arms reductions.

The Need For A Nuclear Age Peace Corps

Publication of *The Cold and The Dark*—along with increasing knowledge of the danger of an accidental nuclear war and the publication of many other reports on the perils of the nuclear age—underlines the need for the formation of a *Nuclear Age Peace Corps,* composed of specially trained leaders who could aid the people of the United States and other countries in developing ways to end the nuclear threat.

Many leaders in many fields are now aware of the fact that action to reverse the arms race "is no longer a political matter, to be left to the wisdom and foresight of a few statesmen and a few military authorities. . . ." Thousands of peace organizations have come into existence in the last ten years—and these organizations have done much to stimulate changes in thinking by millions of people—but a special corps of peace volunteers is needed to bring the latest findings of scientists to the attention of people everywhere.

Advocates of a "nuclear freeze" have begun to use *The Cold and the Dark* report as an additional argument for a weapons freeze. But there are many millions who are not aware of the full significance of "nuclear winter"—and are not aware of the constructive proposals which have been offered to end the nuclear arms race. If humanity is to survive, there must be thousands of peace advocates working day and night to make everyone conscious of an obligation to promote reverence for life—life in all its forms.

A Nuclear Age Peace Corps would have three basic purposes:

1. to provide a thorough background of knowledge necessary to understand how the arms race threatens the very existence of life on earth;
2. to examine carefully the most promising proposals for ways out of the nuclear dilemma; and

197

3. to stimulate dialogues with people of all ages on the fundamental questions of the nuclear age.

Participants in the first training program for the Corps would be drawn from city council members, mayors, leaders of civic organizations, teachers,clergymen and lay leaders of religious groups. These participants would be invited to take part in seminars to be held in major cities.

The seminars would be organized by the Nuclear Age Peace Foundation in cooperation with colleges and universities which would be asked to supply faculty members and seminar facilities. There would also be consultation with leaders from peace organizations and the groups which sponsored *The Cold and the Dark* report. These included the American Institute of Biological Sciences, the American Society for Microbiology, the Canadian Nature Federation, Common Cause, the Ecological Society of America, the International Federation of Institutes for Advanced Study, the National Science Teachers Association, and many others.

The United States Institute of Peace—which was authorized by Congress in 1984—would be asked to aid in developing and funding the Nuclear Age Peace Corps seminars.

The Congress acted to establish a Peace Institute after a nine-member federal commission conducted public hearings in all parts of the United States. Two thousand persons participated in those hearings. It became overwhelmingly clear to the commissioners—and later to the Congress—that many Americans wanted to see this nation take leadership in developing new approaches to the process of making and maintaining peace.

In recommending the creation of a federal educational institution devoted to peace, the commission found that "international peace and national security require use of a range of effective options, in addition to military capacity, to leash international violence and to manage international conflict"—and asserted that "people can be trained in both simple and sophisticated peace-making skills and techniques."

Members of a Nuclear Age Peace Corps—using materials now available—could learn and then demonstrate that a full range of effective options "to leash international violence and to manage international conflict" now exist and can be used with public support.

Making Peace Possible—
Because Nothing Else Is Tolerable

The Cold and the Dark report—as well as other reports on the new weapons systems—can produce positive results for the whole human race by making it absolutely clear to leaders and people everywhere that the prevention of nuclear war is not only possible but essential for the continuation of life on earth.

President Reagan's statement that "a nuclear war cannot be won and must never be fought" shows that he knows the truth of the human situation. (Similar statements have been made by Soviet leaders and by the leaders of other nations.) Shortly after his inauguration for a second term, the President revealed a change in his own thinking. He told a group of religious broadcasters: "In the last four years I've come to believe that we're all God's children—clerks, kings and Communists. We're all made in the image of God."

The interdependence of life on this planet, long known to scientists, has entered the consciousness of people so deeply that the possibility of nuclear war has become intolerable to conservatives as well as liberals, to people of all religious beliefs and people who are agnostics or skeptics. The revulsion against the policy called MAD—Mutual Assured Destruction—has become so strong that President Reagan's advisors have come up with a Strategic Defense Initiative designed to offer a "shield" against nuclear missiles—a "shield" that nobody knows how to build now but one that might be developed in the next twenty years. This plan offers no hope of ending the arms race in the next decade.

Meanwhile, strategists for both of the superpowers admit there are no defenses now capable of giving any protection against nuclear missiles. Yevgeniy Velikov of the Soviet Academy of Sciences put it bluntly: "All kinds of policy positions have become, in the light of what we know now, totally baseless. . . ."

Dr. Lewis Thomas summed up the situation in these terms: "Up to now, we have all tended to regard any conflict with nuclear arms as an attempt by paired adversaries to settle such issues as territorial dominance or ideological dispute. Now, with the new findings before us, it is clear that any territory gained will be, at the end, a barren wasteland, and any ideology will vanish in the death of civilization. . . ."

American and Soviet officials have not yet acknowledged that all kinds of policy positions have become "totally baseless" and it is not likely that they will do so.

It is obviously difficult for many leaders to change their policies or even to consider new initiatives. Before he left office, Canadian Prime Minister Pierre Trudeau traveled around the world in an effort to get political leaders to consider new proposals. He talked with the heads of twenty-four nations. He found these leaders gloomily aware of the rising dangers—but apparently unwilling or unable to contribute much to the development of solutions.

In a speech he gave when he accepted the Albert Einstein Peace Prize, Trudeau said: "Politicians, who once stated that war was too important to be left to the generals, now act as though peace were too complex to be left to themselves. . . . Any government leader who wanted to master the topic completely would have difficulty in discharging all his other duties. . . . Hence the temptation to rely on others, be they ministers, ambassadors, chiefs of staff, technocrats or negotiators. In the last analysis, this means that the nuclear accountants (as NATO Secretary-General Lord Carrington called them) on both sides hold the world to ransom. . . ."

In a recent statement to the Senate Foreign Relations committee, Secretary of State George Shultz made no reference to Trudeau's statements or to the report of the 200 scientists on the climatic and biological consequences of nuclear war, but he did say that "the pace of technological advance now opens possibilities for new ways of strategic thinking—never an easy process."

Shultz told the senators: "During the next ten years, the U.S. objective is a radical reduction in the power of existing and planned offensive nuclear arms, as well as the stabilization of the relationship between offensive and defensive nuclear arms, whether on earth or in space. . . . A world free of nuclear arms is an ultimate objective to which we, the Soviet Union, all other nations can agree." Between 1985 and 1995, the world would remain under the threat of nuclear annihilation.

Can the "nuclear accountants"—the "experts" who attempt to "balance" the offensive and defensive systems of the superpowers—lead us to "a world free of nuclear arms" in ten years or twenty years or in any number of years? The record of the last twenty years, during which the nuclear arms in the world have increased at a staggering rate, does not indicate that they can do so.

So the time is right for a by-pass operation—an operation to go around the clogged arteries of official channels and to bring the people of the world into a full awareness of what they face and what they may be able to do about it. The attainment of peace in a nuclear age is not "too complex" to accomplish—if they have the aid of a Nuclear Age Peace Corps.

In the seminars, the following topics could be explored:

1. The full scope of the findings summarized in *The Cold and the Dark* report.
2. The factors that might lead to an accidental nuclear

war—with discussions of ideas designed to prevent its occurrence, such as the late Senator Henry Jackson's recommendation for a U.S.-Soviet Crisis Consultation Center and Genevieve Nowlin's suggestion for a continuous space patrol manned by members of the United Nations.

3. The recommendations generated by the UN Committee on Disarmament, the special sessions of the General Assembly on disarmament, and the Department of Disarmament Affairs operated by the UN Secretariat. Many of these specific recommendations have high value, but have been generally ignored by the mass media and inadequately considered by officials of the U.S. and the U.S.S,R,

4. Recommendations generated by the Fund for Peace, the Center for Defense Information, the Nuclear Age Peace Foundation, the Interfaith Center to Reverse the Arms Race, and other non-governmental organizations.

5. Reports from the universities and colleges which have begun to redesign programs and develop sources that enhance their understanding of the nuclear arms race and lead to suggestions for positive steps to end it.

6. Proposals for expanding economic trade as well as cultural and scientific exchanges between countries with different political persuasions; such exchanges would promote economic interdependence and social understanding.

7. Ideas offered by independent leaders with significant experience—including former Secretary of Defense Robert McNamara, former Ambassador George Kennan, Admiral Gene La Rocque, former arms control negotiator Paul Warnke, former CIA Director William Colby, and others who are seeking ways out of the nuclear dilemma.

After their participation in these seminars—and passing an examination showing their knowledge of the nuclear situation—the members of the new Peace Corps could carry their knowledge into many organizations and many places. They could speak at meetings of civic organizations such as Rotary Clubs and Kiwanis Clubs, at gatherings of church leaders and women's groups; at committee meetings of both branches of Congress; on television and radio programs; at schools and colleges; in meetings with State Department and White House staff members and in dialogues with leaders of many organizations in other countries.

New leaders are rising to power in many nations. Military dictatorships have yielded to democratic movements in Brazil, Argentina, the Philippines and other countries. Similar movements are underway elsewhere. Members of a Nuclear Age Peace Corps could help the participants in these movements to understand the constructive proposals that might speed up the elimination of nuclear weapons from the earth.

A Nuclear Age Peace Corps could give thousands of people an opportunity to make a creative leap beyond the despair which has afflicted many human beings who have tried and failed to stop the steady growth of the nuclear monsters. Its development would show these people that human beings are not insects trapped on the grinding wheels of the military-industrial systems that dominate the world today.

Dr. Willis Harman, a regent of the University of California and president of the Institute of Noetic Sciences, sees an expanding recognition of human unity which has prepared the ground for a new stage in human development. In his book *Higher Creativity*, Dr. Harman cites two scientific achievements with profound significance: "One is the unleashing of the power of the atom; the other is major progress toward the unfettering of the human mind. The first—leading to the development of nuclear weapons— almost demands the second, advances in the understanding of deeper human motivations and aspirations, values and

203

perceptions, perversities and potentialities, than any previous society has ever achieved."

"Ultimately, our concerns as individuals are meaningless without an equal concern for our human family," Dr. Harman points out. "It is a peculiar fact of life for those of us alive today ... that without a near-future breakthrough into a true realization of our familyhood, there will be no future generations. Let us envision utopia, and thus bring it into existence. There is no reasonable alternative."

Formation of a Nuclear Age Peace Corps would be a long step toward human unity—toward a realization that human beings everywhere are linked together in the web of life and must shoulder the responsibility for working with others to bring a final end to the nuclear threat. That may or may not be utopian. But it is evidently an absolute necessity.

JAN TINBERGEN

14. Revitalizing the United Nations System

Jan Tinbergen has spent his life trying to create a more just and equitable world. He is well qualified to discuss the revitalization of the United Nations. Not only is he one of the world's leading economists (a co-recipient of the first Nobel Prize in Economics), but he spent many years conducting projects for specialized agencies of the United Nations. He is a man well acquainted with the strengths and faults of the United Nations organization, and with the global need for its increased effectiveness.

As an economist, Professor Tinbergen is concerned with finding the optimal organizational level for reaching decisions in a world of sovereign nations. He recognizes clearly that while certain problems can be solved at the national or sub-national levels, others can only be solved at the global level. Among the latter problems are those concerned with population growth, resource depletion, pollution, nuclear weapons, and misuse of the oceans and outer space. If these problems are not solved at the global level, they will continue to intensify and lead to increased conflict among nations.

The United Nations was formed "to save succeeding generations from the scourge of war." So far the organization has failed more conspicuously than it has succeeded in realizing this goal. If it is to become effective in preventing wars, including nuclear war, the U.N. decision-making process must be restructured to better reflect contemporary political power. The organization must also be empowered to enforce its decisions. Professor Tinbergen offers a thoughtful proposal for embarking on a process of revitalizing our only existing organization with the potential for global management.

oday's world consists of a thoroughly intertwined
cluster of nations—more than 150, from very small
and weak to very large and strong—all facing
unprecedented threats. As a consequence of population
growth, exhaustion of certain resources, and new technological developments, problems have arisen with an as yet
unknown impact on human welfare. Pollution of the atmosphere, water and soil, erosion, deforestation and desertifica-
tion threaten the lives of tens of millions of persons and are
getting out of control. Perhaps worst of all are the potential
disasters nuclear energy may bring. Peacetime accidents
have thus far shown only a relatively modest type of danger,
although the potential dangers were demonstrated at Three
Mile Island in the U.S. and Chernobyl in the U.S.S.R. What is
in store in the form of nuclear weapons has been expressed
in words, but does not yet seem to have penetrated into
human conscience.

On the occasion of the fortieth anniversary of the United
Nations many speakers and writers made an attempt to
evaluate its performance. Understandably the evaluation of
the complex and many-sided activities differed depending
upon activities and according to commentators. Activities
in the field of information and documentation were more or
less unanimously praised, while activities in maintaining
peace or preventing war were found to be of very limited
significance. On many other activities, evaluations varied
considerably. Very diverse attitudes were also shown with
regard to the UN's future. Opinions differed widely on the
importance of new tasks for the United Nations institutions—for instance, the creation of a New International
Economic Order, or the introduction of the new Law of the
Sea.

Unfortunately, critics of the UN decision-making methods, or of its failure to establish a peaceful world have not offered a set of carefully selected forward-looking proposals. Rather, they appear not to be interested. They are strong at rejecting new ideas, but have not replaced them by better alternatives. At most, they have elaborated details; useful details, to be sure, such as avoiding repetitive addresses or avoiding the politicization of purely technical subjects. In brief, the critics of the United Nations system have not made positive proposals of the order of magnitude which today's world sorely needs.

Filling Power Vacuums: Historical Examples

In a world consisting of sovereign nations only, without any element of superstructure, a large number of activities will be initiated which, when carried out, would appear to be incompatible. The initiatives of the powerful nations have a better chance to be implemented than those of the weak. If two or more powerful actors want incompatible changes, however, supranational structures will be needed if clashes are to be avoided. Clashes imply waste of energy and massive human suffering and hence a sub-optimal development.

If superstructures to settle conflicts are lacking, we have a power vacuum which must be filled. It may be filled by the conclusion of a treaty, or by the establishment of a common institution. In both cases a portion of a nation's sovereignty is shifted to a supranational level. Such conflict settling institutions save the energy otherwise wasted and prevent the human suffering. They do so by, for instance, gathering information and doing research to avoid future conflicts. In other cases, they may invite a number of weak nations (into an alliance) and thus help to implement a larger part of these nations' aspirations.

To illustrate, I shall mention a few institutions, part of the current system of United Nations institutions, which were created to fill power vacuums.

One of the oldest institutions is the *Universal Postal Union* (UPU). Not long after the organization of national mail services, the international part of this form of communication also had to be streamlined by more uniform national rules and agreements about rates and the distribution of receipts between the nations involved. An international superstructure of mail services became the responsibility of the Universal Postal Union.

The *International Labor Organization* (ILO) was established at the Washington Conference in 1919. During the nineteenth century workers organized themselves in trade unions in order to exert pressure on employers to improve wages and labor conditions, which in the early part of the century were inhuman. During the second half of the nineteenth century a start was made with legislation prohibiting the worst extremes. Prior to World War I a whole system of social legislation was enacted step by step. The end of World War I brought the eight-hour working day. These improvements became possible as a consequence of continued capital formation and technological development. The improved standard of life of workers in developed countries was threatened, however, by the competition of low-wage countries, and it became clear that social legislation had to be internationalized in order to safeguard worker well-being. This internationalization became the task of the International Labor Organization and its secretariat, the International Labor Office in Geneva. Although the ILO was set up to support Western workers' interests, it gradually also contributed increasingly to an improvement of the well-being of Third World workers, so far as economic conditions would permit.

Jumping from the First to the Second World War we find that at the Bretton Woods conference in 1945 two important institutions were created to respond to another set of "vacuums" in the financial field. These were the *International Bank for Reconstruction and Development* (World Bank) and the *International Monetary Fund* (IMF). The Bank helped to finance the reconstruction of war-stricken countries to begin with, and later, increasingly, the development of underdeveloped countries. Its loans are long-term loans made to governments, and so the World Bank is part of a public world infrastructure. Similarly the IMF provides short-term loans to countries in balance-of-payments difficulties and illustrates the existence of a common interest of all member countries in an orderly system of international payments.

Filling Power Vacuums: Contemporary Examples

One of the oldest forms of international discourse, trade between nations is an area where national interests are still given a higher priority than is desirable. A trading partner's interests should be given *equal* weight. In other words, protective forces are still keeping trade at lower than optimal levels. A long-ago proposed *International Trade Organization* (1947 Conference of Havana) was not ratified by the United States. As a second-best solution the *General Agreement on Tariffs and Trade* (GATT) was established, which is only an agreement on how to negotiate, from time to time, tariff reductions. Since the developing countries especially felt that their interests were given low weight, a new specialized agency, the *United Nations Conference on Trade and Development* (UNCTAD) was created in 1964, where Third World interests were given higher weight. UNCTAD is presently suffering from the same lack of power as the United Nations generally and so we may conclude that part of the power vacuum in matters of trade is still waiting for a new approach.

A second contemporary example refers to the rights and duties of transnational enterprises (TNEs). TNEs are able to profit from the absence of some form of world government. An attempt to fill at least part of this vacuum has been the establishment of a UN Centre for Transnational Corporations and a UN Code of Conduct for TNEs and for the governments involved. The Centre collects information on TNE and government behavior.

A third contemporary example relates to the production and distribution of food. The world food economy suffers from a lack of equilibrium: Europe and North America are producing too much and a large part of the Third World is producing too little. So far no solution acceptable to all concerned has been found. There have been only partial solutions, not well coordinated.

A fourth contemporary example concerns the draft Law of the Sea. In a nine-year series of negotiations in the *UN Conference on the Law of the Sea* (UNCLOS) this law has been adapted to a number of new facts, technologies and discoveries. The number of ratifications by participating nations is not yet sufficient for the new Law to become valid. The governments of some important countries,including the United States, have attempted to change the draft law; and it is not yet clear what the result will be. It would be a deplorable setback if the draft law, achieved with such painstaking effort, were to be substantially changed.

A fifth example of an existing power vacuum is found in the field of environmental policies. The *United Nations Environment Programme* (UNEP) Secretariat in Nairobi is the center of information and research that recommends a number of policy activities in order to stop a further deterioration of the environment and to upgrade it. But again there is a power vacuum since UNEP is not endowed with any executive power.

The last, and by far the most important, example of today's power vacuum is, of course, the security issue. As a consequence of a variety of factors we have been forced into a position where two superpowers, the United States and the Soviet Union have available, among other arms, a nuclear destruction capacity enabling them to kill the planet's population several times over. Moreover, they adhere to different socio-economic systems, officially often said to be opposite, or mutually incompatible. Political philosophies of the past, adhered to by many citizens and politicians in both powers and their allies (NATO and Warsaw Pact), when applied by the military and civilian leadership, could easily lead to a third and last world war. In an attempt to introduce the necessary new thinking alluded to by Albert Einstein, the most astute commentators have formulated some basic points. These are (a) a nuclear war cannot be won since it destroys everybody's environment, and hence (b) must not be fought. A prohibition of (nuclear) war lies within the competence of the UN Security Council and it is here that we find the most glaring power vacuum. Decision making by the Security Council is thwarted by the veto power of its permanent members, making implementation of any decision virtually impossible because of lack of consensus.

Having illustrated what power vacuums have been tentatively filled or are in the process or in need of being filled, I now propose to deal systematically with the innovations needed in the UN institutions.

Sources of Inspiration

How can a systematic treatment of the innovation of the United Nations System be undertaken? What, in other words, can be our sources of inspiration? In order to be as realistic as possible we prefer to be guided by two main empirical sources. One is to learn from the history of our own subject, the United Nations. The other is to learn from similar subjects. Their similarity must be derived from the essential features of our subject. We submit that the essential task of the future United Nations is managing our planet. So the other source of inspiration is good management. This may be management of large, well-run enterprises, or management of a successful national government. I will discuss these three sources in succession.

The fortieth anniversary of the United Nations in 1985 gave rise to a large number of evaluations. Many lessons can be drawn from the errors made by the UN system as well as from its successes. Since some types of errors have been, in our opinion, overemphasized, and so are well known, we shall almost automatically apply these lessons.

Other types of errors have not been discussed as much as they should. An example is the recommendation about the amount of official development assistance made in 1969 by the Pearson Commission and in 1970 by the UN Committee for Development Planning. The weak form of decision-making chosen—a recommendation only—clearly is not sufficient and constitutes an error. The governments of the medium-sized and large industrial countries have not taken these recommendations seriously, and actual assistance provided has been about half of the amount suggested by the experts. As a consequence we are now facing the debt problem. If the recommended 0.7 percent of GNP had been made available to Third World nations since 1970, an amount close to the present Third World debt would have been transferred in addition to the official assistance actually transferred. The debt problem is due to that error.

In addition, one success story should be given the attention it deserves. The way the United Nations Conference on the Law of the Sea was chaired and the discussions organized deserves special mention. One illustration is the fact that several quite different drafts were tabled by various participating representatives or groups of countries. The creation, out of these various texts, of a "unique informal negotiation text," was the key to an orderly and efficient discussion.

Learning from errors, therefore, implies that the various improvements in procedures of decision-making that have been mentioned by many commentators are carried out.

Their execution should not only be recommended, but imposed; for instance, by explicitly prescribing them in the regulations and making them part of the task of the chairperson of all meetings.

The idea that in many cases procedures be imposed instead of simply recommended is another example of the need for increased power, the filling of power vacuums which we discussed in a much wider sense.

Learning from well-organized large enterprises means that businesslike approaches deserve attention. These will be forthcoming automatically if the UN institutions are run by persons with outstanding managerial qualities.

An important characteristic of a well-run enterprise is that its staff forms a well-defined hierarchy, with several levels, and clearly defined responsibilities for each level. This latter characteristic implies that for the resolution of each problem an optimal level of decision making exists. This characteristic applies to details as well as to the main tasks and their execution. It applies in particular to the way in which the world's most urgent problems are going to be tackled.

Learning from well-run nations consists partly of modes of action also used by well-run enterprises. But there are some fundamental differences between enterprises and nations. Enterprises can select their "population" of employees; nations are *given* their population, including all sorts of human beings who suffer from old age, sickness or other handicaps, and human beings too young to work and in need of preparing themselves for a job. For a well-run nation efficiency is as desirable as for a well-run firm, but its tasks are different. Clearly the United Nations institutions are more comparable to a nation than to an enterprise. The United Nations organization has to include human beings much more different than in any one nation and so its tasks are more difficult. Whereas one nation can get rid of some less desirable individuals, the world as a whole cannot.

In a sense the commonwealth of all peoples faces prob-

213

lems similar to those of one federal state, and the federal state again faces problems similar to those of one state. The structures repeat themselves "at one level lower." So far the commonwealth of one well-run federal state is better organized than the world at large, and this is why the latter can learn from the former.

National states tend to maintain as much as their sovereignty as possible, and often prefer that the superstructure is weak. They prefer a set of treaties to regulate their common interests. It remains to be seen, however, whether such a weak structure is really preferable. Would it be wise to replace the United States of America by fifty sovereign states linked by treaties? A set of treaties may be a good beginning, but in the long run a stronger structure is more secure. With this picture in mind let us discuss the optimal structure of the United Nations institutions.

Remarks on the General Structure

The UN institutions are operating more or less autonomously, almost as sovereign entities. Where their activities so require they are consulting each other, and their activities are coordinated by bodies such as the *Economic and Social Council* and the *Administrative Committee on Coordination* (ACC). The structure is complicated on the one hand and weak on the other hand. Among the reasons for this state of affairs are that the institutions were created at very different times and their creation served the interests of varying groups of countries, competing for increased power. In contrast to the structure of governments of well-run nations the UN structure lacks strength and needs reconstruction around a set of concrete objectives, together aiming at the management of the planet.

There should be a "World Government," subdivided in "Departments" for separate areas of world governmental tasks, and responsible to a "World Parliament." The Executive should be a board of the heads of the departments of a number of specialized agencies, grouped in a logical way. Some of the smaller agencies, such as the Universal Postal Union or the World Meteorological Organization, should be part of broader departments, such as a Department of Transportation and Communication, or a Department of Agriculture, whose main agencies would be the larger agencies, such as the Food and Agricultural Organization in the latter case.

The tasks of the various institutions will be partly determined by this structure and so will the agency to which they have to report. The complete reconstruction will be a subject to be dealt with by the UN Conference on Necessary Reform, proposed at the end of this essay. It should be clear that world government tasks are only tasks that require a decision at world level; few but important ones.

Reforms of Existing UN Institutions: Representation of Member Nations in Assemblies

Having set out the need for a stronger United Nations system of institutions and the sources of inspiration for its design, I propose to specify a number of reforms in more concrete form. I will do so by, first, discussing the reforms of already *existing* UN institutions (in the present section) and, then, discussing some *new institutions* that should be created.

A major reform is needed with regard to the General Assembly. Countries with a large population should have a larger influence on the decisions made than countries with a small population, and for the time being nations with a high income per capita should also have more influence than countries with a low income per capita since contributions to the total budget must be dependent on these incomes. This latter difference in influence need not persist, however, if the historical development of democratic parlia-

215

ments is followed. This reform should also apply to the assemblies of all specialized agencies.

The credibility and the impact of the United Nations and of any of the specialized organizations depends, to a very high degree, on the composition of the General Assembly or the Assembly of the specialized agency considered. The present system of one nation one vote reduces credibility and impact to a very low level. The way of representation must reflect more clearly the significance to world affairs of the member nations. The history of parliamentary democracy illustrates this. The present situation in Western democracies based on one vote for all adult citizens was preceded by systems where only taxpayers or individuals who had passed an exam were entitled to vote. Similarly the representation of nations in the UN General Assembly or in specialized agencies' assemblies may start with a more limited system and develop in line with the development of the member nations' potential to serve the cause at stake. The assemblies may be characterized by criteria that reflect such potential; criteria adhered to by a sufficient number of experts in all parts of the world.

As a concrete example we shall show the composition of the General Assembly under three possible procedures, each of them with alternatives. Hopefully, this example may serve as a starting point to the official commission in charge of the formulation of a revised UN Charter (see the last section of this chapter). The criteria chosen are: (I) the member nations' agreed on financial contributions; (II) the members' real national product; and (III) the members' population size.

Financial contribution as a criterion is used by shareholders' meetings of corporations and may be nicknamed "one dollar, one vote." It is reflected in the stage of parliamentary democracy where only taxpayers had a vote—although not in exactly the same way: it is more conservative. We will call it the dollar procedure ($).

Real national income as a criterion weights member nations according to what they are contributing to world real product. It reflects the member nations' productivity and will be called the productivity procedure (prod.).

Population as a criterion is used for adults in democratic parliaments and corresponds with "one person, one vote." It will be called the population procedure (pop.).

Since it is agreed upon that nations with a high income per capita should contribute more to the UN than nations with a low income per capita, the dollar procedure (I) leads to a criterion more unequal than the productivity procedure (II) which is more unequal than the population procedure (III) where differences in income per capita do not matter at all.

Income should not be nominal income, expressed in, for instance, U.S. dollars, but real income, expressed in buying power. In other words national currencies should not be converted into dollars with the aid of exchange rates but with the aid of the currency's buying power parity. Fortunately an elaborate study by I.B. Kravis and collaborators made for the World Bank and preceded by an application to more than 100 countries supplies us with exactly the material we need, of an unprecedented quality.[1] Table I is based on this material. This table shows the number of assembly seats given by each of the procedures to the nations whose criterion entitles them to one or more seats. Provisionally an assembly of 200 seats has been assumed (in order to remain close to the present number of 159 member states). Dividing the total, for all countries considered, of the criterion by 200, we obtain the criterion value entitling a nation to one seat. Nations with more than half that value (so the total divided by 400) are also considered to be entitled to a seat.

Table I shows the result of these initial procedures. Some of the most important features are: (a) a large number of member countries do not receive any seat; (b) the dollar procedure gives, for the high-income countries, more seats than the productivity procedure and the latter more seats than the population procedure, for obvious reasons; (c) in contrast, for low-income countries the opposite applies: more seats under the population procedure than under the productivity procedure and more seats under the latter than under the dollar procedure.

TABLE I.

Number of seats in Assembly of (provisionally) 200 seats to be occupied by member nations entitled to one or more seats.

Country	Procedure		
	($)	(prod.)	(pop.)
	Market Economies		
U.S.A.	61	41	11
Japan	16	12	6
Germany FR	13	9	3
France	10	7	3
UK	9	7	3
Italy	8	6	3
Canada	6	4	1
Brazil	3	5	5
Mexico	3	3	3
Spain	3	3	2
Australia	3	2	1
Argentina	2	2	1
Netherlands	2	2	1
Sweden	2	1	.
South Africa	1	2	1
Turkey	1	1	2
Iran	1	1	2
Venezuela	1	1	1
Chile	1	1	1
Portugal	1	1	.
Greece	1	1	.
Finland	1	1	.
Norway	1	1	.
Denmark	1	1	.

218

	$	prod	pop
Austria	1	1	.
Switzerland	1	1	.
New Zealand	1	.	.
India	.	7	31
Indonesia	.	1	7
Pakistan	.	1	4
Nigeria	.	1	4
Thailand	.	1	2
Philippines	.	1	2
Egypt	.	1	2
Burma	.	.	2
Nepal	.	.	1
Afghanistan	.	.	1
Zaire	.	.	1
Tanzania	.	.	1
Uganda	.	.	1
Sudan	.	.	1
Kenya	.	.	1
Sri Lanka	.	.	1
Morocco	.	.	1

	Central Planned Economies		
USSR	29	23	13
Poland	3	3	2
Romania	2	1	1
Yugoslavia	2	1	1
Czechoslovakia	1	1	1
German DR	1	1	1
Hungary	1	1	1
Bulgaria	1	1	1
China PR	.	21	42
Vietnam	.	1	3
No. of nations represented	36	46	50
Not represented	123	113	109
Alt. no. of seats	319	299	294

$: dollar procedure; prod: productivity procedure; pop: population procedure.
Source materials is derived from I.B Kravis, *et al.* "Real G.D.P. Per Capita for More Than One Hundred Countries," *The Economic Journal*, 88 (1978), pp. 215-242.

219

It will be clear that the results under the dollar procedure strongly depend on the assumptions made with regard to the regime of contribution assumed. Our assumption has been that this "tax" exempts per capita real incomes under $1000. With the figures for 1975 this exemption applies to 64 nations. Ecuador would be the lowest-income country supposed to make a contribution. The "tax" rate applied to 1975 income per capita above $1000 was assumed to be 0.0005 or .05 percent, since that results in a revenue near today's revenue of international organizations of roughly $2 billion (in 1975 dollars), of which the United States paid $581 million or 29 percent. This matches with the roughly 30 percent of the seats the United States would occupy under the dollar procedure.

The features of Table I require further procedures. It is not acceptable that any member nation is not represented in a future world parliament. There are several alternative further procedures to solve this problem:

   I. Member nations may themselves form groups which are entitled to one (common) seat, and so occupy the remaining seats.

  II. As a minimum all member nations are entitled to one seat. This would require the creation of additional seats: 119 under procedure (I), 99 under procedure (II) and 94 under procedure (III). The definitive number of seats would then become 319, 299 and 294.

 III. The provisional number of seats of the Assembly may be set higher, for instance 500. This warrants a seat to countries with lower criterion values; for 500 seats down to 0.001 × the total.

 IV. Different weights may be given to the member nations' votes, based on the exact values of the criteria; the additional seats and several of the other seats would have a weight below 1. This system may be used also in the present one seat for all members system.

  V. Still another alternative is that the smaller countries (in the sense of the criterion used) are grouped into larger units entitled to one or more seats and the groups created have one or more seats in the (General) Assembly. The process of grouping should be organized by the UN Secretariat and discussed with, as well as accepted by, the countries concerned. The groups should have their own assemblies in which the member countries are all represented. As an example, all Spanish speaking Latin American countries (excluding the Caribbean and Central American countries) may be taken. These ten countries as a group are entitled to seven seats under the dollar procedure, to nine seats under the productivity procedure and to eight seats under the population procedure.

Such grouping could be called the system of "indirect representation." It will be more difficult to obtain consensus on grouping in other parts of the world. This requires more research and political discussion, but might contribute to new forms of cooperation so far impossible. This system might be used to drastically reduce the number of seats of the General Assembly and so contribute to more intensive discussions and better decision-making.

Whatever the procedure followed, the criteria (or weights) must be recalculated at regular intervals. In the long run a shift from the dollar procedure to the productivity and eventually to the population procedure must take place, in the spirit of the New International Economic Order formulated in 1974.[2]

Since the reform in representation of member states constitutes a rather fundamental reform it seems useful to compare the procedures proposed with one existing institution of a regional character (at a lower level, to use the language of our general orientation), namely, in the European Community. Table II compares the composition of the European Parliament with the number of seats calculated in our productivity and population procedures.

TABLE II.

Number of seats in the European Parliament (EP) of the 12 member states of the European Community and according to our productivity (prod) and population (pop) procedures.

Country	Seats in EP	Seats acc. to (prod)	Seats acc. to (pop)
France	81	103	87
Germany (F.R.)	81	127	103
Italy*	81	81	93
United Kingdom	81	94	93
Spain*	60	38	59
Netherlands	25	24	23
Belgium	24	18	16
Greece*	24	10	15
Portugal*	24	8	16
Denmark	16	11	8
Ireland*	15	4	5
Luxembourg	6	1	1
Total	518	519	519

*Less productive countries

There is a clear similarity between the actual composition of the European Parliament and our procedures, in particular if the "further procedures" discussed are kept in mind. The actual composition of the EP clearly favors small countries and less productive countries. The small countries are those in the lower part of the table. The less productive countries are indicated by an asterisk. A distinction should be made between less productive countries disfavored by natural factors and those less productive as a consequence of less appropriate policies. We don't claim to have succeeded here; more analysis is needed. The distinction is important if we want to avoid undesirable impacts of our procedures on nations' policies.

The overrepresentation of small countries is based on a

country's right to be represented and to have a particular identity. But it may reduce the country's willingness to integrate into larger units. In the world at large—more than in Western Europe—there are too many very small countries, hardly viable and economically very much in need to integrate to larger units. The clearest example is the Caribbean and Central American region; but also the island states in the Pacific and parts of Africa suffer from too much nationalism.

The *secretariats* of the UN institutions should be managed efficiently and more weight should be given to efficiency in comparison to other criteria, such as the nationality of staff members. Changes in this respect should not be made suddenly, but stepwise so as not to harm the existing rights of persons already engaged. Various ways and means to raise efficiency have been set out by a number of authors and this subject need not be elaborated on.[3]

With regard to the *World Bank Group* the most important reform is in the way of deciding on capital increases. A decision on this subject should be made by the directors (in the same way as other decisions are made), and not depend on the decisions of single nations. Since the existing decision-making procedure is one of as much consensus as possible, preferences of single governments are given adequate consideration; they should not have the right to make independent deviating decisions. In the meeting of World Bank directors a gradual increase in the number of votes of low-income countries should be projected. For the IMF similar reforms apply.

The *United Nations Environment Programme* (UNEP) needs to be endowed with the power to carry through environmental policies to stop further deterioration and to improve the quality of air, water and soil to levels it considers necessary. One way in which a more desirable form of decision-making may be gradually attained is to enumerate a list of subjects on which national governments have to decide in consultation with UNEP, and stepwise to raise the number of votes in such consultative meetings given to UNEP.

The most important set of coherent reforms needed must have as its central theme the elimination of violent settlement of conflicts between nations and its replacement by peaceful change. Changes in the international order will remain necessary, and a vital role will be played by the International Court of Justice. To that effect the Court may need not only legal expertise which by definition it has, but also a wider, let us say sociological, basis in order to deal with questions not yet legally covered or covered by obsolete or contradictory legislation in various parts of the world.

The most important institution involved at present is the *Security Council,* but it is also the institution most in need of reform. Its decision making capability is thwarted by the veto power of the Council's permanent members. This must be eliminated if we are serious in our desire to manage the planet. Imagine the United States if California and New York had a veto power; or the Soviet Union if some of its republics had a veto power! Such a structure would not be acceptable to the other states or republics.

Without the veto power, the Security Council would become capable of making more effective decisions. However, decision-making may be improved by some form of weighted voting here also. Even a different composition may be considered, e.g. a composition equal to that of the General Assembly. The present composition reflects the overwhelming power of the nuclear powers, and so of the superpowers, which constitutes discrimination against the nonnuclear powers.

The next point is how to implement such decisions—which, at the level of a well run nation are decisions by its federal government. In order to make the nation follow the federal decisions there is that nation's police force and its system of courts, headed by the Supreme Court. Whereas the Supreme Court has its analog at the world level, the police force does not. This brings us to the new institutions to be added to the UN system of institutions.

New UN Institutions Needed

In order to become familiar with the idea that the addition of new institutions is something natural, I shall remind the reader of some additions already under way, or suggested. The most innovative addition is the new *Law of the Sea.* Its necessity follows from a number of technological developments and a major development in our world understanding of the necessity of peaceful coexistence. There is no way back to isolation; our economies are too intertwined.

A second addition to the UN set of institutions, discussed by others, is an institution dealing with the peaceful uses of outer space. The establishment of a corresponding *Law of Outer Space* has been proposed, and it may be implemented similarly to the Law of the Sea.

A third addition of a new institution was proposed by this author, and is called a *World Treasury.*[4] Again it is the example of a well run nation which clarifies at once the central role a Treasury has to play.

These three examples—present in different phases of their existence: almost created, seriously proposed and suggested for consideration—illustrate how natural it is for new institutions to be added to an existing set. It is natural for any social organization.

Creation of a World Treasury

In a well run nation the most important financial institution is the Treasury or Ministry of Finance. It is a serious lacuna in our international structure that a comparable institution at the world level is lacking. Therefore one of the agencies to add to our present structure is a World Treasury. Out of the World Treasury the various UN agencies should be financed.

This would allow considerable saving on discussions about each member nation's contributions, where such repetition of arguments now occurs in the deliberations in each of the specialized agencies. For some of the very important agencies such as the World Bank the present situation may be maintained, but for a large number of other specialized agencies one central discussion at the World Treasury would be much more efficient.

The existence of a World Treasury is a logical corollary of the idea of a real management of the world community. So is the introduction of a tax system instead of the system of voluntary contributions to the UN system, and this is of particular importance to the World Bank Group and the International Monetary Fund. No policy worth that name is possible if it is left to the taxpayers to decide how much tax they pay!

Another aspect concerns the amounts spent on different recipients. These amounts must be determined by the General Assembly in a process of setting priorities in the way the current operation of the world community is best served. Alongside the current operation, development investments may be financed from the current budget without using a capital transfer. Current financing has the advantage that no agreement is needed on the rate of interest to be paid and on a repayment schedule. This saves much time and effort that in a number of cases—when the debtor is unable to stick to the original agreement—was made in vain, because new negotiations are necessary anyway. Recent experience with the heavily indebted countries of Latin America provides an eloquent example.

Technically the World Treasury will hardly need the introduction of new approaches. The type of activities has been performed by the UN Secretariat and the secretariats of the specialized agencies.

The independent international commission on the reform of the United Nations or the *UN Conference on*

Necessary Reform that I propose at the end of this essay may wish to elaborate on a number of details of the World Treasury mode of operation.

A World Police

A United Nations system to manage the planet needs the power to implement its decisions. This implies the power to prevent illegal behavior of its member nations. The institution in charge of this task may be called police. Among the tasks of this World Police will be inspection or verification of the member states' behavior.

The instruments to be used to prevent illegal behavior should be geared to the nature of illegal activities. Thus, if that behavior consists of a backlog in payments of financial contributions, instruments of economic policy, for instance financial or trade policy, may be appropriate. If illegal behavior consists of the use of violence, the appropriate instrument will be the use of armed police forces. So far the United Nations has used armed forces only in UN Peace Forces, mobilized temporarily for special purposes. *The World Police Force* should be a permanent institution, however. Even so its organization may profit from experiences of the UN Peace Forces in the past. In order to minimize the Police Force's dependence on the superpowers it may be better not to recruit troops from these countries. Preferably forces of small or economically less developed countries known for their contribution to worldwide thinking should be invited, such as India, Sweden or Guyana, among others.

Part of the World Police may be the *World Disarmament Organization* proposed by the Netherlands. This organization would be charged with implementing and monitoring disarmament treaties. Another part of the World Police may be the *International Satellite Monitoring Agency* (ISMA) proposed by France. This Agency would make the observational capabilities of satellites available to the international community for monitoring troop movements, military exercises and disarmament agreements. An even more far-reaching idea for monitoring the earth from space would be the establishment of a *United Nations Space Station* which would allow for immediate human observation and verification of military and arms-related activities.

A question to be studied more closely is under which "Department" the World Police will reside. One possibility is that it would be part of a "Justice Department," under which the International Court of Justice may also be placed. The question then arises whether or not the Security Council should be part of the same "Department." Such a structure corresponds to the usual structure of democratic countries.

Another possibility is that the armed Police Force can only be used when the "Government" as a whole decides to do so, or even a special session of the General Assembly is required.

These questions are a few more examples to be studied by a UN Conference on Necessary Reform proposed below.

Where and How to Start

Although the United Nations Charter indicates an official procedure for its revision, its application must be, for all practical purposes, prepared outside the United Nations in order to achieve a smooth process of change. As a result of informal discussions of a limited group of interested participants some degree of consensus should first be reached. The "Independent Commissions" on international development issues (Brandt Commission) and on disarmament and security issues (Palme Commission) may serve as models.

The Brandt Commission was established at the initiative of Mr. Robert S. McNamara. Its predecessor, the Pearson Commission, was established by the World Bank, when Mr. McNamara was its President. The Palme Commission was established by its chairman and a few members, inspired by the work of the Brandt Commission.

The next step may be the establishment of a *United Nations Conference on Necessary Reform* to consider the recommendations of the Independent Commission. The Conference should follow the example of the (third) United Nations Conference on the Law of the Sea. If the same imaginative initiatives are available as in that Conference, a good deal of success in reforming the United Nations system is possible. This is what we must aim at and work toward achieving if we are to develop a set of global institutions capable of effectively managing planetary problems.

15. A United Nations Space Station

A WAGING PEACE PROPOSAL

A dramatic step to halt the perilous arms race in space and to guarantee the security of nations would be the establishment of an *unarmed multinational manned space station*. This concept, emphasizing the importance of humans working in space rather than relying entirely upon fallible computerized mechanisms, has been successfully demonstrated. The rescue and repair of failed satellites by human know-how in space is convincing. The creation of an unarmed United Nations Space Station would provide every nation, rich or poor, with the necessary security and technical information to turn its human and economic resources from an extravagant military buildup to the improvement of its citizens' lives. The scientific and technical expertise is already available in advanced nations; the political mechanisms (existing UN agencies and ratified treaties and agreements) are in place; and the organs for funding through the UN are accessible. The establishment of a manned space station is feasible.

The scenario for the launching of such a project could be as follows: the United Nations Security Council, mandated by its Charter to maintain the peace and security of all nations, would authorize the International Atomic Energy Agency (IAEA) and the International Satellite Monitoring Agency (ISMA) to implement the 1963 General Assembly's Resolution 1884 (XVIII) to strengthen its supervisory powers. In addition, to insure "the peaceful use of outer space," the Agencies would be asked to carry out the provisions of Articles III, IX, X, and XI of the Outer Space Treaty, ratified in 1967, by placing in orbit an unarmed manned space station. This observatory-laboratory's sophisticated multi-national crew, in continuous communication with nationally established UN centers in every country wishing to participate, would consist of experts, skilled in political sciences as well as all scientific and technological fields, who would operate the equipment on board. Each member would represent, proportionately, the United Nations Security Council (i.e., one member from each of the five permanent nations and one member from each of the ten rotating nations chosen every two years from the General Assembly). The truly multi-national composition of the unarmed manned space station would be a key factor in winning trust and confidence of governments and their peoples.

An international observatory-laboratory has important advantages over the proliferating clutter of national and regional satellites. With the Security Council's trained liaisons on board, the recurring fear of accidental war due to computer-generated false alarms would be eliminated. Insistence on verification of alleged breaches of agreements would have immediate expert attention on board. The dread of nuclear proliferation would be alleviated and wasteful rivalry between nuclear and aspiring non-nuclear powers would be replaced by collaboration for mutually beneficial scientific and economic enterprises. The threat of terrorist pirating of satellites would be greatly diminished. Best of all, the universally shared expense of the space station would cost a fraction of the extravagant arms race into space while providing shared rewards. The cooperative development of space industries and related world economies under the multi-national shield of the United Nations could guarantee an unprecedented era of benefits for all humankind.

There are further persuasive elements for adoption of this proposal. *Politically:* In the absence of threat to the present balance of power within the UN, the "big five" would remain secure; the "in-between" nations would be included in the creative process and decision-making. The superpowers would have the opportunity to gracefully bow out of their self-destructive arms confrontation. *Psychologically:* The image of human beings working together in space to develop resources and preserve peace would have dramatic symbolic value. *Economically:* The opportunity to share in new resources under secure skies would allow governments to convert funding for unproductive military arsenals to the needs of their citizens.

At this crucial crossroads in human destiny there is an urgent need for courageous leaders to make the fateful decision between suicidal militarization of space and the exciting prospect of exploring a new world of infinite possibilities and benefits for all peoples.

SEYMOUR MELMAN

16. Converting from a War Economy to a Peace Economy

In this chapter Professor Melman argues that "if the present trend of U.S. military buildup continues, if the intense use of capital for the Pentagon prevails, it is entirely likely that the competence of U.S. industry will be irreparably destroyed. . . ." The way to change this situation is to begin converting the plants now producing military related goods to civilian production. This would allow the workers to continue working and the plants to continue producing, but to do so on civilian rather than military related products.

Conversion would be healthy for our economy, good for our workers, and would enhance the prospects for arms control and disarmament, thus improving the conditions for national and international security. It would allow us to restore a more reasonable balance to our national budget by cutting back on the 63 percent of the budget now devoted to current or past military expenditures, thus reducing our gigantic national deficit. It would allow us to compete again abroad and at home with products other than sophisticated weapons, thus reducing our growing trade imbalance. Finally, conversion would put more Americans to work since each billion dollars spent in the military sector provides only 76,000 jobs as compared with 100,000 per billion dollars spent on construction, 139,000 on health projects, or 187,000 on education.

Economic conversion is the changeover of factories, research laboratories, bases and related facilities from military to civilian applications. After enduring a warlike economy for more than forty years the American people need to plan for economic conversion for the following vital purposes: (a) To make possible the physical reconstruction of U.S. industry, infrastructure and environment that have been depleted by the war economy. (b) To give confidence in the ability to carry out the production cutbacks that would be a core part of any agreed disarmament process. (c) To make disarmament an opportunity rather than a penalty for the large number of people whose working lives will be converted to civilian skills and tasks.

Economic conversion is dramatically different from what was called *reconversion* at the close of World War II. At that time factories that had turned from civilian to military production for the duration of the war reverted to their former activities. They were able to reapply the old machines and more often than not the former workforce to the production system that had been there before, turning out familiar products, getting raw materials from familiar suppliers, selling to familiar markets.

The situation now is altogether different. Factories and laboratories producing military goods and services were for the most part brought into being for those purposes; they have no civilian history. This refers, of course, to overall organizations and physical entities, not necessarily to particular individuals. But it is also true that a large part of today's work force have spent their entire careers in military-serving operations.

Economic conversion has three functions. One is to change production facilities from military to civilian use, thus directly diminishing the power base of war-making institutions. Another is to reverse the erosion of competence in civilian industrial production that has been caused by the spread of cost-maximizing practices from military to the civilian sphere. Lastly, conversion offers economic opportunity to the people of the war economy institutions while the reversal of the arms race proceeds.

The Managerial Power Base of the
War-Making Institutions: About 120,000

What is the meaning of "the power base" of the war-making institutions? In the United States, about 120,000 persons comprise the central administrative office of the U.S. military-serving industrial system, located in the Department of Defense. It is an office equivalent to the top decision-making entity of a multidivision, multiplant firm; it formulates general policy, designates the principal managers of main subdivisions, and polices compliance with policy among the divisions. The central administrative office of the Department of Defense stands in relation to 37,000 prime contractors as does the central administrative office of General Motors to the divisions of General Motors. It is the largest such central administrative office in the American economy and very possibly the largest such body in the world. The war-making institutions have mobilized the largest labor force under one management. They have the largest research and development staffs subject to one management. The R&D sections of the Department of Defense and its allied agencies consume from 70 percent to 75 percent of the total R&D budget of the federal government.

We are indebted to President Eisenhower for calling attention, in his farewell address of January 7, 1961, to the fact that during every year of the previous decade the fresh capital resources made available to the Department of Defense exceeded the cumulative net profits of all American corporations. That relationship has continued from 1961 to the present day. Hence, the war-making institutions have been wielding the largest finance capital fund in the American economy. From 1946 to 1980 the budgets of the Department of Defense totaled $2,001 billion. The budgets executed and projected for the period 1980-1988 were to be $2,089 billion. If control of finance capital is a means of exerting decision power—economic, political and other—then it is only too clear that the war-making institutions of the United States have enjoyed, and do enjoy, an unprecedented measure of decision power.

Costs to Society of the Military Product

A modern military budget is a capital fund. Capital in an ordinary industrial enterprise is of two sorts: fixed and working. Fixed capital is the money value of the land, buildings, machinery. Working capital is the money value of all other resources that must be brought to bear to set the enterprise in motion. A modern military budget, the funds as they are applied, provides precisely the set of resources that are conventionally identified as fixed and working capital. And they do that on behalf of a set of products that have a unique characteristic: They contribute nothing to ordinary consumption (i.e., to the level of the living), nor can they be used for further production.

And because of that peculiarity of the military product, the aggregate cost to the whole community of the capital resources so used is almost entirely overlooked in our economic textbooks. The cost to the whole society is *first* the money-measured by direct resources allocated to the military function. A *second* cost is measured by the civilian use-value of goods and services for consumption or for production that are foregone when the resources are used for military products. For the whole community that value foregone is approximately equal to the cost of the direct inputs from the military budget. There is a *third* cost: when capital resources are used for new civilian production on a continuing basis, there is usually improvement in the design of the means of production which becomes more competent, more efficient and more productive. Economists call this an increase in the marginal productivity of capital. But when capital resources are used for purposes that

236

cannot be applied to any further production, that increment of productivity of capital is lost, forever.

There is yet a *fourth* kind of social cost to the whole society. A large part of knowledge that is generated on behalf of the military has unique application to military technology alone and is not relevant elsewhere. So the possibility of the knowledge being used elsewhere (which would be likely if the R&D were carried out for civilian purposes) is foregone. A *fifth* kind of cost, while unmeasurable, is quite important. As a large labor force is trained for the military, it becomes habituated to working not with an eye to minimizing cost but to maximizing cost, and to offsetting that maximized cost with maximized subsidies. Such practices are possible only when carried out by a ward of the state, with almost unlimited resources made available by tapping the income of the whole society. A labor force so trained develops what Thorstein Veblen genially called a trained incapacity—in this case for civilian work. To my knowledge no one has yet attempted an aggregate measure of the social cost of the military in the categories I have identified.

How the Military Depletes the Civilian Sector

Returning to the basic idea of the military budget as a capital fund, it is important to compare that budget with another capital fund, the Gross Domestic Fixed Capital Formation. The simply means the money value of new civilian capital items put in place in a given year—school buildings, factories, machinery, roads, waterworks, libraries, and the like. From data on national income assembled by the staff of the United Nations one can calculate the capital fund made available for the military in a number of countries for a given year as a ratio per hundred dollars (or francs or yen, etc.) of capital represented by new civilian capital formation (whether privately or publicly funded). For the last year of such available data, 1983, here are the ratios: in the United

States for every $100 of civilian gross fixed capital formation, $40 was separately expended for the military; in the United Kingdom the ratio was 31; in France 16; in Sweden 12; in West Germany 13; in Japan 3.3. For the U.S.S.R. there are no official data. My estimate, which I will be pleased to discard when proper data are offered, is 66. These relationships are informative. The very low ratio of military to civilian use of capital in Japan and West Germany is a fundamental clue to the modernity of industrial plant and equipment, to the rapidly developing civilian technologies in those countries, and to the ability of those countries to sustain a rapid rise in wage rates together with competitive competence.

A further estimate in this area is truly startling. It is based on the U.S. military budget as planned to 1988. For the military there is a five-year budget plan (five-year plans being as American as apple pie when prepared for the Pentagon). I compared that 1988 budget with an estimate, derived by simple statistical extrapolation, of the Gross Domestic Fixed Capital Formation in the same year. And the U.S. ratio I arrived at for 1988 is 87:100. If the present trend of military buildup continues, if the intense use of capital for the Pentagon prevails, it is entirely likely that the competence of U.S. industry will be irreparably destroyed, that the quality of the civilian production system will be so degraded as to be an important factor in reaching what I described in *Profit without Production* (Alfred A. Knopf, 1983) as a point of no return.

Allied to the military budget as a capital fund is its influence on productivity growth. The United States, during the century 1865-1965, paid the highest industrial wages in the world, and its industries were able at the same time to turn out products of a quality and at a price that made them salable both domestically and abroad. That was possible because high wages were offset by progressive mechanization of work and improvement in the organization of work. As a result, there was growing output per man-hour, an

238

increase in productivity. But after 1965, following a period of growing military budgets, productivity growth of the United States dropped sharply. According to a December 31, 1984, report of the U.S. Bureau of Labor Statistics on trends of manufacturing productivity and labor cost, eleven countries, including Canada, Japan, Belgium, Denmark, France, Germany, Italy, the Netherlands, Norway, Sweden, the United Kingdom, during the period 1960 to 1983, all had higher average rates of productivity growth than the United States, whose average annual increase was only about 2.6 percent.

The ratio of military to civilian use of capital therefore has profound consequences for mechanization of work and modernity of the industrial plants are the basic requirements for substantial improvement of productivity growth. But as cost-minimizing was replaced in the military industry by cost-maximizing, the classic process whereby endless detailed improvements were made in manufacturing productivity was stalled. The mechanism of cost minimizing in U.S. industry used to work as follows: the wages of labor, a major cost item, would rise for various reasons—market forces, union bargaining, whatever. The users of labor in cost-minimizing firms would move to offset the wage increase by mechanization of work, by better organization of work, by redesign of product. When this took place among the firms that produced industrial machinery, it meant that the wages that they and their customers paid could rise more rapidly than the prices of their product-machinery. In turn, this meant that the users of machinery were being offered new, more efficient equipment at prices that were progressively more attractive. So a continuing process invited the broader, more intensive use machinery in place of manual labor. The automatic derived effect was an improvement in the average productivity of labor.

In an earlier study, *Dynamic Factors in Industrial Productivity* (1956), I showed this pattern as characteristic of the United States, and of Great Britain until 1950. Now that pattern has been essentially transformed. The following table shows percent changes in average hourly earnings to industrial workers and percent changes in machine tool prices 1971-78.

	Worker Earning/Hour	Machine Tools Prices
United States	+72	+85
West Germany	+72	+59
Japan	+177	+51

(Source: *Profits Without Production*, p. 174)

In Japan average hourly earnings to production workers rose 177 percent while machine tool prices rose only 51 percent. There is the classic pattern. The producers of machine tools contrived to offset the wage increase with internal plant efficiencies so that the prices of their product only rose 51 percent. The West German differential—72-59—is lesser, but one still inviting further mechanization of work. While U.S. average hourly earnings rose as much as those in West Germany—72 percent—U.S. machine tool prices rose 85 percent, thus discouraging widespread mechanization of industrial work.

By 1978 the United States had the oldest stock of metalworking machinery of any industrialized country. To be sure this was caused not only by the fact that the Department of Defense had become a major purchaser of machine tools and a major sponsor for machine tool R&D, thus causing cost-maximizing to infect the interior operations of the machine tool industry. The Pentagon's erratic bursts of production orders have been a major contribution to an unstable market for machine tools. There was also a general transformation in the emphasis of U.S. industrial management, away from competent production and toward straight making money by all manner of financial devices.

How a Permanent War Economy
Counters Productivity Growth

There is a definable set of conditions that favor productivity growth. They are: cost-minimizing within the machinery-producing industries; cost-minimizing among machinery users; wages of labor rising faster than machinery prices; the availability of finance capital at modest interest rates; R&D to innovate new means of production; stable rates of production; a management oriented to production; and the availability of a competent surrounding infrastructure as a production support base. The effect of military economy in its normal operation has run counter to every one of these requirements for productivity growth. As a result, American firms have become less able to offset cost increases from whatever source and therefore unable to supply even the domestic market at acceptable levels of price and quality. By 1980, 27 percent of all automobiles were imports, so too were 25 percent of machine tools (by 1986 it was 49 percent), 15 percent of steel mill products, 87 percent of black and white TV sets, 47 percent of calculating machines, 22 percent of microwave ranges and ovens, 34 percent of integrated micro circuits, 24 percent of x-ray and other irradiation equipment, 74 percent of motion picture cameras, 51 percent of sewing machines (by 1984, 100 percent of the household type), 100 percent of radios, 22 percent of bicycles, 50 percent of shoes (by 1987, 86 percent). Every one of these percentages also means that the same percentage of domestic employment in those industries has disappeared. That is what accounts for the several million jobs lost in the U.S. industrial economy.

Misleading Statistic

There is a discrepancy between the national employment figures issued by the government and the details of life in particular industries, cities, and regions. An aggregation effect obscures the diversity of experience in U.S. economy and society. The military economy prospers; there are boom conditions in the industries and in the regions that seek to employ engineers and skilled workers for the Pentagon's needs. The evidence may be seen in job announcements in the newspapers of Los Angeles, Boston, and New York City. But there is no boom condition in Homestead, Pennsylvania, where the works of the U.S. Steel Corporation are blacked out and where the neighboring works of the Mesta Steel Company, once supplier of steel mill equipment to U.S. industry, have been dismantled.

Again and again, it is essential to differentiate among the published aggregate figures for economic activities. For example, on December 22, 1984, an AP dispatch reported that, according to the Commerce Department, orders for durable goods posted their biggest gain in more than four years—an 8.3 percent November increase. Next paragraph: more than half the gain was attributed to a 99.4 percent increase in the volatile military orders category. In other words, the headline read "Durable Orders Surge 8.3 Percent," but the small type tells us more than half was in readily manipulated Pentagon orders.

Depletion has occurred not only in the so-called smokestack industries, but also in the highest tech of all the high tech—the computer industry. An instructive example is one of the most popular, fastest-selling and important of computers, the IBM Personal Computer. On the back of the cathode ray tube box is printed "Made in Taiwan" or "Made in Korea." The label on the lower box says "Made in the U.S.A.," but the disk drive is made in Singapore or Hong Kong, and the chips, made in Japan, are also assembled abroad. The keyboard and power unit are made in Japan. What is left for production in the United States is the outer case and the assembly of the main working components. Indeed, for the R&D-intensive industries as a group, the 1980s saw a sharp reversal of position. In 1980 the high-tech industries group showed a balance of payments that was favorable for the U.S. By 1986 that had become a net deficit.

This situation troubles me, not for some nationalist reason, or for belief in the desirability of economic autarchy, but because in order to live a community must produce. There is no theory or experience from which to infer that it is possible on any sustained basis for a community to have its production done for it by someone else.

There is a further problem for which the military economy is responsible. The military trains engineers and production workers to accept product unreliability. Military products have been made increasingly complex, to the point that the complexity necessarily reduces reliability. That happens because the reliability of a set of linked components is the product of the reliability of each of the separate components. Since no man-made device is ever 100 percent reliable, the coupling together of more and more components degrades the reliability of the mechanism or system.

It is normal in military experience that of a hundred F-15s, the first-line fighter plane of the U.S. Air Force, 45 of them have, on the average, been in repair at any given moment. If a set of M-1 tanks are on maneuvers, they can be kept running only by heroic efforts of maintenance staffs, and by the immediate availability of spare parts and abundant fuel—3.86 gallons being required per mile of tank travel. On the anti-aircraft Aegis cruiser, software is crucial to the operation of the computer-control systems for the weaponry involved, but the software has a high failure rate. And other parts of the system can be expected to function only 45 percent of the time. Such unreliability, which has become acceptable in the military, is completely unacceptable in civilian operation.

If a trolley car or subway goes out of service 45 percent of the time, if it fails frequently on the tracks, it will block the right of way; it will inconvenience a whole community; it will immediately come to the attention of many witnesses. There will surely be a great public outcry for relief from an intolerable situation.

When aerospace technology and modes of organization were applied to the production of trolley cars (as was done by the Boeing-Vertol Co. outside Philadelphia; the full details are in Chapter 13 of *Profits Without Production*), it becomes clear why the military-industry approach won't work in civilian economy. Boeing-Vertol had to drop out of the trolley car business because it was confronted by massive lawsuits from the Massachusetts Bay Transit Authority. The trolley was handsome; it was a pleasure to ride in when it functioned, but it had a remarkable array of things that went wrong. The things that went wrong were built-in weaknesses, the result of the mode of organization and operation that is systematically pursued in military industry, and notably in the aerospace industry. That is why economic conversion, which includes retraining personnel from military to civilian competence, is essential.

One of the standard practices of the military industry is called concurrency. In the civilian economy, when a new product is projected, it customarily goes through a set of functional stages: the concept; research; something is designed; a prototype is used; the prototype is tested; faults are discovered; it is redesigned, retested—perhaps several times. Only after the prototype meets the desired performance standards is the order given to produce. Not in the land of the Department of Defense. There, concurrency is practiced; indeed, ordered by the regulations of the Secretary of Defense. Concurrency means carrying out all these steps in parallel. Then when you have produced and used the product you discover defects, whereupon you change the design for items yet to be produced and retrofit those already made.

This is probably the most expensive way of building anything ever formulated. As this becomes the habitual behavior of military engineers and managers, and to some degree production workers, they become incapacitated for functioning in civilian economy. This is why occupational retraining for economic conversion is not an arbitrary idea. It is indispensable if the persons engaged in military economy are to function competently in a civilian environment.

Planning For Economic Conversion

What are the strategic components of economic conversion? *First,* it must be planned well in advanced. To establish an alternative civilian use for a military industrial enterprise of size, one needs a lead time of at least two years. This period is required for selecting new products; for selecting new production equipment; identifying sources of raw materials; and retraining the labor force. For firms (or divisions of firms) with an all-military background, the selection of new products is crucial. What marketable civilian products can be produced most competently by people or equipment hitherto employed entirely by the military? *Second* economic conversion planning must be decentralized. If attempted from a national center, it will fail because it is not possible to oversee from a remote headquarters the myriad specific data that must be taken into account in a plan devised for a given enterprise. *Third,* the whole activity must be carried out without subsidy to the managements involved. A continuance of subsidy means a continuance of cushioning for what in the civilian realm would be gross incompetence. *Fourth,* it is essential that every military-serving factory and base be obliged by law to set up an alternative use committee, half of its members being selected by management, half by the working people (all grades), with responsibility and authority for planning alternative products, production and marketing systems for the plant, laboratory, or the base facility. It must be made mandatory because otherwise the managements involved, and even some of the engineers or production workers, would be massively reluctant to engage in such planning.

Fifth, managers and engineers must be retrained. Military-serving managers are expert in the politics and diplomacy of dealing with the Department of Defense; they couldn't sell a folding bed to Sears, Roebuck to save their lives. Engineers who have been trained to create products of escalating intricacy, without regard to cost, must be taught a new approach to product design that seeks cost-minimizing simplicity within the limits of reliable performance. Research and development must be disciplined so that people who had been accustomed to making lavish use of resources paid for out of the federal pocket will discover economical ways of doing their work in a civilian environment. Some of the production workers need to be retrained, but probably a smaller proportion than engineers and managers.

Sixth, economic conversion planning must also include funds for relocation, because parts of typically oversized administrative and engineering staffs will have to be moved to other locations. *Seventh,* even with the most thorough advance planning, there is bound to be a lag between the end of the military production and the start of civilian work. Some income support will therefore be required.

What can ex-military-serving firms produce? For a start they could examine the list of manufactured products now being imported to the United States, asking: which of these products are producible in our facilities; could that work be done at acceptable price and quality? There is also a challenge to compete against competent producers already in the field. Also, agendas for large capital investment are required. American industries will require vast capital investment. The same applies to American infrastructure. In 1982, the editors of *U.S. News and World Report* reckoned that the crumbling infrastructure of the United States could be repaired at a price of $2,500 billion. U.S. military budgets (spent and planned) 1980-1990 exceed $2,900 billion. A Labor-Management Infrastructure Task Force reported (Oct. 1983) "A Consensus on Rebuilding America's Vital Public Facilities." The study was coordinated by Arnold Cantor, Assistant Director, Department of Economic Research, AFL-CIO, and Russel S. Davis, Vice President Strategic Planning, Union Pacific Corporation, and stressed highways, bridges, urban water supply and wastewater treatment facilities. Enormous new markets are defined here.

House Resolution 813

The set of requirements for conversion planning that I have enumerated here are incorporated in the text of a bill proposed by Congressman Ted Weiss, and supported by more than fifty colleagues. In 1987 it is designated H.R. 813, a bill to "facilitate economic adjustment of communities, industries, and workers through reduction or realignment of defense or aerospace contracts, military facilities, and arms export and for other purposes."

The importance of H.R. 813 is twofold. First, it outlines a coherent, urgently needed, constructive approach that is an economic alternative to the arms race. Second, politically, with planning for economic conversion both the government and the people will have fresh confidence for negotiating and implementing the reversal of the arms race.

With a combined address to disarmament and economic conversion we can strike at the heart of the single most dangerous political process of our time. That is the antagonistic cooperation whereby the war-making institutions of the United States and the U.S.S.R. have reinforced each other

247

and generated larger budgets, larger military economies, larger stocks of more dangerous weapons, and in doing so have justified more centralism, more authoritarianism in each society. I know of no single public issue that is as crucial for the survival of society than disarmament and economic conversion.

FRANK K. KELLY

17. A Planetary Project for Peace with Jobs

A WAGING PEACE PROPOSAL

Millions of people in the industrial nations of the world are engaged in a vast web of activities related to the production of weapons and military supplies. The economic situation now existing can be described as a "war economy"—in which the bread and butter, the everyday existence of these millions of workers and their families, depends upon preparations for war and the production of supplies for the many wars now raging on the Earth.

Information about the catastrophic effects of a nuclear war has been circulated in every country. Yet this widespread knowledge has not yet led to an effective demand for an end to the nuclear arms race. To a large degree, many of the people of the most powerful nations are afraid to "let go" of these monstrous weapons because no clear-cut picture has been presented to them on how they would survive economically in a demilitarized world.

Until recent times, many leaders in the United States and the Soviet Union assumed that steps toward disarmament must precede planning for conversion of economic activities from military production to civilian purposes. Recently, however, economists, engineers and planners in America and in the Soviet Union have agreed to explore ideas for moving toward conversion as rapidly as possible.

The announcement that Soviet and American representatives will meet in the United States—with participation by members of the Soviet Institute on the U.S.A. and Canada and the American Council of Learned Societies—has sent a signal to the people of the world that leaders of these two great nations are willing to try to develop cooperative programs. Everyone working for peace must hope that these meetings will produce constructive results.

In an article in the *New York Times* on March 21, 1987, Professor Seymour Melman of Columbia University, the American coordinator of the projected symposium on economic conversion, declared: "There are two main links between conversion planning and disarmament. First, with workable economic conversion plans in place, a mutually agreed upon reversal of the arms race can be made into an economic opportunity and not a penalty for the people involved. Second, growing confidence in the practicability of conversion will, I think, encourage disarmament negotiations."

Agreements on conversion programs by the Soviet Union and the United States would remove the fears of millions of citizens that disarmament would bring widespread unemployment. Millions of skilled workers would be able to turn their energies to civilian jobs in many fields, ranging from the construction of housing, schools, and health facilities to repairing cities and getting rid of the pollution now damaging the air and water of the world.

In addition to the United States and the Soviet Union, many other nations are wasting their resources in the production of weapons and instruments of destruction. It seems to me that what the world needs now is a *Planetary Peace With Jobs Project* developed by leaders from all nations, working together in an international organization with headquarters in Geneva.

A Planetary Project for Humanity

The nuclear arms race threatens the whole human race. The whole human race would benefit from a *Planetary Peace With Jobs Project*, involving the leading thinkers, organizers, economists, management specialists, architects, labor leaders and elected officials in all the countries which now belong to the United Nations.

I suggest the formation of a World Assembly for Peaceful Production, to be convened in Geneva by a committee of Nobel Laureates. Members of the Assembly would be nominated by all the countries willing to participate. From these nominations, the Nobel Laureate Committee would choose the participants in the first meeting of the Assembly.

At that meeting, fifteen directors of the *Planetary Peace With Jobs Project* would be chosen—each to serve for a term of three years. Sixty members of an Advisory Board—twenty from socialist countries, twenty from capitalist countries, and twenty from non-aligned nations—would also be selected. In consultation with the Advisory Board, the directors would choose an Executive Director, who would be responsible for organizing the Project and expediting its work.

The Project should have funding for ten years, at a rate of $5 billion a year, to be provided by the members of the United Nations in proportion to the annual contributions made by these members to the UN for its support.

The Project would have five phases:

1. A world-wide survey of the economic adjustments that would be necessary to shift from a war economy to a peace economy;
2. Provision of grants from the Project's capital fund to aid creative projects demonstrating the feasibility of shifting to a peace economy;
3. Presentation of awards and incentive grants to indus-

251

tries and countries making the most rapid and effective changes from war production to peaceful projects generating large numbers of jobs;

4. Development of retraining programs in all countries, to enable workers to acquire new skills or to use old skills in a new way, and to move with a minimum of problems into peaceful projects;

5. Creation of a Job Information Bank in Geneva, with information about job opportunities in all countries and sufficient funds to aid workers in moving on a voluntary basis into the areas where such opportunities may be most plentiful.

Comparison with the Manhattan Project

The Manhattan Project—the name given to the American effort to develop an atomic bomb—was undertaken by President Franklin Roosevelt on the recommendation of Albert Einstein to make sure that humanity could be saved from the scourge of Hitlerism. Einstein and other scientists believed that Hitler's Nazi regime was developing an atom bomb to be used for the conquest of the world.

The project to develop the American bomb was called the Manhattan Project because its headquarters were located in Manhattan Island, in New York. But the project eventually engaged the services of more than 100,000 men and women. President Truman noted later: "It was the achievement of the combined efforts of science, industry, labor and the military, and it had no parallel in history."

The release of nuclear energy was made possible by a series of bold steps—new insights by scientists, new technologies, and new factories that were fully automated and operated by remote control. President Roosevelt and President Truman believed that these discoveries and techniques could be kept secret. They underestimated the ability of Soviet scientists and did not realize that the Soviet Union had launched a project to develop atomic energy in 1942—at about the same time as the Manhattan Project. When the Soviet Union produced atomic bombs, many American leaders were astounded.

In the development of a *Planetary Peace With Jobs Project*, the cooperation of the two superpowers is absolutely necessary. There will be no necessity for secrecy in this Project. There will be no need for competition between the two great nations.

The people of the Soviet Union and the people of the United States are reaching out to one another—calling for friendship, calling for joint efforts to advance the welfare of humanity. People around the world are calling, too—calling for an end to the nuclear terror, calling for a time of peace with jobs for all.

The Project can be far greater than the American Manhattan Project or the Soviet Nuclear Project. It can enlist the participation of people over the entire planet. There are tremendous obstacles, tremendous problems to be solved—just as there were obstacles and problems in the long struggle to release atomic energy—but these obstacles can be overcome.

It is time for the people and the leaders of all nations to commit themselves to another effort without parallel in history—the effort to help humanity to move from an era of war (and fighting wars) to an era of productive peace.

IV. FRIENDS AND FELLOW COSMONAUTS

The leaders of the Nuclear Age Peace Foundation have traveled widely to speak and share ideas on achieving peace in the nuclear age. This section contains examples of Foundation leaders speaking out for peace.

Frank Kelly, senior vice-president of the Foundation spoke to seventy-nine Soviet leaders in Moscow on April 26, 1983 on "The Role of the Public in Preventing Nuclear War and Limiting the Nuclear Arms Race." In his speech, Mr. Kelly suggested that the Soviets might take the initiative in stopping the arms race by publicly dismantling 50 percent of their nuclear weapons. A Soviet official said that he thought it was "an interesting idea" but might be interpreted as "a sign of weakness." Later the idea of a 50 percent reduction in nuclear arms was put forward by Mr. Gorbachev, and is now being seriously discussed as a next step after the elimination of short and intermediate range nuclear weapons in Europe.

In October 1985, Foundation president David Krieger, spoke at a conference of Nobel Laureates on "Peace—the Best Environment." He addressed the dangers of accidental nuclear war and the work of the Foundation in promoting prevention measures. One of the Nobel Laureates at that meeting, George Wald, a member of the Foundation's Advisory Council, presented the appeal drafted at the conference to General–Secretary Gorbachev prior to the Geneva Summit meeting with President Reagan. Although many attempts were made to reach him, Mr. Reagan would not receive the Conference statement. In his article, Professor Wald discusses his meeting with Mr. Gorbachev.

In 1987 the Nuclear Age Peace Foundation coordinated the world-wide activities of the second International Peace Week of Scientists. In connection with Peace Week activities in Spain, which also commemorated the fiftieth anniversary of the bombing of Guernica, David Krieger spoke in San Sebastian on "The Responsibility of Scientists." He

255

encouraged scientists to take greater personal responsibility for what they produce and to cease "justifying work on the most inhumane and wasteful weapons systems imaginable."

Foundation vice-president and treasurer Wallace Drew represented the Foundation at the fortieth anniversary of the bombing of Hiroshima in August 1985. He also traveled to the Soviet Union in 1987 as did Board Member Ethel Wells, who helped pave the way for the Santa Barbara-Yalta Sister City relationship.

FRANK K. KELLY

18. The Role of the Public in Preventing Nuclear War

(An address given in Moscow, April 1983)

We are all travelling on the Spaceship Earth at high speed toward the stars. What we do on this beautiful ship in the coming years may determine the fate of the earth—and the future of life in this universe. We are challenged to rise to the highest levels that humanity can attain.

Twenty-two years ago a Soviet cosmonaut circled the earth in outer space and showed us that we live on one small world. In the *New York Times* at that time, I proposed that the American people should give a great sculpture to the people of the Soviet Union, clearly celebrating man's leap toward the stars. My proposal was not adopted, although some of my fellow Americans saluted it as a step that might have brought two great peoples close together. The Statue of Liberty, given to the United States by the French, has long been symbol of what friendship can mean.

The Americans who landed on the moon in 1969 transmitted pictures of the fragile blue ball on which we live. So we know that we share a small globe—a single spaceship. How can we, as citizens of the two most powerful nations on earth, permit the continuation of a nuclear arms race which may lead to the destruction of our home in the universe? We know that we must work together to prevent such a catastrophe.

Those of us who believe in God feel that the Creator did not design this magnificent planet, so full of life, so marvelous in many ways, to be destroyed by human folly. Those who do not believe in God still strive to preserve life for themselves and for their children.

In the United States, in Europe, in all parts of the world, millions of people are now demanding an end to the nuclear arms race. In the U.S., 11.6 million people voted in 1982 to endorse a proposal calling for a verifiable freeze on the development, testing, and deployment of nuclear weapons. In Europe, millions of people have taken part in demonstrations against the ceaseless production and deployment of nuclear arms.

In his book, *War and Peace*, Leo Tolstoy wrote: "The movement of nations is caused . . . by the activity of *all* the people who participate in the events. . . ." In our time, with the oneness of the world brought home to us by our space explorers, more and more people are awakening to the fact that all of us *do* participate—one way or another—in the shaping of events. If we are passive, if we shrug our shoulders and say that the nuclear arms race is beyond our control, then we are succumbing to fatalism, we are surrendering our power as human beings.

Leaders of the freeze movement interpreted the results of the voting in November 1982 as "a clear public mandate to end the nuclear arms race now." Randy Kehler, national coordinator of the campaign, declared: "It was the closest equivalent to a national referendum in the history of American democracy." Nearly 20 million Americans voted on the proposal, with 60 percent favoring it and 40 percent against it. Since it is rare in American elections for 60 percent of the voters to approve any proposal, the margin of victory for the freeze was highly significant.

President Reagan and his advisors, however, continued to insist that a freeze agreement with the Soviet Union under existing conditions would simply lock the United States into a position of inferiority. Mr. Reagan insisted repeatedly that the huge increase in Soviet military strength in the last ten years was a threat to American security. His program for large increases in American arms spending continued to hold the support of large numbers of Americans.

Pubic opinion polls taken for the President showed that his speeches denouncing the freeze and calling for more arms had a major impact in swinging many Americans to his side. Polls taken by the *Los Angeles Times* during the same period, however, indicated that 47 percent of the voters wanted to spend less money on arms, compared to 43 percent who favored higher spending for military projects.

American attitudes toward arms spending have been deeply affected by Soviet actions. President Lyndon Johnson was prepared to make a joint announcement with Leonid Brezhnev of steps toward a Strategic Arms Limitation Treaty (SALT) in 1968. But the movement of Soviet tanks and troops into Czechoslovakia caused a sharp reaction in the American public, and the SALT negotiations did not get underway until 1968, when Richard Nixon had become President.

The views of the American public can shift with astonishing speed. The treatment of news events by the broadcasting media and the newspapers—often used by Presidents to sway public opinion—may swing millions of citizens from one position to another. When President Reagan took office in January 1981, a poll taken for him by Richard Wirthlin indicated that 76 percent of those questioned by the pollster favored a massive increase in arms spending, while only 13 percent wanted cuts in the Pentagon's budget. Wirthlin's polls helped Reagan to gain Congressional approval for enormous increases in military appropriations.

Actually, of course, the American build-up in arms began under President Jimmy Carter, who had been told by his advisors that the Soviet Union had increased its military budget substantially for fifteen years while the United States

259

had fallen behind in the arms competition. At the Vienna summit meeting in 1979 between President Carter and General Secretary Brezhnev, Mr. Brezhnev asked: "Why speed up the arms race? Let us limit weapons, not increase them." Mr. Carter replied that each side would have to face the inevitability of military parity with the other, but he acknowledged that there could not be "any superiority or victory in a nuclear war."

Although he was deeply troubled by the increasing peril of a nuclear holocaust—and his religious faith compelled him to work for peace—Mr. Carter decided in 1980 that the political situation in the United States made it impossible for him to obtain ratification of the SALT II Treaty signed by the Soviet Union and the United States. He said he was told by former President Gerald Ford and other Republican leaders that he could not get enough republican votes in the Senate to ratify the treaty. In the election campaign of 1980, Ronald Reagan attacked the treaty, calling it "fatally flawed."

What happened to the SALT II Treaty illustrates the severe problems confronting American leaders and the American public in attempting to limit the nuclear arms race. Peace efforts by the political party which holds power are sometimes denounced by political opponents as "appeasement" or based on dangerous concessions to a cunning and powerful adversary. The Soviet Union is depicted in the worst possible light—described as ruthless, untrustworthy, determined to dominate the world. The fears of millions of Americans are aroused, and millions are persuaded again that national security depends upon building more rockets and nuclear bombs.

In spite of the recurrent waves of fear, however, a strong movement against nuclear weapons has developed in the major churches in the U.S.A. The bishops of the Episcopal church have denounced weapons of mass destruction as contrary to the laws of God and man. The Presbyterians, the Methodists, the Baptists, Churches of Christ, the Congregationalists, and others now have active peace fellowships. And there is an increasing awareness of the nuclear danger as a result of the statements issued by many Roman Catholic bishops.

In the past, many wars have developed as a result of conflicts among religious groups. Now, at last, the church-goers in the United States are facing up to the fact that Jesus of Nazareth said that peacemakers would be especially blessed, because they would be called children of God. All of the great religions have called for peace among men. Today that call is being heard by millions of people with varying faiths.

The Roman Catholic bishops in the United States—leaders of the 50 million Catholic citizens—released a pastoral letter to all Catholics urging them to work actively for an end to the arms race. When the third draft of this letter became known, a spokesman for the U.S. State Department said: "We are pleased that the letter explicitly endorses many of the far-reaching objectives which the administration seeks—notably, negotiated agreements for substantial, equitable and verifiable reductions in nuclear arsenals."

Archibishop John R. Roach of St. Paul-Minneapolis, president of the National Conference of Catholic Bishops, and Cardinal Joseph L. Bernardin of Chicago, chairman of the Bishops' Committee on War and Peace, immediately commented: "We could not accept any suggestion that there are relatively few and insignificant differences between U.S. policies and the policies advocated in the pastoral letter. . . ." Referring to differences between the positions taken by the bishops and "current U.S. policy," Cardinal Bernardin and Archbishop Roach said: "The basic moral judgment of the document is, we believe, summed up in these two sentences: 'A justifiable use of force must be both discriminatory and proportionate. Certain aspects of both U.S. and Soviet strategies fail both tests.' "

It is evident from the drafts of this pastoral letter that the

261

bishops did not see how the use of nuclear weapons capable of destroying whole cities—and perhaps the whole earth—could be justified under any circumstances. There can be no doubt that this letter from the bishops, which will be circulated and studied in Catholic churches all over the United States, will have a significant effect in stimulating millions of Catholics to take part in public efforts to end the nuclear arms race. As a Catholic myself, I am greatly encouraged by the action of the bishops. (Ten days after this speech was delivered, the Catholic bishops released the third draft of their statement, calling for a halt in the nuclear arms race.)

There is another public effort going on in the United States which may help to limit the arms race and prevent a nuclear war. This is the National Peace Academy Campaign, in which I have been participating for the last four years. The Campaign now has members in all of the states, and it has been endorsed by religious and civic organizations with millions of members.

As a result of the Peace Academy campaign, the U.S. Congress created a U.S. Institute of Peace—a signal to the world that the United States is dedicated to the peaceful resolution of conflicts. I am grateful to the people who elected me to serve as a director of that campaign—and to the many thousands of citizens who publicly supported it.

There are now thousands of peace organizations in the United States. There are dozens of them in the city of Santa Barbara, where I live just a few miles from president Reagan's ranch. The Nuclear Age Peace Foundation, of which I am an officer, is a newly formed educational group, engaged in bridge-building between individuals, organizations, and nations. We base our program on statements by Abraham Lincoln and Albert Einstein. Einstein said: "The unleashed power of the atom has changed everything save our modes of thinking, and we thus drift toward unparalleled catastrophes." Lincoln said: "We must think anew and act anew."

While I am speaking of the role of the public in the prevention of nuclear war, let me express my appreciation to the founders of the U.S.-U.S.S.R. Citizens Dialogue Committee. In the years to come, I hope that many Soviet and American citizens will participate in the essential work of this committee. Through our dialogues we will come to understand one another better—and perhaps to love one another. As a Christian, I know that all human beings are made for love.

In addition to love, we need more respect for the power of reason. We must not drift year after year toward an unparalleled catastrophe. We must do what Lincoln advised us to do: "think anew and act anew."

Long ago, the prophet Jeremiah warned the people of the wrath that would come upon them if they did not change their ways. Some heeded him; some did not. And when the wrath came, there was weeping and lamentation in many places.

There are prophets today, crying aloud, calling upon the people of the great nations to save the earth. A friend of mine in Santa Barbara—George Hall, an Episcopal priest, a conservative man—said to me: "The only way out that I can see is for one of the two giant powers to take the initiative for disarmament without waiting for the other. I hope my country will take the lead. If not, I hope that the Soviets will do it."

What a great thing it would be if one of the giant nations, the United States or the Soviet Union, would announce that it was dismantling half of its nuclear weapons—and inviting representatives of all the nations to come and witness that dismantling! What if one of these countries would invite the television networks, the newspaper correspondents, members of parliaments, leaders of churches, to come and see this great act for the future of humanity? It could be the first step toward disarmament.

Would not the people of the world respond with a tremendous cry of joy?

We know they would.

Would not that giant nation still have plenty of power to defend itself if it should be attacked?

Of course it would. But who would dare to attack it, with the eyes of humanity upon it? Other countries would have to respond favorably.

Would not that nation open a new era in history, with humanity set free from the nightmare of a nuclear war?

It would. We know it would.

As I stand here now, I think of Mr. Brezhnev's words to President Carter: "If we do not succeed, God will not forgive us." I do not believe we can set limits on the forgiveness of God. Perhaps the divine love is so encompassing, so everlasting, that God could forgive us for destroying our earth. He could make a new earth, a new heaven—and when He wills it, that will certainly come to pass.

But could the survivors of a nuclear war—if there are any—forgive their leaders and their fellow human beings and themselves for devastating the earth?

I do not know whether Andrei Gromyko was serious or jesting when he said to President Carter: "Yes, God above is looking down at us all."

But I believe there is a God above us and a God around us and a God within us—a God who suffers and calls to us—a God who will lift us with His love to meet the greatest challenge humanity has ever faced.

DAVID KRIEGER

19. Address to Nobel Laureates

(Given in Maastricht, Holland, October 1985)

I would like to begin my remarks with a poem. I think that it is very important that art and peace be joined, and perhaps particularly that they be joined in the hearts of scientists. This poem was written by a women in California, Debra Turner, and is included in a collection published by the Nuclear Age Peace Foundation entitled *Reflections on the Sacred Gift of Life.*

This Bright Morning

This bright morning
And now,
Between the tides' changing,
When the water is like glass,
Between the winds and the waves,

Somewhere there is war.

War being fought.
War being planned.

I only know one thing
Beyond here and now
On this bright morning:

Nowhere is there war being won.

I am very pleased to return to Holland to participate in this meeting. Five years ago I worked with a foundation here in the Netherlands, the RIO Foundation; the acronym stands for Reshaping the International Order. The honorary president of the Foundation was Jan Tinbergen whom I am very happy to meet here again. My work at the RIO Foundation was to coordinate a study on Disarmament and Development, but before the end of the project it was changed by necessity to a study on Disarmament, Development and Environment. We examined the impact of seven high level technologies on each of these three areas. For example, we studied the impacts and potential impacts of nuclear, chemical and biological, environmental modification, space and ocean technologies on the general areas of disarmament, development and environment. The simple conclusions of our study were:

1. All of these high technologies are transnational in their effects. That is, their effects cannot be contained within national boundaries.
2. Each of the technologies is a dual-purpose. That is, it can be put to peaceful or warlike uses.
3. The uses to which these technologies are put are largely the result of political decisions within individual nations despite the fact that their effects, for good or evil, will be multi-national or even global in scope.
4. To achieve effective disarmament it will be necessary to have international control of the warlike uses of the technologies.
5. It is also necessary to have international management of the peaceful uses of these technologies both to maximize economic development ends and to prevent transnational environmental destruction which can result from uncontrolled peaceful uses.

In sum, our study underlined the theme of this conference, that peace is indeed the best environment, and suggested that to achieve a peaceful environment it would be necessary to have an institutional framework for the

266

international control and management of dual-purpose technologies.

Underlying the concept of dual-purpose technologies is the understanding that human beings are dual-purpose. We can choose to use our technologies, our tools, for ends which are beneficial or detrimental to the common good. In short, humans are dual-purpose because they can choose to act for good or for evil. But never before in history have we had the tools to act with so much power in either direction. As we are well aware, the future of civilization, humanity and even life on earth is dependent upon our success in achieving the necessary control and management of our technologies, and to do this we must gain control of our impulses toward selfishness and self-destruction. We must live by values which are suitable for achieving this control if we are to be successful.

I would like to suggest to you the extreme importance of considering the issue of an accidental nuclear war. I think that people today generally are coming to understand that nuclear war is more likely by accident than by design. Even Richard Nixon, that old Cold Warrior, has suggested that among the ways a nuclear war was most likely to begin, an accidental war was the highest likelihood.

As we think about accidental nuclear war we should keep in mind that accidents do not just happen. There are *predispositions* to events which we call accidents. Often we call an event an accident because we cannot recognize its causes or predispositions. When accidents in the workplace are studied, however, predispositions such as lack of sleep, drug use, boredom, and poor machine design turn up to "explain" the event we have called "accidental."

Even when we attempt to be redundant in our safety measures with dangerous technologies, still accidents occur. Examples include the near melt-down at Three Mile Island nuclear power plant, plane crashes with nuclear weapons aboard, and the incident of a workman dropping his wrench into a Titan missile resulting in a fuel explosion blowing the lid off of the missile silo.

Misperceptions hidden in language may be important predispositions to accidental nuclear war. Let me give some examples. We speak of *defense* as if such a thing actually existed in relation to nuclear weapons. It does not. Defense in a physical sense is no longer possible. Instead, we have deterrence which is a psychological concept based on fear. Now, although it is obvious that a psychological barrier cannot be as effective as a physical barrier, we still talk about defense as if the two were synonymous. This is very dangerous because it is not an accurate assessment of reality.

A second misperception in our language is the concept *nuclear war*. War traditionally has involved battles and strategies and soldiers fighting against one another. Nuclear war does not resemble this in any way. What we call nuclear war would, in fact, simply be massive genocide. It would be the undifferentiated slaughter of human beings without consideration of their military or civilian status, or concern for gender or age. The use of nuclear weapons might be a holocaust, but it would not be a war.

A third misperception in language is our use of the word *terrorist*. As I understand this word it means threatening to kill innocent people in order to achieve a political end. While most people are rightly indignant about the use of terrorism, they do not perceive that the use of nuclear weapons by all nuclear weapons states fits the definition of terrorism exactly. It is a "gun to the head" policy. For a long time it has been the policy of nuclear weapons states to threaten the use of nuclear weapons against the innocent civilians on the side of their perceived enemies. Despite the sanction of these policies by national leaders, they should be recognized for what they are—terrorism of global dimensions.

We may have an accidental nuclear holocaust because we deceive ourselves with our language, and because we humans are imperfect and fallible. That is our nature, and we should be doing everything we can to reduce the risk of so great a catastrophe.

Instead, however, we have been taking steps which actually make nuclear war by accident more likely. Here are five examples of factors increasing the likelihood of accidental nuclear war:

1. Nuclear weapons are becoming more numerous. The more weapons there are, the longer the chain of command there must be for controlling them. Each link in the chain of command makes control more tenuous.

2. Delivery systems have become more accurate. This creates a fear of first-strike, and increases the possibility of first use in time of crisis.

3. Warning time has decreased. Warning time is only a matter of a few minutes now, and this is not sufficient for reasonable decision-making.

4. Systems for warning have become increasingly complex and subject to error. There is growing experience with computer generated false alarms of attack, but there may not always be sufficient time to adequately check out a false alarm.

5. The know-how and materials for construction of nuclear weapons has spread to an increasing number of nations. If additional nations develop nuclear arsenals the problems of control will increase significantly. Right now the nuclear weapons powers are teaching other nations by their example that nuclear weapons are valuable additions to a nation's military power and prestige. The nuclear weapons powers may be saying that they don't want proliferation of nuclear weapons, but at the same time they say so they are developing ever more lethal and powerful nuclear weapons for themselves.

What can be done about this situation? First, let me

emphasize that the Hot Line is not enough. The Hot Line is for crisis management, and once a crisis is underway there may be precious little time for sound decision-making.

The emphasis needs to be on methods of prevention as a first and most important line of protection against accidental nuclear war, and only secondarily on methods of crisis management. Here are several suggestions for prevention:

1. We need to develop *Accidental War Assessment Centers.* We need to subject weapons technologies and strategies to assessment for their accidental war implications before they are developed and deployed. Those weapons and strategies which increase the danger of accidental war should obviously not be implemented. Similar analysis must be given not only to proposed new systems, but to existing systems as well.

2. We need *U.S.-Soviet Risk Reduction Centers* which will engage in joint evaluation of potential crises, and work out plans for averting crises.

3. We need to have *abstention from first-strike oriented technologies.* This could be done by each side unilaterally, or by agreement. It is based upon the idea that it is in the interest of each side not to threaten the other with a first-strike potential.

4. We need *major reductions in the numbers of nuclear weapons.* This would help both to tighten control of remaining weapons and to set the proper example for other nations as one measure to prevent proliferation. Major reductions is also promised by both the United States and the Soviet Union in Article VI of the Nuclear Non-Proliferation Treaty.

5. We need to *prevent the extension of the arms race into outer space.* Instead of an arms race in outer space, the U.S. and Soviet Union could create a joint effort for dramatic cooperation in space. Instead of "Star Wars" we could have 'Star Wonder." A member of the Nuclear Age Peace Foundation, Genevieve Nowlin, has deve-

loped a wonderful concept for a *multinational, unarmed, manned space station.* It would be an observatory-laboratory to be used for the advancement of all nations by providing open reports on issues of troop movements; treaty and false alarm verification; and agricultural, ecological, weather and pollution information. In short, it would be a cosmic observatory-laboratory of global cooperation with the purpose of contributing to the earth's disarmament, development and environmental enhancement. It would be a major step toward the international control and management of dual-purpose technology.

At this meeting we are working to develop a statement to present to Mr. Reagan and Mr. Gorbachev prior to their summit meeting. If I were in the same room with either or both of these men I would ask them: first, *to reassess security in light of accidental war dangers:* second, *to recognize the historic opportunity they have to improve world security, lessen tensions, and save their economies:* third, *to think as grand-parents, that is, as humans in the nexus of our human family, and to consider the moral implications of threatening to kill hundreds of millions of people:* and finally, *to realize how much it is in their own and their nations' self-interest to reverse the nuclear arms race and take the necessary steps to minimize the threat of accidental nuclear war.*

I would like to conclude by suggesting some corollaries to the Golden Rule which are applicable to today's nuclear armed world.

—What we threaten unto others, *will be threatened* unto us.

—What we threaten unto others, *may be done* unto us.

—What we *do* unto others, *will be done* unto us.

GEORGE WALD

20. A Message to
Gorbachev and Reagan

was working at my desk at Harvard about noon on
Veterans Day, Monday, November 11, 1985 when I had a
telephone call from Amsterdam. An appointment had
been arranged with Soviet General Secretary Mikhail Gorbachev in Moscow for Wednesday afternoon, November 13.
Would I go? After about ten minutes of concentrated
thought and feeling I called back to say that I would.

What had happened is that in October 25-27 a conference
on the arms race had been held in Maastricht, a town in the
south of Holland where there had been a lot of fighting in
World War II. A Mr. Alois Englander had originally invited a
large number of Nobel Laureates to meet in Vienna on this
theme, but at the last moment unforeseen difficulties had
transposed the meeting to Maastricht. It was hastily put
together there by an Amsterdam publisher, Theo Knippenberg and his partner, Susan Gabrielle. It was a mixed
gathering that included five Nobel Laureates: Ilya Prigogine
(Chemistry) from Brussels; Richard Synge (Chemistry),
Scotland; Jan Tinbergen (Economics), Rotterdam; Sir Peter
Medawar (Physiology or Medicine), London, represented by
his wife, Jean; and myself. Claire, the daughter of the late Sir
Martin Ryle (Physics), Cambridge, England also took part in
the discussions.

A statement was drawn up as of October 27, addressed to
President Reagan and Mr. Gorbachev, looking toward their
approaching meeting in Geneva. It called upon them to

agree upon a comprehensive framework for disarmament that included the following five immediate steps:

1. A pledge of no first use of nuclear weapons;
2. A comprehensive nuclear test ban treaty;
3. The progressive de-militarization of outer space;
4. Deep cuts in the present nuclear weapon stockpiles, as a first step in their early elimination; and
5. Establishment of a joint framework to prevent the accidental initiation of nuclear war.

The first four points are the altogether familiar ingredients of opinion and efforts to cool and eventually stop the arms race and prevent the outbreak of nuclear war. Only the fifth point is unusual, though greatly needed. It was the contribution of David Krieger, founder and president of the Nuclear Age Peace Foundation in Santa Barbara, California.

Mr. Englander at once distributed this statement to a wide array of Nobel Laureates, and by November 12 had collected the signatures of fifty-two Nobel Laureates from eighteen countries, including thirteen from the U.S. Next day we added the signatures five Soviet Nobel Laureates, bringing the total to fifty-seven.

On November 4 Mr. Knippenberg in Amsterdam began a simultaneous effort to have an American and a Soviet Nobel Laureate deliver this statement in person to President Reagan and Mr. Gorbachev. He began by working through the American and Soviet embassies in Amsterdam. On Monday, November 11, he was called by the Soviet Ambassador to say that an appointment had been arranged for Wednesday afternoon with Mr. Gorbachev. He immediately cabled this news to the U.S. embassy, asking that it be transmitted to Washington. It was then that he called me at Harvard.

On Tuesday I flew Pan Am overnight to Paris, and on Wednesday went on by the Soviet airline Aeroflot to Moscow. It wasn't all that simple, for there were no exchange relations between American and Soviet commercial airlines, and Pan

Am had written my ticket. One good outcome of the Geneva summit is that such relations began again.

So as my plane began to load I was left waiting for something to be done. At the last minute a young man appeared from the Soviet embassy to straighten things out. He went aboard with me and on the plane before take-off wrote me a Soviet visa.

I landed in Moscow at about 4:00 p.m. (8:00 a.m. Boston time!) having spent sixteen hours on and off planes, badly needing sleep, a wash, a shave. To my amazement as I emerged into the airport there, waiting for me, were not only Knippenberg, Gabrielle and Englander, but a covey of Soviet officials. We piled into four black limousines, with a car up ahead with rotating flashing lights to speed us through traffic, and were whisked into the Kremlin.

There, after a few minutes of introductions and photos, we were shown into a big room. Mr. Gorbachev sat at one end of a long table, with me opposite. Next to Mr. Gorbachev sat Anatoli Alexandrov, the President of the Soviet Academy of Sciences and member of the Central Committee; and next to him Eugene Velikhov, the Vice-President of the Academy and one of Mr. Gorbachev's principal advisors on arms control. Next to me sat Alexander Prokhorov, a Soviet physicist and Nobel Laureate; then Susan Gabrielle and Theo Knippenberg, publishers in Amsterdam of the new bi-weekly Kaos (Chaos) and Alois Englander who had collected the Nobel signatures. Since I was spokesman for the Nobel Laureates the conversation was almost entirely between Mr. Gorbachev and me.

We had been told beforehand that Mr. Gorbachev could spare us twenty-five minutes to at most a half hour. As it turned out, the conversation lasted two and a half hours.

It began with predictable formalities. I read our statement in English, a translator read it in Russian. Then Mr. Gorbachev began by thanking us. He said that it was a most important statement for all mankind, that his government

274

would give it most serious attention. We live, he said, in a period of radical transformation. Arms control is growing ever more complicated and difficult, as new technologies are introduced. He inveighed particularly against the militarization of space; and made the interesting point of asking whether deploying weapons in space over the territory of another nation does not constitute a violation of national sovereignty.

He said that the Soviet Union had proposed for negotiation at the United Nations a program for international, peaceful cooperation in outer space, involving not only planetary exploration, but the technological development of space, perhaps its eventual industrialization. "If we can stop the arms race," he said, "what enormous resources that would be free for other things needing to be done. What great strides in science might occur."

At that point I interrupted to say, "Mr. Gorbachev, science can wait. But this cannot wait!"—slapping our statement. "What brings me here is not to promote science. What brings me here more than anything else is the thought of children—your children, ours, all the world's children. How much longer will they be permitted to live: one year? two years? five? No one knows."

"Yes", he said, "Of course, that's what matters most. Those children are humanity's future."

I think that interchange warmed up the discussion. In any case it went on for another hour. Mr. Gorbachev put most weight on the U.S. not developing Star Wars. Unless that stopped, he said, there could be no reductions in the nuclear stockpiles. On the contrary, they would increase. He said that he was puzzled that the U.S. clung so tenaciously to going on with Star Wars. Was it the influence of our military-industrial complex?

Finally all that came to an end, already an hour past our original limit. It was time to go. But right then, because our discussion had been so warm and friendly, I made a split-

second decision. I said that I was going to introduce a
painful subject, that it had not been discussed with the
others in our party nor with the Nobel Laureates; that I was
speaking on my own.

And I brought up human rights. I said that all over the
world there were persons who wanted to think the best of
the Soviet Union, but were deeply embarrassed by the
harshness with which the Soviet government treats its
dissidents. I said that I thought that this was doing a great
harm to the public image of the Soviet Union. I could name
off-hand a dozen such cases that were arousing wide concern; but would begin with only one, Yuri Orlov, who has
spent nine years in Soviet labor camps, and by our information would soon be dead if he were not released.

What was going to happen? I have read in our press that
this subject excites great irritation and anger in Soviet
officials. Would Mr. Gorbachev respond that way? Would he
walk out?

No, nothing like that. He began to explain carefully the
Soviet point of view. And to our amazement, our conversation continued on that theme for another hour.

Mr. Gorbachev said first that the Soviet Union is a nation
of 270 million people, and he cannot know them all. He
implied that he had not heard of Yuri Orlov. I replied that
Orlov's case is well known in many parts of the world.

He said, "The Soviet Union is a nation of law. It is not for
me to put people in jail or to take them out of jail. These
people have offended against our law. They have had their
trials, and been judged. They are serving their sentences."

I said that Orlov's crime, as well as I remembered, was to
have formed a small Helsinki Watch committee, to monitor
Soviet compliance with the Helsinki Agreements, which the
Soviet Union had signed. That we found it hard to consider
such activity criminal. I said that it was a centuries-old
tradition in Russia—not in my country, where intellectuals

tend to go about their own business, but in Russia—for intellectuals to take responsibility for their entire society.

At this point Alexandrov, President of the Soviet Academy of Sciences, broke in. What's all the fuss about Sakharov? he said. Sakharov is perfectly comfortable in Gorky, he said. We haven't expelled him from the Academy. He gets his salary. He's writing scientific papers. Where's the trouble?

Besides, said Mr. Gorbachev, he's an up-and-down person. First he designs our H-bomb, now he wants to get rid of nuclear weapons. He's a brilliant and inventive scientist. What if we let him out and he went to work for the other side? Better to have him in Gorky.

I think it was Velikhov who brought Shcharansky into the discussion—a young Jewish computer scientist who was tried for treason. A few days later in Geneva I met his wife, Avital. She held a press conference there in which I took some part.

At the last, Mr. Gorbachev issued three block-busters. He said that he thought Soviet citizens had better access to their government than in any other nation. He said that they had more chance to criticize their government than in any other nation. And then he said that in his opinion the Soviet Union is now the most democratic nation in the world.

Needless to say, these are startling statements to an American. They were to me. But he went right on to explain what he was talking about. I have heard it spoken of as "economic democracy." Instead of emphasizing such things as multi-party politics and the concerns expressed in our constitutional Bill of Rights, Mr. Gorbachev went on to say, that the Soviet Union has no unemployment, provides free medical care for all, child care for working mothers and care for the aged.

I then said that I thought we would get no further with that discussion, but that I wanted to end with two questions:

1. How would I have been dealt with were I a Soviet citizen who had spoken to the American government as frankly

and openly as I had spoken with him?—and

2. What did he think the effect on world opinion would be if he were to say, okay Professor Wald, you can take Yuri Orlov and his wife home with you? (A short time after, they came to New York where I visited them. Orlov is now at Cornell.)

With that, Mr. Gorbachev thanked us again for our statement, and our meeting came to a cordial end.

I have been asked frequently my impressions of Gorbachev, the person. They are good. The impression is of a warm human being, anything but a rigid, impenetrable bureaucrat. His facial expressions are lively and responsive. He smiles frequently, a characteristic smile flickers frequently over his face. There I was, tired, unshaven, in a jersey and corduroys, yet at ease and enjoying our conversation. I can only conclude from our two-and-a-half-hour session that perhaps he did too.

Next morning, every newspaper in the Soviet Union had this as its front page story, pictures and all. In general, it was not presented as a dialogue, but as a statement by Mr. Gorbachev to the Nobel Laureates. There was no mention whatever of the hour spent on human rights.

On November 4, simultaneous with his first approach to the Soviet government, Mr. Knippenberg had appealed to the U.S. embassy in Amsterdam to arrange an opportunity for us to deliver our statement personally to President Reagan. Having pursued this fruitlessly in Amsterdam, he continued in Moscow with repeated telephone calls to the White House. I also pleaded for such an opportunity at the U.S. embassy in Moscow.

I set out from Moscow for Geneva on Sunday, November 17, already reconciled to the realization that it was now too late: I was not going to see Mr. Reagan.

Arriving in Geneva around noon on Monday, November eighteen—incidentally my seventy-ninth birthday—I called the U.S. Mission at once to ask for a chance to deliver our statement. Could I give it to Secretary of State George Schultz?—Security Advisor Robert McFarlane? Not a chance. Next morning I was trying again, dealing with U.S. officials who were affable, interested, but not very productive. It was my last day. The statement should have been delivered before the Summit Meeting, and that was passing. Finally a young man came to receive the statement. He was Joe Lehman, a minor public relations person on the staff of the Arms Control and Disarmament Agency. By that time it was a relief to give him the statement and the list of Nobel Laureates who had signed it.

I think from this experience and others of a similar nature that the Reagan administration does not receive communications that are not strictly in line with its policies. On the other hand, as it happens, the first four points in our statement were in complete accord with Soviet positions. No-first-use has been a unilateral Soviet position since 1982, then joined by China, but rejected by NATO. The Soviet Union has repeatedly asked for an end of testing of nuclear weapons, and Mr. Gorbachev announced on August 6, 1985 a unilateral test ban for the rest of that year, to extend indefinitely if the U.S. joined in. Eventually it was continued for nineteen months with no U.S. response. The Soviet insistence on stopping the militarization of space—both the Strategic Defense Initiative (Star Wars) and the closely related anti-satellite (ASAT) program—was brought to the Geneva Summit as an absolute condition before proceeding to cut the nuclear stockpiles of both powers by half. So the first four points of our statement were in complete accord with stated Soviet positions.

Why was that so?

It was because, entirely regardless of Soviet positions, these are the familiar, day-to-day tenets of people everywhere who are deeply concerned to cool the arms race and eventually stop it, so to relieve humanity of the growing threat of nuclear war. These are the positions of almost all

279

American Scientists not working for government or the weapons industry. They are the position of the Federation of American Scientists, the Union of Concerned Scientists, and such major American organizations as the

American Friends Service Committee, the Women's International League for Peace and Freedom, the Mobilization for Survival, among others. These are also the expressed positions of some top members of former U.S. Administrations including four former Secretaries of Defense. They are equally supported by scientists and peace groups in the other NATO nations. They come directly out of the logic of trying to cool and eventually stop the arms race, and trying to prevent nuclear war. That is why we could so quickly collect the signatures of fifty-seven Nobel Laureates to our statement.

Let me explain point by point what I have called the logic of our statement. It is so straightforward that a child could understand it.

1. *No First Use.* The U.S. government and NATO have declined to pledge no first use of nuclear weapons on the ground that were the Soviet Union to launch a massive tank attack on Western Europe, since their tank forces are said to greatly exceed NATO's, our only recourse might be to meet it with nuclear weapons. The trouble is that that would take a lot of nuclear weapons—probably thousands. The Warsaw Pact would of course respond with nuclear weapons. As Vice Admiral John Marshall Lee, USN retired, explained to a NATO group on May 3, 1985, "The problem is that wrecking a conventional attack with nuclear weapons simultaneously makes the conventional battle irrelevant. The war becomes a nuclear war ... Our Allies are not defended; they are only destroyed ... Conventional deterrence and defense must be provided by conventional means." Once nuclear weapons have begun to be used, no one can say where that would end. Robert McNamara, U.S. Secretary of Defense under two Presidents, has stated: "It is inconceivable to me, as it has

been to others who have studied the matter, that 'limited' nuclear wars would remain limited . . . Any decision to use nuclear weapons would imply a high probability of the same cataclysmic consequences as a total nuclear exchange."

2. *A Comprehensive Test Ban Treaty.* There is now a virtual consensus among all the world's peace movements that the most feasible first step toward containing the nuclear arms race would be a comprehensive test ban treaty. The first arms control treaty, the Partial Test Ban Treaty of 1963, banned nuclear tests in the atmosphere and underwater, but permitted them to continue underground. If that had been a comprehensive test ban treaty the entire world, including the two superpowers, would be enormously more secure than now. We would have no MIRV's, no first strike weapons, no neutron bombs or cruise missiles, and problems of verification would long since have been settled. Glenn Seaborg, who led the isolation of plutonium and was for many years chairman of the U.S. Atomic Energy Commission, (Nobel Prize in Chemistry, 1951), issued the call for a Comprehensive Test Ban in 1983, saying that "A CTB would halt that aspect of the arms race that is most threatening, the qualitative improvements in nuclear weapons."

3. *De-Militarization of Outer Space.* The so-called Strategic Defense Initiative ("Star Wars") and the associated Anti-satellite (ASAT) programs represent together the most destabalizing development that has entered the arms race in many years. They represent an infinitely more sophisticated anti-ballistic missile (ABM) system, in direct violation of the 1972 ABM treaty between the U.S. and the Soviet Union, which remains the bulwark of any effective system of mutual deterrence. An Appeal to Ban Space Weapons issued by the U.S. Union of Concerned Scientists has been signed by 720 members of the U.S. National Academy of Sciences and 57 U.S. Nobel Laureates. Scientists in over 50 American universities have signed a pledge not to "solicit or work on" Star Wars research because the program is "ill-conceived,

281

dangerous and will only serve to escalate the nuclear arms race."

4. *Significant Cuts in the Present Stockpiles of Nuclear Weapons.* These become possible only if Star Wars is given up. The reason is obvious. Star Wars is intended to be a system for destroying nuclear weapons on their way to their targets. No such system, if feasible at all—which is very doubtful—can be completely effective. The cheapest and easiest way to counter it is to launch more nuclear weapons. One can be confident that the result of instituting a Star Wars program will be, not to decrease, but to *increase* the stockpiles of nuclear weapons.

5. *Avoiding the Danger of Accidental Initiation of Nuclear War.* This is the new element in our statement, and I should like to explain it. In October, 1980 U.S. Senators Gary Hart and Barry Goldwater issued a report to the Senate Committee on Armed Services on "Recent False Alerts from the Nation's Missile Attack Warning System." There are four stages in alerts:

1. routine, non-threatening;
2. Possibly threatening;
3. Definitely threatening: the Chairman of the Joint Chiefs of Staff is involved and the nuclear bombers put on alert.
4. Missile Attack Conference: involves all senior personnel, including the President.

This would conclude whether or not to launch the missiles—major nuclear war. The report covered 1979 and the first half of 1980. SIPRI, the Stockholm International Peace Research Institute has since brought this information up to May, 1983. It turns out that the first stage in false alerts come at the rate of 10–12 per day; the second stage, starting at 2–3 per week, in 1979-80 rose steadily to 7.6 per week in 1983. The third stage, the last antecedent to launch, involved two incidents each in 1978, 1979 and 1980; and none since. An intensive investigation of the two incidents in 1980 showed that they were "caused by a bad chip in a communications processor computer."

It must be understood that nuclear missiles launched between the Soviet Union and the United States would take about thirty minutes to reach their targets, thirty minutes in which to decide whether or not an attack has been launched. On the other hand the Pershing II missiles being deployed in West Germany are only six to eight minutes from their targets. The same would be true of missiles launched from offshore submarines. That leaves hardly enough time for conferences. What we have come to fear is that this situation will drive one of the powers to go over to Launch on Warning (i.e., turning the decision over to the computers). For, as the above data show, and as every computer specialist knows, computers are not altogether reliable, they make mistakes. It is to try to deal with the possibility of such mistakes that the fifth point of our statement was introduced.

It would be utter nonsense to allege that our statement was following the Soviet line. It had nothing to do with the Soviet line, or indeed any other political line.

Our agreement with the Soviet position means something else, of very great importance. It means that the Soviet government too really wants to cool and perhaps to stop the arms race. That is not only, as for us a matter of survival, but because the Soviet Union is in trouble politically and economically. In Afghanistan it is in a morass comparable with our Vietnam War. It faces big industrial and agricultural problems. I believe it is still true now as it was four years ago that every day on the average two 20,000 ton vessels leave American ports loaded with grain sold to the Soviet Union. The Ukraine used to be the breadbasket of Europe; now the Soviet Union cannot adequately feed its own people and livestock.

Under these circumstances, I believe it is altogether true that the Soviet government finds the arms race a heavy

283

burden, and would gladly be rid of it. For that reason I do not doubt Mr. Gorbachev's sincerity in espousing his present positions.

When I got back to the United States I set about at once trying to tell my story. There were press and TV interviews. I wrote an account that I sent around, but to my dismay none of the main-line media seemed inclined to use this material. For about three weeks after the Geneva summit there seemed to be no space for anything but adulation of the President. It reached extraordinary lengths. After the second week an issue of *Time* magazine, looking back upon the Summit encounter, said that President Reagan had had the advantage throughout: height, hair, and straightness of back.

While I was still struggling with this situation, the first freeze came to New York. In a front-page story the *New York Times* announced that the police were scouring the city in force to try to round up ten thousand homeless persons, who might have frozen trying to sleep in the streets. In Boston the figure was six thousand.

Also a special Physicians' Task Force together with the Harvard School of Public Health had just completed a careful survey of hunger in the U.S. It found twenty million chronically hungry Americans—people who, with their families regularly missed a meal because they had no food or money to buy it.

That made me think again about Mr. Gorbachev's startling remarks on the "economic democracy" that he said obtains in the Soviet Union. The four things he claimed to be provided to the Soviet people—full employment, free universal medical care, child care for working mothers, and care of the aged—are not available to all Americans. We are proud of our multi-party politics and the freedoms expressed in our Bill of Rights. But what if one asked one of those twenty million hungry Americans, which would you rather have, food or free speech?—what do you think he/she would say? Which would *you* choose? It is of course an unfair question: one needs both. But clearly also Mr. Gorbachev had a point.

An Appeal To President Reagan And General Secretary Gorbachev[†]

You have an unparalleled opportunity to change the course of human history.

We call upon you not to leave Geneva until you have agreed to a concrete plan for comprehensive disarmament, including the following immediate steps:

1. Pledging No First Use of nuclear weapons;
2. A Comprehensive Nuclear Test Ban Treaty, starting with a mutual moratorium on nuclear explosions;
3. Progressive de-militarization of outer space;
4. Meaningful reductions in present nuclear stockpiles as a beginning toward their early elimination;
5. Establishment of a joint framework for assessing the dangers of the accidental initiation of nuclear war.

As President Eisenhower said, the arms race is daily taking food from the mouths of the hungry.

Today security can be found only in disarmament and meeting the needs of a dignified human existence. The future demands a cooperative redirection of scientific and technological know-how.

World peace will require less emphasis on ideologies and more on tolerance as well as on the solution of problems which depend upon international cooperation.

Courage today is required not in war, but to make peace.

We call on you to begin the *PEACE RACE.*

[†]Statement drafted at conference for Nobel Laureates, *Peace—The Best Environment,* at Maastricht, Holland, October 27, 1985.

DAVID KRIEGER

21. The Responsibility of Scientists

(Address given in San Sebastian, Spain, December 1987)

We need more to merge compassion with our curiosity. Science stands in need of humanistic directing... A basic part of philosophic or scientific concern for ethics is concern for human betterment.... Truth for truth's sake must be wedded to truth for humanity's sake.
　　　　　　　　　　　　　　　　　　　　　　　　—Ted Lentz

Events connected with the second International Peace Week of Scientists took place in some thirty-three countries, and included scientists from East and West, North and South speaking on a wide variety of topics. These events in Spain are the final events of this year's Peace Week. As Chairman of The International Coordinating Committee of this year's Peace Week one thing I can tell you with certainty is that there is a fraternity of good-willed and dedicated people working throughout the world on issues of making this a more decent and peaceful world.

The goals of the Peace Week are:

1. To improve the climate for arms control and disarmament, and the application of science for peace and human betterment;
2. To increase awareness of the impact of scientific developments on international security;
3. To encourage scientists to work for constructive rather than destructive objectives; and

4. To involve scientists and citizens around the world in a public dialogue on the great issues of our time.

Over fifty major organizations endorsed the Peace Week, including UNICEF, the International Association of University Presidents, the International Union of Students, the International Physicians for the Prevention of Nuclear War, Greenpeace International, the U.N. University for Peace, the Federation of American Scientists, the Union of Concerned Scientists, the Soviet Academy of Science, the Brazilian Association for the Advancement of Science, the Institute of Nuclear Research of the Hungarian Academy of Science, and Scientists Against Nuclear Arms (SANA) in Australia, New Zealand and the United Kingdom.

Individual endorsers of the Peace Week included distinguished scientists from around the world, university presidents, and some twenty Nobel Laureates.

I would like to express some simple ideas to you based upon many years of working for peace, along with my recent experience in coordinating the International Peace Week of Scientists.

• Scientists seek to know the truth, but they are often biased in their positions on social issues because they are human like all of us. Therefore, scientists should be careful to make clear to themselves and others when they speak on the basis of scientific methodology, and when they express opinions that are not based on scientific methodology. And, of course, citizens must be careful to evaluate the perspective from which a scientist speaks.

• Scientists are specialists, and therefore generally are very focused in their knowledge. They know a lot about a little, and perhaps a little about a lot. Specialists often miss the big picture because of their focus on the particular.

• We live in a time badly in need of generalists who see the big picture, for example, who see the Earth as one unitary body which we all share.

Archibald MacLeish, the poet, wrote:

to see the Earth
as it truly is
small and blue and beautiful
in that eternal silence
where it floats
is to see ourselves
as riders on the Earth together
brothers
on that bright loveliness
brothers who know now they are
truly
brothers.

The poet's wisdom is often overlooked in the specialization of the scientist.

● The boundaries on our Earth are made by humans, exist in our minds, and can only be broken down by our actions. These boundaries are invisible, in fact, figments of our imaginations.

● Tragically, scientists often spend their entire working lives developing, enhancing, or perfecting weapons to threaten people who live within some other invisible boundaries.

● Now the arms race has reached a new level of absurdity. Scientists are attempting to develop invisible shields that will protect the people who live within certain invisible boundaries.

● Scientists act out of self-interest. Most will work for the highest bidder. Very few exceptional human beings, who may also happen to be scientists or engineers, will place the greater interest of the common good before their own self-interest.

● Today we have enough weapons. One scientist, Victor Weisskopf, has calculated that the explosive power in today's arsenals is equivalent to 6,000 times the entire firepower used in all of World War II. Thus, the explosive power of today's weapons is equivalent to 6,000 World War IIs.[1]

• The obsession of our societies with war and war preparation has directed science toward destructive rather than constructive objectives. The Soviet leader, Mikhail Gorbachev, recently wrote: "Our rockets can find Halley's comet and fly to Venus with amazing accuracy, but side by side with these scientific and technological triumphs is an obvious lack of efficiency in using scientific achievements for economic needs."[2]

• All of our great technologies are dual-purpose, that is, they can be employed for good or evil. The responsibility of scientists does not end with the creation of a technology. They must also take some responsibility for the use of their creation.

• Most great technological achievements these days are team projects, what I would call "corporate science." These are scientific projects mobilized toward achieving a given objective. Perhaps the first great effort of "corporate science" was the Manhattan Project to create the atomic bomb during World War II. We badly need to mobilize scientists in new projects of the scope of the Manhattan Project, but directed toward human betterment rather than mass annihilation.

• All technologies carry with them the risk of accident. This was underlined for the world by the Challenger and Chernobyl tragedies.

You are perhaps aware of the accident in Palomares, Spain on January 17, 1966 in which a B-52 carrying nuclear weapons had a mid-air accident while refueling and dropped four nuclear weapons. There was fortunately no nuclear explosion, but there was a detonation of high explosives in two of the bombs which resulted in spewing plutonium over a wide agricultural area. It was necessary to ship 5,000 barrels of contaminated soil to a waste burial site in North Carolina. The clean-up cost was $50 million.

• At the Nuclear Age Peace Foundation we have done a lot of research on the dangers of accidental nuclear war, and we believe that the dangers are significant and increasing. This is primarily because decision time for evaluation of nuclear attack has decreased significantly, and the decision to launch nuclear weapons has become increasingly dependent upon technology. There is also the important factor of human error, and the fact that many weapons handlers and national leaders have been found to have drug and other psychological problems.

• It has been suggested that in any fool-proof system the fool will always prove greater than the proof. A few years ago a faulty 46 cent computer chip signaled that the United States was under nuclear attack, and led to U.S. forces going on alert.

I recently read that at an Air Force base in Cheyenne, Wyoming an armored car was parked on top of a minuteman III silo which had given off signals that it was about to launch itself.[3] Another article discussed an emergency procedure at the Sequoyah Nuclear Power Plant which required an engineer to sledgehammer toilets and seal the holes in the floor with tape to keep radioactive gases from escaping in the event of an accident.[4] The lesson here is that technology is not always as sophisticated as it may seem.

• In many respects it is scientific arrogance which is threatening our environment. Scientists promised answers to the problem of nuclear waste disposal which they could not deliver on. The waste remains an enormous threat to this generation and hundreds of generations to follow.

The problem is compounded because nuclear power plants are subject to attack by conventional weapons. Recently Iraqi planes bombed an Iranian nuclear plant. This is an action which can equalize disparate opponents. It is an action which someday may be taken by terrorists.

Science has become extraordinarily militarized in a time when human needs cry out for attention.

We spend nearly $1,000 billion for military purposes in a

world in which 40,000 children die daily of starvation and preventable diseases.

In developing countries some one billion people are below the poverty line. 780 million people are undernourished. 850 million persons are illiterate. 1.5 billion persons have no access to medical facilities. One billion people are inadequately housed.[5]

It would seem that scientific vision has been constrained by the voracious appetites of the military. According to Carl Sagan, in the 1960s the United States sent twenty-four space missions to other worlds, and in the 1970s it sent fourteen such missions. However, since 1978 it has not sent a single spacecraft to the Moon or the planets. Sagan pointed out that "in 1982, for the first time in American history, military expenditures in space exceeded civilian expenditures. Today they are about twice as large."[6]

Despite all of this, in the twentieth-century science has for many become godlike, occupying a position of great importance in our modern societies. And with this near deification of science, scientists have gained in stature and authority. We might ask why science has assumed so important a role in modern society. The answer, it seems to me, is that science, as a method of knowing, has been successful and Western civilization has always been enthralled with success. Science has driven the engines of discovery and understanding, and therefore change.

Science is, of course, not the only method of knowing our world. There is also the intuitive, the artistic, the experiential and the spiritual. We need only look back to the time of Galileo and the Inquisition to know that science has not always been accorded the preeminent place in society that it holds today. In our time, science has prevailed because it has demonstrated most dramatically the power of its discoveries. Science has allowed us to split the atom and to travel into outer space; to transplant a human heart and to prevent polio and other dread diseases. The discoveries of science have affected every area of our lives—our eating patterns, our health, our travel, our communication, our security and our view of ourselves and our world.

In societies that honor power, as do Western cultures, it should not be surprising that scientists have an honored place. In many respects scientists have become the high priests of modern societies. With enough funds and mobilization of resources they are often able to deliver feats of seeming magic such as linking up two vehicles in outer space or developing bombs capable of destroying whole cities.

Some of you will undoubtedly say that these Herculean feats are not those of science, but of technology. Of course, technically this is correct. Science is a methodology for discovering truth, and fitting it into a theoretical format which allows for predictability and authentication by repetition. Technology, on the other hand, directs knowledge toward an objective. The objective may be the creation of a satellite or a submarine, a new strain of corn or a solar energy system.

Most of what the public thinks of as science today is, in fact, technology—science directed toward a given objective. And, more than that, it is team technology. The lone, pioneer scientist, Einstein being an example, has been replaced by the team technologist or "corporate scientist," exemplified by Edward Teller. Einstein created a theory of relativity, what we know in shorthand as E+mc², a theoretical formulation which changed our view of the world. Teller, on the other hand, is known for his work as the "father of the H-bomb," a technical triumph of some magnitude which undoubtedly also changed our view of the world.

It is not surprising that our corporate societies would organize and elevate corporate science to provide technological responses to social problems. How we deploy our scientists, what projects we give to them, is indicative of our

292

priorities as a society. In the United States most federal government research money for scientists, approximately 70 percent, goes toward military projects. In Japan, perhaps most resources for scientific discovery go toward perfecting consumer electronics. Each society makes explicit choices about how it will use its scientifically trained men and women, and it dangles the carrots of money and prestige in the direction it wishes them to move.

In a perfect society, which allocated its scientific resources where there was the greatest social need, the system of corporate science could be very beneficial. But in a less than perfect society—that is, the real world—the system moves scientists in directions that may serve narrow and/or dangerous interests rather than the greater good. As one example, in the United States many health and disease prevention projects suffer while exorbitant funding goes into developing x-ray lasers as part of the so-called Strategic Defense Initiative (SDI), a concept riddled with dangerous flaws.

I watched on television news recently as President Reagan told a group of Strategic Defense Initiative workers, presumably scientists and engineers, at the Martin Marietta Corporation that the work on SDI would continue and he would never use SDI as a bargaining chip in negotiations with the Soviet Union. The corporate scientists responded to this promise with a rousing round of applause and cheers, demonstrating, I believe, their concern with their personal job security. As a general rule, support for SDI is strongest among scientists who are receiving or hope to receive some personal benefit such as job security or research funds from the program.

It is important to state that scientists need not be pawns of any system. Scientists, like all other members of our species, are blessed or cursed (depending upon one's viewpoint) with the capability of choice. That is, scientists, like other mortals, may choose how they will spend their time and energy. It may be social custom to gravitate toward the projects with the greatest monetary rewards, but it is not one's only choice. It is always possible, as Nancy Reagan never tires of reminding us to "just say No." Scientists, for example could say No to lending their talents to developing ever more lethal and omnicidal weapons systems.

Scientists without a vested interest in the SDI program have been far more critical of its faults. In fact, more than 7,000 American scientists have signed a pledge never to work on SDI related projects. Five thousand scientists outside the United States have also signed this pledge. An Appeal by American Scientists to Ban Space Weapons, signed by many distinguished scientists including fifty-seven Nobel Laureates, called upon the United States and Soviet Union "to negotiate a total ban on the testing and deployment of weapons in space" and further asked the two countries "to reaffirm their commitment to the 1972 ABM Treaty, which prohibits the development, testing, and deployment of space-based ABM systems."[7]

I would like to give three examples of scientific professionals who have demonstrated exemplary courage during their careers by saying No when they did have a vested personal interest in a project, but chose to act on conscience rather than self-interest.

John Gofman is a nuclear physicist and medical doctor. His credentials as a scientist are extremely impressive. He worked with Glenn Seaborg, a Nobel Laureate in Physics, in developing plutonium isotopes. Later, he was asked by the Atomic Energy Commission to head up a study on the biological effects of radiation. He concluded that nuclear power plants in the United States would result in an additional 32,000 cancer and leukemia deaths a year. The AEC did not like the results of his study, and insisted that he not publish them or speak publicly about them. Dr. Gofman felt that the AEC's position was unconscionable, and refused to go along with this repression. Instead he spoke out, and exposed his findings to the full light of scientific debate. As a result, he lost his support at the Lawrence Livermore Laboratory for the heart and cancer research he was engaged in, and was forced to resign his position. John Gofman would not allow a government agency to dictate or suppress his research findings. He has been a world leader in pointing out the biological dangers of radiation that are inherent in the generation of nuclear power.

Robert Aldridge is an aerospace engineer. He worked for sixteen years for the Missile Division of Lockheed Corporation as a design engineer for the Polaris, Poseidon, and Trident missile systems. When he came to believe that the United States was attempting to develop a first strike capability, he resigned. He did so despite the fact that he had a wife and six children still at home. Bob Aldridge is the author of *First Strike! The Pentagon's Strategy for Nuclear War.* He has devoted his full time since leaving the missile design business to writing, consulting for peace organizations, and educating the public on technical aspects of nuclear strategy and security.

David Parnas is an expert in the organization of large software systems. He was hired by the Strategic Defense Initiative Organization (SDIO) as an advisor for a salary of $1,000 per day. He served on a panel with this interesting name, "SDIO Panel on Computing in Support of Battle Management." Parnas wrote that the first assignment for the members on this panel was to prepare position papers on the problems that they saw with the SDI system.

After spending weeks writing up his views, Parnas became convinced that SDIO supported research could not solve the technical problems he had identified. He wrote: "I could not convince myself that it would be useful to build a system that we did not trust. And if SDI is not trustworthy, the U.S. will not abandon the arms race. Similarly the USSR could not assume that SDI would be completely ineffective; seeing both a 'shield' and missiles, it would feel impelled to improve its offensive forces to compensate for the defense.

295

The U.S., not trusting its defense, would feel a need to build still more nuclear missiles to compensate for the increased Soviet strength. The arms race would speed up. Even worse, because we would be wasting an immense amount of effort on a system we couldn't trust, we would see a weakening of our relative strength. Instead of the safer world that President Reagan envisions, we would have a far more dangerous situation."[8]

Parnas resigned his lucrative position, and has become an active opponent of the SDI program. He articulated these reasons for his decision to resign. "As a professional," he wrote, "I am responsible for my own actions and cannot rely on any external authority to make my decisions for me. I cannot ignore ethical and moral issues. I must devote some of my energy to deciding whether the task that I have been given is of benefit to society. I must make sure that I am solving the real problem, not simply providing short term satisfaction to my superior."[9]

Parnas' statement about personal responsibility for his actions provides a good starting point for consideration of an ethical code for scientists, a code that is perhaps long overdue. Should there not be for scientists something similar to the Hippocratic Oath for doctors? Should there not be limits beyond which no reputable scientists would go in contributing his or her skills? Are there not projects which are simply beyond the bounds of not only scientific, but basic human, morality? We can look back upon the depths to which the Nazi doctors stooped in performing experiments on human subjects during World War II.

I believe that there should be ethical guidelines for scientists, and that scientists themselves should take the lead in formulating these guidelines.

Scientists, it seems to me, have a basic responsibility to work for constructive rather than destructive ends. It is a major purpose of the International Peace Week of Scientists to engage scientists and citizens throughout the world in

296

discussions of what constitute appropriate projects for scientific effort. There are certainly many important areas in need of additional scientific expertise. Victor Weisskopf has listed the following ten areas for scientific cooperation between the U.S. and Soviet Union, but they would seem equally applicable to scientists everywhere.[10]

1. New energy sources.
2. Conservation of planetary resources.
3. Atmosphere problems, such as the increase of CO_2, the dangers to the ozone layer, the dying of the forests.
4. Pollution of the oceans.
5. Problems concerning our planet, earthquake warning, polar exploration, weather and crop predictions.
6. New sources and distribution of food, famine prevention.
7. Health problems, epidemics, birth control.
8. Uses of space for communication and industrial processes.
9. Collaboration in large scientific enterprises, such as particle accelerators and planetary exploration.
10. Third world support.

This is an agenda that could keep scientists constructively employed for a long time. There is much to be done, and much need not to waste our scientific and technological expertise on the development of weapons of indiscriminate mass destruction, weapons that can only be used at peril to all humanity.

A very important point about science is that it must be done in the light of day; that is, it must be exposed to peer review. This is part of the scientific process. Science without exposure to criticism or science limited to bureaucratically defined criticism is not science. It may be expedient; it may fit well with the corporate structure of scientific projects; but it is not science. Science and secrecy are not compatible. Scientists jeopardize their integrity when they work under conditions of classification of information.

Scientists must take greater personal responsibility for how they work and what they produce. Scientists, of course, are also humans and citizens, and they must of necessity view the world from these perspectives as well as from a scientific perspective. If we want to have scientists capable of seeing the bigger picture in which they work, we must educate scientists to be philosophers with high ethical standards as well as specialists in their fields. In a recent report issued by Sigma Xi, a scientific research society with over 100,000 members, member responses to a question on scientific education included the following:

"Most scientists are woefully ignorant of the true nature of science, its history and its place in society. By and large our training is exceedingly narrow."

"One problem in graduate education is that universities turn students into moles who spend all their time on one very limited area and discourage these moles from developing themselves in a broader sense."

" ... The newer products of our graduate schools are blind to much that surround them because of an insufficiently humane grounding."[11]

In our world today we badly need humane citizens, and that includes citizens who also are trained to be scientists. Scientists today seem capable of justifying work on the most inhumane and wasteful weapons systems imaginable. This must change. And it would be best if scientists could initiate these changes from within their profession. In a larger sense, as citizens we must speak up and act to assure that our corporate societies direct their resources, including their scientists, toward humane goals.

I would like to conclude with these thoughts written some twenty-five years ago by Robert Maynard Hutchins, the great educator and founder of the Center for the Study of Democratic Institutions:

298

The leading phenomena of our time exhibit a curiously ambiguous character. Technology may blow us up, or it may usher in the paradise of which man has been dreaming every since Adam and Eve got kicked out of the first one. Bureaucracy may stifle democracy or be the backbone of democratic government. Nationalism may disrupt the world or prove to be the necessary precondition of a world community.

Unfortunately these ambiguities do not lend themselves to scientific procedure. Our essential problem is what kind of people we want to be and what kind of world we want to have.

Such questions cannot be solved by experiment and observation. But if we know what justice is, which is not a scientific matter, science and many other disciplines may help us get it.[12]

V. THE RESPONSIBILITY OF CITIZENS

This book is about Waging Peace. In our view, that means an active commitment to achieving peace—a commitment which has become essential in the nuclear age. Waging Peace means not passing on to someone else the responsibility for achieving peace, but rather accepting this responsibility personally.

Consider this question: If there were a nuclear war, which unleashed the tremendous destructive power of even a small portion of the world's nuclear weapons, who would be responsible for this tragedy?

Would it be the political leaders who, forced by the constraints of time and pressure, made the decision to launch the missiles?

Or the military leaders who argued for ever more complex and frightful nuclear weapons systems?

Or the soldiers who obeyed their orders to fire the missiles?

Or the Congressmen who appropriated the funds for the weapons year after year?

Or the industrial leaders who profited from the arms race and lobbied to expand it?

Or the scientists and engineers who lent their brain power to the creation of increasingly powerful and accurate weapons?

Or the "enemy" who competed in the arms race?

All of these will share in responsibility, but major responsibility will lie elsewhere. It will lie with each of us who has not acted to reverse the nuclear arms race as we've moved closer and closer to the precipice. It will lie with the parents and grandparents who did not choose by their actions to secure the future for their children and grandchildren. Responsibility will lie with citizens—those who failed to exercise their important responsibilities as citizens to keep their governments acting humanely.

After a nuclear war it will not much matter, of course, where blame is placed. What does matter is for each of us to accept responsibility now for preventing a nuclear war by actively working to reverse the nuclear arms race. With dedication, courage and energy we might never again need to experience (as at Hiroshima and Nagasaki) the horror of nuclear war.

At the Nuclear Age Peace Foundation we believe that accepting this personal responsibility for reversing the nuclear arms race is the greatest and most necessary challenge of our time. It is the cornerstone of a future that carries civilization, and human life, forward.

THEODORE BECKER

22. Mediating the Nuclear Stalemate

Many people think of peace as a goal rather than a process. They think that peace is something to be achieved rather than a way of being in the world. The belief that peace is a goal rather than a means allows, even encourages, the violent settlement of disputes.

By definition and logic, as long as disputes are resolved with violence, there will not be peace. One act of violence, as history teaches us, will only sow the seeds for the next—and the vicious and repetitive cycle will continue.

A.J. Muste, an American non-violent activist, said "There is no way to peace; peace *is* the way." To live peacefully requires that an individual or a country use peaceful methods of resolving conflict. These methods might be thought of as "tools" of peaceful conflict resolution.

We can take as a given that there will always be conflict among individuals and among nations. Our choice is whether we use and support peaceful or violent methods to resolve that conflict. Among the "tools" of peaceful conflict resolution available to us is mediation. In this chapter, Professor Becker not only explains mediation in simple terms, but also puts forward a thoughtful and creative proposal for citizen mediation of the nuclear stalemate.

Just as politics is too important to be left to politicians and war is too important to be left to generals, so is peace too important to be left to government, diplomats or professional peacemakers. The modern interpersonal mediation movement in America has proved that ordinary citizens make excellent mediators in complex, difficult, violence-prone disputes; they have the necessary compassion, empathy and listening skills to fuel the processes of human intercommunication and understanding that will—in John Lennon's words—"give peace a chance."

Peace is not just the absence of war. Peace is not a nuclear stalemate. It is not a holocaust waiting to happen by accident or design. Peace is the consequence of human harmony.

Mediation is the best process developed in humankind's history to end the nuclear stalemate. But it must be redesigned and expanded as never before to include the dedicated participation of millions and millions of private citizens all around the world using the most advanced modes of human communication. Then, and only then, will the U.S. and Soviet governments understand that they must end their MADness and seriously adopt the sane ways of peace pondered, discussed and agreed upon by the peace-loving citizens of the world community.

Conflict is Natural

Conflict between people is as natural as disease, storms and earthquakes. Even though violence, illness, hurricanes and volcanic eruptions cause great pain and suffering, they are currently unavoidable. Nevertheless, despite the fact that these natural disasters have rained havoc on humankind throughout history, many researchers work on ways to lessen or even prevent these destructive natural forces.

The field of medicine has had some great successes, almost eliminating such diseases as bubonic plague, polio, and yellow fever from the face of the earth. Modern technologies like space satellites and computers are helping meteorologists understand how typhoons are spawned and new instruments are helping vulcanologists understand what causes earthquakes. There is still a long way to go before the human race will see the end of these catastrophes, but modern science has developed warning systems that have eliminated the damage caused by major storm systems.

The field of conflict resolution has had only modest success in learning about the causes of human violence toward other human beings and in developing new techniques to help lessen the amount of fighting and wars. But one of the major recent advances has been the rediscovery and development of *mediation* as a technique of peacemaking.

What Mediation Is And How It Works

When children fight with their parents, or sisters are angry with their brothers, or neighbors don't like what is going on next door, or husbands and wives don't get along, how is this handled?

1. They may continue to squabble forever—making life even more difficult for themselves.
2. They may move away from one another for a time or forever.
3. Either or both parties may use violence to get their way.
4. They may go to court and let a judge decide who is right.
5. They may sit down and discuss (negotiate) a solution where each feels they get something by giving something.
6. They may ask a third party to help them come to a fair agreement.

This last method is called *mediation*—and although it is relatively unfamiliar to most modern Americans, it is not unusual. In fact, mediation was the major way social and personal conflict was solved in early America and is the major way to resolve conflict in most of the world even today.

A mediator is a third party to a dispute, a go-between, someone who is neutral and impartial and whose goal is to help feuding parties come to some settlement of their differences. A mediator does not play the role of a lawyer, judge, counsellor, social worker, or arbitrator. The mediator makes no decision for the parties like judges and arbitrators do. There is some difference of opinion as to whether or not mediators are supposed to generate ideas about how to resolve the dispute. Some mediators give advice; others don't. The basic idea, though, is for the mediator to:

1. help the parties clear up misunderstandings they have about the other;
2. convey how the parties feel about the situation;
3. transmit messages from one party to another; and
4. use a variety of techniques that will help the parties understand that it is better to resolve the dispute peacefully and quickly rather than continuing it indefinitely or resorting to more antagonistic means of settling the problem (like going to court or to war).

Mediation works very well in most cases where it is used. It is usually considered to be a non-confrontational and non-adversarial method of dispute resolution. What this means is that when people who are disputing about something decide to let a third party act as a mediator, they are willing to think about ending the dispute in some other way than by fighting or threatening to fight. In a fight, someone wins and someone loses. It's the same way when people hire lawyers to fight for them in court: someone wins and someone loses. Mediation is often called a "win-win" type of process because when the parties agree to a settlement, each gains something. Thus, each wins. Sometimes this is done by a "compromise," where each gives up something to get something. Sometimes it is done by "creative problem solving," where each thinks up entirely new ways where each gets something without having to give anything up.

This may sound odd to Americans. Americans put a strong value on individualism, competition, and personal rights. So, when Americans think they are right about something and that someone has done them wrong, they immediately think they should overcome their opponent in some way: argue them down, beat them up, take them to court, prove that they are right and the other person is wrong. This is one reason why America has more lawyers per capita than any other country in the world and more lawyers than doctors.

In international relations, America (like many other nations, including the Soviet Union) does not recognize the mandatory power of the International Court of Justice. Instead, the U.S. government simply decides what it thinks is right and then tries to argue with the opposition to come to its side (diplomacy or negotiations), or relies on the amount of military power in America's arsenals ("Speak softly, but carry a big stick," "Gunboat diplomacy," "Send in the Marines," etc.) to get its way.

In much of the rest of the world, though, there is a stronger value placed on getting along with others in their society and in trying to maintain peace and harmony among individuals for the good of all. China and Japan are two good examples of this approach. Thus, there are very few lawyers in those countries and many mediators. So, when people get into a conflict in those countries, their first reaction is not to continue the strife indefinitely or to get a lawyer or a gun. Their first reaction is to seek the help of a third party in clearing up any misunderstandings of thinking their way out of their predicament.

Whom do the parties seek as a mediator? That varies from place to place. Mediators may be a friend to both parties; or they may be people in the neighborhood that both parties know or respect; or in China there are official mediators in every neighborhood who can be called upon to help resolve conflict. The mediator's role in these decisions is not to decide who is right and who is wrong; it is to help the parties themselves restore balance and harmony among themselves and to end the conflict situation. Mediators are peacemakers.

About the only field in which modern Americans have heard about mediation's success is that of labor disputes. Most conflict between labor unions and corporate management is resolved by mediation, and it has been this way throughout most of the twentieth century. However, in the 1970s, some labor mediators and professors wondered if mediation could be reintroduced into American daily life and began to set up some experimental "Neighborhood Justice Centers," or NJCs.

Neighborhood Justice Centers have grown a lot in the past 16 years or so. They usually have a number of trained volunteer mediators who handle all kinds of conflicts, that is: between husband and wife; among family members; between neighbors; between landlord and tenant; etc. Many times, the police or the courts send cases to the NJCs since they have found that mediation will produce a quicker, cheaper, and more durable resolution than will the legal system.

Due to the great success of these mediation centers, the court systems in some states have begun to tell people who have come to court that they *must* first go to mediation before they can continue in court. In others words, there is a movement in America today to make mediation mandatory in some kinds of cases (for example, divorce and child custody). When people are forced to go to mediation, though, they are not as likely to come to an agreement as when they go voluntarily. In cases where people go to mediation on their own, the rate of success is between 85 percent and 95 percent. Where courts force people to mediate, the rate of success is somewhat lower, approximately between 60 percent and 70 percent. Thus mediation is most likely to be successful when people voluntarily decide to give it a try.

There are other lessons that have been learned in the

present development of mediation in America in addition to its success rate. For example:

1. Mediation works best when the parties have an ongoing, continuing interdependent relationship.
2. When parties come from different backgrounds, it helps to have a panel of mediators (rather than one person) who vary in terms of sex, age, race, etc. Thus, there is a better chance that each party can find some trait in one or more of the mediators with which they can identify.
3. All persons who are part of the dispute should have the opportunity to participate in the mediation.
4. Mediators need to be good listeners, have lots of patience, and should have a warm and compassionate nature.
5. When the parties themselves come up with a mediated solution to the problem that they consider reasonable and just, they are very likely to keep to the agreement and not violate its provisions.

Mediation In International Relations

Obviously, if mediation works so well in interpersonal disputes around the world, one might ask if and how well it works at the international level in disputes between nations. After all, the nuclear stalemate that hovers over all citizens of the world is a problem between two gigantic nations, not between two ordinary people. Just because mediation works well in interpersonal relations doesn't mean it will work equally well in international relations.

Sad to say, the evidence to date seems to back those who would be skeptical about the success of mediation in helping resolve international disputes. Since the International Court of Justice cannot compel nations to bring disputes to it, clearly there is no way to compel nations to mediate, either.

309

There are, however, various international organizations that are set up to provide mediation services to nations that want to use them (The United Nations is the best example.) Just as governments make binding agreements to submit certain types of disputes to decision by the International Court of Justice, so do they agree to mediate other types of disputes. In conflicts involving border disputes, or trade or fishing rights, etc. where established international mediation organizations do the mediating, the success rate is pretty good. Roughly 50-60 percent of such mediations end in an agreement among the parties. Obviously that is much less of a success rate than in interpersonal dispute resolution, but it shows that nations willing to utilize mediation can help themselves end conflict.

On the other hand, when questions of ideology are at the root of conflict, or the two superpowers are directly or indirectly involved, the rate of success in mediation falls to around 15 percent—which is not too good. Why is this so?

The United States has frequently tried to pose as a mediator in the violent and bloody wartime situation that continues to characterize the Middle East. The best example of this was the Camp David mediation between Israel and Egypt with the U.S. (President Carter) acting as the "mediator." But the U.S. is hardly impartial in this case: it has a stake in the outcome and it favors the view of one party (Israel) that a major actor in the dispute (the Palestine Liberation Organization) should be excluded. A substantial part of the current Middle East conflict is rooted in ideological conflict between the U.S. and the Soviet Union, which at this point in time makes it unrealistic to have the U.S. try to act as a mediator, since it is a major party in the dispute.

The situation in Central America in the mid-late 1980s is similar. The Reagan Administration sees Nicaragua as a puppet state backed by the U.S.S.R. to further its strategic aims in its struggle with the U.S. The Soviet government would profit tactically by having a friendly nation just north of the Panama Canal. But many Central American and South American nations do not wish to see Nicaragua, El Salvador and Honduras turned into a battleground between the superpowers. So they have backed a mediation group called the Contadora Process, consisting of Latin Americans exclusively. The group has worked out an agreement among all the Central American parties. The U.S. government, however, has ignored the mediators and continued to back CIA-funded guerillas whose goal has been to overthrow the leftist ("Sandinista") Nicaraguan government.

There are many people around the world who see the global situation as it really is, and realize that something needs to be done to break the nuclear stalemate between these two ideological foes—an impasse between superpower governments who support open and covert warfare all around the world (Central America, the Middle East, Africa, Afghanistan), wars that defy the successful use of mediation. Yet, no one calls for a mediation between the Soviet Union and the United States. After all, what form could it take? Who could possibly mediate it?

Mediating And "Media-ating" The Nuclear Stalemate

Obviously, a traditional type of mediation to break the nuclear stalemate would be impossible. No one will be able to get the two governments to sit down at a table with mediators. In fact, these two governments wouldn't be able to agree on who would be suitable to mediate their grievances. Moreover, the U.S. and Soviet governments have amply proved how little they accomplish in face-to-face negotiations carried out by seasoned negotiators and lasting many years. Finally, there is substantial proof that both these governments go to great lengths to deceive one another, deceive their allies, and even lie to their own citizens about their true objectives and sinister tactics in foreign affairs!

This last point is crucial to understand if there is to be a successful mediation of the nuclear stalemate—that there is a great gulf between the governments of both superpowers and their own citizens. (In the 1960s, this was commonly known as the "credibility gap" in the United States.) There is not the slightest doubt that the overwhelming majority of American and Soviet citizens do not want a nuclear war. But each country has been persuaded by its government that the only way to peace is to continue the nuclear arms race or to leave negotiations to government officials. Each government says it only wants to maintain a rough parity of weapons with the other, yet each tries secretly to develop new weapons to give it superiority (while denying that to its own citizens).

The Communist Party in the Soviet Union controls the mass media and thus controls what the Soviet citizenry sees, hears, and thinks about the United States. Little good is said about America, if anything. This may change under Soviet Premier Gorbachev's policies of openness ("glasnost"), but at best this will allow the Soviet media to approach the American media's freedom to expose its own government's deceptions to the American public: President Johnson's lies about what happened in the Tonkin Gulf in order to get the public to support an all-out American military involvement in Vietnam; President Nixon's lies about his illegal bombing of Cambodia for well over a year; President Reagan's lies about not swapping arms for hostages with Iran and his permitting the National Security Council to spread "disinformation" to the American public in order to mislead Libya's Kaddafi about American government intentions.

Both governments continually deceive their own citizens even though their adversaries usually know the truth. The reason for this is that both these governments have their own agenda: to continue the Cold War and the nuclear arms race. Both the United States and the Soviet Union are dominated by "military-industrial" complexes that profit greatly by the nuclear stalemate while impoverishing and retarding many other social groups and movements in their own countries.

Thus a successful mediation process between the Soviet and American people will not primarily involve their governments—at least at first. It can only develop from a groundswell of popular opinion and an outpouring of private support, an overwhelming public demand and willingness to take the risk of mediation by people of the United States and the Soviet Union.

Clearly, these two huge populations cannot sit around a table with a mediator or two. The solution is to mediate the nuclear stalemate by vastly expanding a process of "mass media-ation" that has already begun in America and between groups of American and Soviet citizens. The goal of this "media-ation" is to utilize modern communications systems and techniques (a) to convey mutual feelings of the desirability and necessity of peace; (b) to clear up misunderstandings that each society has about the other; (c) to discuss specific issues that divide the two countries; and (d) to explore the workability of fragments to some future agreements between the two societies. The major actors are and will continue to be private citizens acting individually, in groups and with various elements of the mass media. At this point, both governments are relatively powerless to impede these first steps, and even lend some cosmetic support by agreeing to various official "cultural and scientific" exchange programs.

Initial Steps

Some initial steps taken by private citizens toward "media-ating" the nuclear stalemate have been:

1. In the early 1980s, the people of eight states put "citizens' initiatives" on the ballot in their states asking the President of the United States to negotiate a "nuclear freeze" agreement with the Soviet Union that would provide for some kind of system where each side could

check-up on the other to make sure each was keeping its word.

Millions of citizens voted in favor of this in these statewide initiatives, as well as in hundreds of New England Town Meetings on the subject, putting the President on notice of their desire. The event got strong media coverage in the U.S. and elsewhere and became a loose national "electronic town meeting" on one way to begin the ending of the nuclear stalemate.

2. The Esalen Institute of California has developed the "space-bridge" technique utilizing satellites to link groups of private citizens in the U.S.S.R. and the U.S. in cross-cultural television through large-screen simulcasts.

3. Beyond War, a citizens' association, has made impressive use of the space-bridge technique for worldwide presentations of their annual award for peace, linking up speakers and audiences in many parts of the world.

4. An important American television personality, Phil Donahue, and an equally important Soviet television personality, Vladimir Posner, developed a series of "space-bridges" over U.S. and U.S.S.R. television between studio audiences in both countries criticizing each other's political system. Only a few hundred people (not experts) were involved, but these events demonstrated the feasibility of much larger, network sponsored space-bridges between much larger audiences on issues directly related to the nuclear stalemate.

5. In early 1987, this was done when the Union of Concerned scientists sponsored a "Satellite Summit" between two audiences, one in Hamburg, West Germany and the other in Washington, D.C. Each audience watched groups of experts from the U.S., U.S.S.R., West Germany, etc., discuss ways of ending the nuclear arms race and were in touch with each other via space

satellite. This was broadcast live to the American public via the Public Broadcast System (PBS).

6. Ted Turner, founder and owner of Cable News Network (CNN) developed a series of extensive athletic events with the Soviet government called the "Goodwill Games." The first of these was held in the summer of 1986 in Moscow. Although not an "official" meeting between American and Russian athletes, it provided opportunities for American and Soviet media and athletic professionals to develop an understanding of each other and to work together in a cooperative enterprise.

An even more visible and valuable cooperative enterprise might be to implement the vision of the U.S. Senator from Hawaii, Spark M. Matsunaga. His idea, called "The Mars Project" is a joint space exploration exercise between the U.S. and the U.S.S.R. designed to maximize humankind's knowledge of the universe and minimize wasteful competition in that pursuit. In addition, this would provide a positive, ongoing, continuing, interdependent relationship toward a "common purpose" (space exploration)—a basic building-block for successful mediation.

7. An unofficial group of American scientists (Natural Resources Defense Council) who were familiar with earthquake detection went to the Soviet Union in 1986 to test devices that would be able to tell whether or not the Soviet government was detonating nuclear weapons in underground tests. The Soviet government was trying to demonstrate that it would allow foreigners to come onto its territory to use such instruments, and the American scientists were trying to show that American citizens were more interested in this type of arrangement than was the American government.

As popular columnist Ellen Goodman put it: "The point of this scientific project is to prove that a private citizens' group with a budget of $2 million can do what the Pentagon with its $300 billion says we can't: verify nuclear tests."

These are some of the basic building blocks of successful international peacemaking initiatives at the individual citizen and private group levels and they, of necessity, underlie a future successful mediation of the nuclear stalemate. Obviously all of these together are not enough to comprise a serious, formal mediation between the U.S. and U.S.S.R. over the nuclear stalemate. But they are a start and show what private American citizens can do to move in the proper direction.

Big Questions Remain

A very big question still remains whether private Soviet citizens can do anything without the permission of their own government and thus without it being a policy and/or ploy of the Soviet government and Communist Party. Another big question is what role governments and/or citizens of other countries can and must play in furthering the U.S.-U.S.S.R. mediation process. For if they do not play an intermediary role, then we will be back to a narrow two-party negotiation process, which has paid little in dividends in the forty years of the Cold War.

There are many countries each superpower trusts to some degree and some that each considers relatively neutral in the U.S.-U.S.S.R. rivalry. These nations need to create independent organizations designed and devoted to mediating the nuclear stalemate. One example of a start in this direction is "The Five Continent Peace Initiative." This is a group of six national leaders from six unrelated and unaligned countries: Argentina, Greece, India, Mexico, Sweden, and Tanzania. They have met several times (including Mexico City in 1986) and issued statements on the desirability of ending the nuclear stalemate. However, the American and Soviet media have not given their efforts major coverage.

Such mediational organizations must not be exclusively

comprised of government officials acting on their own, but must enlist broad national support in their own countries to underwrite and boost this major international effort. When possible, they would best link up with private organizations also dedicated to ending the nuclear stalemate.

Perhaps the key component to a successful third-party international mediation enterprise will be to develop major media programs capable of penetrating the media networks of both the Soviet Union and the United States. These cannot just be extravaganzas or official pronouncements. Their content must:

(a) include messages that will objectively and fairly portray the other side to each country's population;

(b) realistically show the price each side must pay if it continues the nuclear arms race on earth and in space; and

(c) imaginatively propose alternative ways of verifiable disarmament and ways of mutual cooperation on earth and in space between two superpowers.

But most of all they must avoid even the slightest appearance of being for or against the national security interests of either superpower.

In other words, citizens of other countries in the world have a lot to gain by stopping their present course of either blindly going along with their superpower ally's reliance on the "MAD" road to "peace" and by starting to play an active role in mediating and/or "media-ating" the nuclear stalemate. Together with citizens in the U.S. and U.S.S.R. who try to move their society into active communication with citizens in the other society, these countries, as "media-ators," can help construct an unprecedented international mediation process necessary to end the present, unprecedented "nuclear stalemate."

There is no guarantee that this will happen or that it will be successful. However, given the alternative that presently exists, it seems to be very little to lose with an awful lot to gain: a truly peaceful future in which all nations share equitably in the development of this planet and in the exploration of the universe.

23. Councils for Non-Violent Solutions

A WAGING PEACE PROPOSAL

I believe we Americans should form ourselves into groups I call 'Councils for Non-violent Solutions' to develop new and viable alternatives to offer our representatives. In fact, I see such Councils as a necessity for a self-governing nation.

To create such Councils we would need to decide that the responsibilities of citizenship demand new efforts from us and that we must create new policies. Milton Mayer once wrote that the American Citizen is the highest official in the American government. I believe it is time for us to don the mantle of our office and get down to the business of governing.

"We should move past disarmament as a primary strategy and past peace as an immediate goal," wrote Robert Fuller, former president of Oberlin College. "We should not look to halting the arms race or war in terms of arms control treaties, although ultimately these are needed. We should view U.S.-Soviet conflict as a situation between people having to do with their relationships, their psychologies, and their spiritual backgrounds."

We should realize that the Soviets threaten us because they're afraid of us. And we threaten them for the same reason. "The threat," according to Robert Fuller, "isn't that they're hoping to conquer our land—they couldn't govern it if they had it—nor we theirs. The greatest threat is our fear of each other. We must interrupt this cycle of fear. When nations have nuclear weapons, to be feared is to be in jeopardy. By making others afraid of us, we diminish our own safety. To be safe, we must protect the safety of others."

Our greatest safety in relation to the Soviets lies in being committed to saving their lives. To do this we must encourage our representatives to be, in Fuller's words, "people who specialize in introducing different cultures to each other," that is, people who will describe our values and lifestyle without discounting that of the Soviets ... inviting the Soviets to do the same. Our representatives must also, in Fuller's view, be "people who develop the skill to hold in check their ancient, familiar impulse to fight."

There is a Buddhist practice: If you feel anger and aggression against someone, give that person a gift. You cannot continue to feel anger and aggression while you're thinking about giving a gift. What gift could we give the Soviets?

The Soviets suffer severe food shortages for a variety of reasons. We could assure them that we will sell them wheat at a fair price into the indefinite future. We will not allow their people to go hungry. Some of us are familiar with the concept 'win-win.' Some of us believe there can be no successful peace conference unless both sides feel they have received equal benefits from it.

Sharing and exchange is a gift of peace. It is beneficial to both sides. There are many areas where we can share and exchange with the Soviets—many areas where we both need help from one another.

This would require a new effort to perceive Soviet life in fresh ways, finding what we can love about their way of life. If we are open to seeking this new perception, surely we can find better ways to meet human needs than either nation is now practicing. Obviously, it would be best if this examination were reciprocal.

For example, on the domestic scene the Soviets have a high alcoholism rate and they acknowledge this. So do we. We could pool our combined knowledge to help sufferers in both countries. The Soviets have a very high divorce rate— so do we. We could examine our lives together to see where the threats to enduring relationships lie and help sufferers in both countries.

Both nations have housing problems; both nations have working mothers. Both nations need new and innovative ideas on shelter, and on child care for working mothers.

Both nations have land areas subject to 'perma-frost'—an area so cold the ground never thaws out: Alaska and Siberia. Both nations are seeking ways to make these areas livable, are experimenting with ways to feed and house people in these frozen norths.

Surely we could meet to discuss our common problems and share what each has learned.

24. Three Steps My Family and I Can Take Now to Encourage Peace

Each year the Nuclear Age Peace Foundation conducts an essay contest on a peace-related theme and awards $3,000 in prizes to the winning entrants. The contest is open to all high school students.

This essay contest was made possible by a generous gift from Gladys Swackhamer, a ninety-four-year-old retired social worker, and is named in honor of her parents, Austin H. and Florence Anderson Swackhamer.

This chapter contains the winning essay for the 1987 contest. Sonia Weaver, a graduate of Bluffton High School in Bluffton, Ohio, is currently attending Bethel College in Kansas.

The question of what my family and I can do to encourage world peace is far more pressing than we can imagine. Full comprehension of the danger to our planet would render it impossible to live a normal life. But, fortunately, there are many things we can realize about the state of the world and what we can do to save ourselves. The survival unit of the 1980s is no longer a person or a country, but the entire human race. Current levels of nuclear weapons make it possible to obliterate everyone hundreds of times. Nuclear war is a statistical probability.

Knowing that the end could come at any time is having a devastating effect on today's high school students, and on our attitudes, values, and goals. Many young people seek instant gratification because the future to them seems out of control. Thinking that the planet is only going to be destroyed in a nuclear war, many find it hard to care about the environment or inhabitants of Earth. We are way behind schedule if we want to save the planet.

It is past time to realize that not only our morality but also our technology demands that we abandon war as a way of solving problems. For these reasons, it is very important that we find ways of promoting peace.

The first step my family and I could take to encourage peace is to say an emphatic "No" to the system which makes it impossible. President Eisenhower was right when he warned us that the military-industrial complex could get out of hand. Our government now operates under a system called the Iron Triangle. The sides of this triangle are Congress, the Pentagon, and private defense contractors. Countless examples show that there is a revolving door among these three institutions, and when people leave jobs in one side of the triangle, they are more likely than not to be found in another. Linked together by a chain of money, power, and skilled lobbyists, the Iron Triangle works to keep power in the hands of the military-industrial complex, and away from the people. Congress approves ridiculously high military budgets for the Pentagon, which through slanted contracts and huge cost overruns, allows private industry to make incredible amounts of money. Private industry, in turn, provides the money for Congresspersons to get re-elected.

Obviously, a system like this will not be easy to fight. But there are effective steps that my family and I can take. Letting defense contractors know how we feel about their actions is one thing we can do. General Electric is the only one of the top ten defense contractors to make most of its money from non-defense products. This means that a boycott would hurt GE the most. The war industry thrives because it is so profitable. By letting General Electric know that we refuse to buy any of their products until they stop making money from the destruction of human life, we would begin to take the profit out of war. Granted, almost all corporations have defense holdings, and granted, five people not buying a GE iron is not going to stop the Iron Triangle. But where would the civil rights movement be if Rosa Parks had said to herself that one woman refusing to ride in the back of the bus would not end racial discrimination?

The answer to world peace is that each of us has to start somewhere, even if it is with one corporation, and one family, in one small town. From this point we can begin to broaden the impact of the boycott. If your friends and neighbors join, and together we spread the word through churches, newspapers, and demonstrations, then maybe two and two and fifty really will make a million, GE will get rid of its defense holdings, other corporations will take notice, and one link in the Iron Triangle will be broken.

Another step my family and I can take to free the world for peace is to become involved in the movements for equality and economic justice. All too often these issues are not recognized as peace concerns. Poverty is the ideal breeding ground for violence. Our country's urban problems prove this without a doubt. Murder is now the leading cause of death for black males in many of our cities. And the infant mortality rate in the impoverished sections of Washington, D.C., the same city which approves $500 toilet seats for the military, is higher than the infant mortality rate in some Third World nations. Poor babies die at three times the rate of babies born above the poverty level. Urban problems should be of concern to people of peace, not only because of riots and violent crime, but because lives are being lost in other ways. Babies are not being given a chance to grow up. Those that do manage to live, often are not given a chance for a good education, career opportunities, or the framework to make positive decisions for their lives.

The inescapable conclusion is that poverty kills. This fact has implications for what my family and I need to work for, not only in United States domestic policy, but in our foreign policy as well. We need to let our leaders know that fighting poverty in Central America deters communism far more effectively than any gun. And in South Africa, where the black population is kept impoverished through the cruel racial caste systems of apartheid, there will only be more violence unless the government opens itself to economic and social reform. Poverty makes people feel desperate, without a sense of control of their lives. Where nonviolent evolution seems impossible, violent revolution becomes inevitable. Encouraging our government to follow a policy of meeting people's basic needs is a step my family and I can take to promote peace in the world.

But perhaps the most important part of working for world peace is achieving peace on the personal level. Becoming happy with who we are makes it easier for the members of our family to spread the message of peace throughout our lives. Individual acts of kindness have a multiplicative effect. Children, given lots of positive encouragement, feel good about themselves, and may feel less of a need to cut others down in order to build themselves up. On a larger scale, if our world leaders relied more on who they are as people, and less on weapons and threats to make themselves feel powerful, the policies of the world would change dramatically for the better. Becoming aware of one's own humanity makes it easier to see the personhood of others. The military teaches its recruits to view certain people as subhuman enemies. But if we truly recognize that people of all nations belong to the human family, and that we are all in this together, we will be unable to kill each other any more.

There are two kinds of power—power over others and enpowerment. The first kind of power comes from external things like having more money, or more physical strength, or more weapons than the people you want to control. The second kind of power is the power that we can find within ourselves. It is the power that Martin Luther King used in the civil rights movement, and the kind of power that Jesus had. By working to become attuned to the strength within us we realize that peace can be achieved. This is the kind of power that gives people the courage to end abusive relationships, to protest injustice, and to refuse to be part of the endless cycle of threats and destruction.

In conclusion, establishing world peace is not an easy task. The money and power in the world today are stacked against peace, just like they were stacked against racial and sexual equality. But we have hope because the women's and civil rights movements are succeeding, just like the peace movement will. But in a larger sense, no matter what happens in the world, we cannot fail. After all, we can only get a glimpse of what God is like. There are many things in the world we do not understand or understand only partially, but peace is not one of them. Everything I have ever learned and felt about God tells me that God is for peace. Once we align ourselves with the Source, we have already succeeded.

FRANK K. KELLY and DAVID KRIEGER

25. Twenty Positive Steps You Can Take to Help Reverse the Nuclear Arms Race

1. Examine the overwhelming evidence which proves that the building of nuclear arms does not defend the United States. Nuclear arms can only be used for retaliation—not for defense. After a huge arms build-up, the U.S. is just as vulnerable to a nuclear attack as it was ten years ago.

2. Make a note on your calendar every day reminding yourself that your life—and the lives of your family members, your children and grandchildren, your friends and neighbors—depends upon ending the nuclear arms race. It does! Don't be shy about speaking out on this fundamental fact. President Reagan has declared: "A nuclear war cannot be won and must never be fought." All the Presidents who preceded him in office since 1945 have known this fact.

3. Refuse to be swayed by fear. Note and remember this statement by General Douglas MacArthur, made in 1957: "Our government has kept us in a perpetual state of fear—kept us in a continuous stampede of patriotic fervor—with the cry of grave national emergency. Always there has been some terrible evil to gobble us up if we did not blindly rally behind it by furnishing the exorbitant sums demanded. Yet, in retrospect, these disasters seem never to have happened, seem never to have been quite real." Remember that we have been stampeded into spending trillions of dollars on arms—and we are now told that we must spend trillions more in search of "security" which we never attain.

4. Read and discuss with your friends and neighbors President Dwight D. Eisenhower's farewell address to the American people. President Eisenhower—a graduate of West Point, one of the great generals in American history—declared that a nuclear war could destroy our civilization. He knew there could be no such thing as victory in such a war. Eisenhower said: "Disarmament, with mutual honor and confidence, is a continuing imperative. Together we must learn to compose differences, not with arms, but with intellect and decent purposes." President Eisenhower's farewell address should be available in your local library, or you can write to the Nuclear Age Peace Foundation for a copy.

5. Consider seriously the disarmament proposals made by leaders of the Soviet Union. Do not assume that these proposals are simply made for propaganda purposes. It is true that the Soviets like to present themselves as peace advocates—because they know that peace advocates are deeply admired by people all over the world, who are sick of war and preparations for war. But the Soviets need peace and disarmament for their own survival. William Colby, former director of the CIA, and many other American leaders have pointed out that the Soviets can be trusted to advocate survival. Their leaders are well aware of what a catastrophe a nuclear war would be for their people.

6. Examine the disarmament proposals offered at the United Nations by the leaders of many nations. Many countries regard the U.S. and the Soviets as equal threats to the survival of humanity. Their leaders—particularly the heads of Canada, Sweden, India, France, Greece, and other countries—have offered ideas which Americans should consider.

7. Read, discuss and circulate the booklets in the *Waging Peace* series prepared by the Nuclear Age Peace Foundation. These booklets deal with some of the most significant topics in this age. Most of the chapters in this book were first published in the *Waging Peace* series.

8. Analyze and compare the points made by religious leaders in the statements issued by major denominations in the United States on the morality of "nuclear deterrence." Each of these statements took years to prepare. The leaders of the Episcopal, Methodist and Roman Catholic churches consulted many experts on arms control. They decided that the arms race is—in the words of the Methodist statement—"a social justice issue, not only a war and peace issue."

9. Organize an educational program or work with others in developing such a program. Plan or suggest a program on the subject of reversing the nuclear arms race at your church or synagogue, or through an educational, professional, or social organization to which you belong. Whether you are a church member or not, you can use the statements issued by religious leaders as starting points for discussions. Contact the Nuclear Age Peace Foundation or a local group in your area for help in finding qualified speakers.

10. Use the materials available from many organizations to develop a series of meetings. Work with members of these organizations—such as supporters of the Center for Defense Information, Citizen Diplomacy, Common Cause, Council for a Livable World, Federation of American Scientists, Grandmothers for Peace, Greenpeace International, Nuclear Age Peace Foundation, Peace Links, SANE/Freeze, Search for Common Ground, Union of Concerned Scientists, Uited Campuses to Prevent Nuclear War, United Nations Association, U.S. Peace Institute Foundation, and Women's Action for Nuclear Disarmament.

11. Join one of the groups working to reverse the nuclear arms race—the Nuclear Age Peace Foundation or one of the other organizations mentioned above—or join a professional group such as Physicians for Social Responsibility, Educators for Social Responsibility, or others. Contribute your ideas as well as your money to one or more of these groups; attend their meetings; find out about local affiliates in your area.

12. Support innovative proposals offered by legislators or others. Examine the proposals offered in the California Legislature for a "Peace Day," for an Exchange for Peace Program (which would involve an exchange of students between California and the Soviet Union and other nations), and for the awarding of California Peace Prizes to citizens active in developing peaceful solutions to human conflicts. Encourage legislators in your state to develop similar proposals or other innovative ideas.

13. Write letters to editors, radio broadcasters, television commentators, and circulate copies to your friends. This is an important way of sharing your views. A Santa Barbara teacher persuaded the General Assembly of the United Nations to pass a resolution she advocated—simply by writing letters to delegates of all the countries represented at the United Nations. Make your letters short and constructive.

14. Circulate petitions sponsored by the Nuclear Age Peace Foundation and Grandmothers for Peace, calling upon parents and grandparents (and other friends of children) to urge President Reagan and General Secretary Gorbachev to take further steps to reverse the nuclear arms race as rapidly as possible.

15. Urge members of your City Council or County Government to adopt resolutions condemning the arms race and send copies of these resolutions to Washington and Moscow. Suggest that these local leaders support the U.S. Institute of Peace, and endorse the petitions circulated by Parents and Grandparents calling for a reversal of the nuclear arms race.

16. Commend Senators and Representatives who support arms control or vote to cut back spending on nuclear arms. Ask your local newspapers and broadcasting stations to give full reports on how your representatives in Congress vote on these issues.

17. Telephone the White House on major issues. The President's office keeps track of telephone calls. If you want to register your views, call 202-456-7639 and express yourself vigorously. All Presidents change their positions from time to time—often in response to telephone calls and letters.

18. Support a Comprehensive Nuclear Test Ban Treaty (CTB)—and an immediate cessation of nuclear tests. Many authorities are convinced that a verifiable ban on all nuclear testing would be the biggest single step toward a reversal of the nuclear arms race. More than 100 nations belonging to the UN have voted in favor of a Comprehensive Test Ban. Nobel Prize winner Glenn Seaborg wrote: " . . . a Comprehensive Test Ban Treaty is the simplest and quickest way of moving forward to lessen the constant threat of nuclear war. A CTB would halt that aspect of the arms race that is most threatening—the qualitative improvement of nuclear weapons."

19. Urge leaders of Congress, the Defense Department and their science advisors to cooperate in creating Accidental Nuclear War Assessment Centers. We need national and international centers for analyzing and reporting on the accidental nuclear war dangers created by the increased computerization of weapons systems, warning systems and nuclear strategies.

20. Vote and support only those candidates for national office who speak out for reversing the nuclear arms race and make this a top priority of their campaign for office. Encourage candidates for Congress and the Presidency to offer positive proposals for reversing the nuclear arms race.

Notes

CHAPTER 1

1. *Santa Barbara News Press,* August 5, 1987
2. *New York Times News Service,* April 26,1987.
3. Defense Information Center, *Defense Monitor,* Vol. XV. No. 7, 1986, "Accidental Nuclear War" pp. 1-17.
4. Eisenhower, Dwight D., *Waging Peace,* Garden City, New York, Doubleday & Co., 1965, Vol. 1 p. 446.
5. *Ibid,* Vols. 1 and 2.
6. Defense Information Center, supra, Vol. XVI, No. 3 1987, "No Business Like Arms Business," pp. 1-7.
7. Richard John Neuhaus, ed., Clergy and Laity Concerned, *CLC Reports,* New York, April, 1987.
8. Institute of Soviet-American Relations, *Surviving Together,* November, 1986.
9. *Ibid,* Index to Soviet-American Organizations, pp. 118-119.
10. Lown, Bernard, International Physicians For Prevention of Nuclear War, Cambridge, Mass., Letters, April and July 1987.
11. Institute For Soviet-American Relations, supra, March, 1987, "Excerpts From Gorbachev's Speech to Plenum of Central Committee," pp. 13-17.
12. Shipley, David K., *Broken Idols, Russia, Solemn Dreams,* New York Times Books, 1983, p. 281.
13. Cousins, Norman, *Pathology of Power,* Kennan, George F. Foreword, pp. 10-11, W. W. Norton Company, 1987.
14. *Ibid,* p. 208.
15. United Nations Association, Santa Barbara Chapter Newsletter, Summer, 1987.

CHAPTER 2

1. Walsh, R. 1984. *Staying Alive: The Psychology of Human Survival.* Boston: New Science Library/Shambhala.
2. Das, Ram and Gorman, P. 1985. *How Can I Help?.* New York: Knopf.
3. Elgin, D. 1981. *Voluntary simplicity.* New York: William Morrow.
4. Schumacher, E. 1977. *A Guide for the Perplexed.* New York: Harper and Row.

CHAPTER 3

1. In 1971 The Department of Health, Education and Welfare published an "Institutional Guide to Policy on the Protection of Human Subjects." Informed consent was defined as the agreement obtained from a subject, or from an

332

authorized representative about the terms and conditions of participation in an activity of the Department. The components of informed consent were: (1) a fair explanation of procedures, (2) a description of risks and discomforts, (3) a description of benefits, (4) disclosure of alternative procedures, (5) an offer to answer inquiries about the procedures, and (6) an instruction that the subject is free to withdraw consent and discontinue participation at any time.

2. The freedom to care for one's health and person is an activity that falls within the privacy right. Justice Douglas in Doe v. Bolton, 410 U.S. at 211-13.

3. The idea that lawful government must be based upon the consent of the people is found in Plato, and was later developed by English political philosophers of the 16th and 17th century, particularly John Locke.

   "If the supreme authority be conferred on the magistrate by the consent of the people ... then it is evident that they have resigned up their liberty of action into his disposure." Gough, *Locke's Political Philosophy,* 63, 1647.

   The first American use of the term reflects the influence of English philosophers. The pattern for later use is in the variations of the phrase in the Declaration of Independence.

   "That to secure these rights, Governments are instituted among Men, deriving their just powers from the consent of the governed." *Declaration of Independence, 1776.*

   "The fabric of American Empire ought to rest on the solid basis of the consent of the people." *The Federalist,* No. 23, 1787.

   "Resolved, that in our opinion, the true cause of the trouble in Louisiana is to be found in the fact that the people have no confidence in the present usurping government, which does not command their obedience, and which fails to give protection because it is not founded upon 'the consent of the governed.' " *Appleton's Ann. Cyc. 479/1, 1874.*

   "The doctrine of the 'consent of the governed,' the doctrine previously enunciated by Jefferson in the Declaration of Independence, was not held by him or by any other sane man to apply to the Indian tribes in the Louisiana territory which he thus acquired." *Roosevelt Letters,* II. 1401., 1900.

4. The wishes of the governed are communicated to representatives who have agendas of their own which often take precedence over obligations to the governed. For a discussion of how and why lawmakers and bureaucrats make decisions to advance their own self interest rather than that of the public, see discussion by Nobel Laureate in Economics (1986), James M. Buchanan in *The Calculus of Consent,* University of Michigan Press, Ann Arbor, Michigan, 1962. These ideas are developed in later books and articles under the topic "Public Choice Theory" and most recently in *Liberty Market and State,* Wheatsheaf, 1985.

5. See "Statement on the Illegality of Nuclear Warfare," by the Lawyers Committee on Nuclear Policy, 225 Lafayette Street, N.Y., N.Y.

6. The eighteenth century philosopher Thomas Reid, in talking about intentional action said, that whatever a man had done without will and intention cannot be imputed to him, i.e. "what I never conceived nor willed I never did." American citizens believe that they themselves do not intend to incinerate

millions, and want to believe that the government does not intend to use nuclear weapons either. However, any examination of the conditions of "intention" forces the conclusion that our government does indeed intend to use nuclear weapons because its activities meet all the logical criteria for intentionality, i.e., we have developed the strategy, tactics, plans and blueprints for the execution of the plan.

7. *Docket Report 1986-1987,* the Center for Constitutional Rights, 666 Broadway, N.Y., N.Y.

8. We wonder whether the military have advised the servicemen who sit at the consoles controlling initiation of a nuclear weapons launch that they will be personally responsible for mass murder.

9. The medical literature overflows with statements that subjects and patients are not qualified to 'really understand' that to which they consent. These statements imply that full autonomy is the only instance of real autonomy. In other words how short of the ideal of full understanding and full independence from the control of others does a decision have to be to qualify as informed consent. Insisting on complete autonomy, or complete understanding sets a different standard for informed consent than for decisions made in the rest of life where substantial understanding or substantial autonomy are the practical rule. From *A History and Theory of Informed*

   Consent by Faden and Beauchamp, New York: Oxford University Press, Oxford, 1986.

10. Jay Katz, in *The Silent World of Doctor and Patient* (New York: Free Press, MacMillan Inc., 1984) claims that any meaningful legal pronouncement on informed consent is only 25 years old, although consent to surgical interventions is an ancient legal requirement.

11. Henry E. Sigerest, *On the History of Medicine,* (New York: MD Publications Inc., 1960).

12. Rush, Benjamin, "Medical Inquiries and Observation," See Faden and Beauchamp, op. cit.

13. Faden and Beauchamp, op. cit.

14. Donald C. Konold, *A History of American Medical Ethics, 1947-1912,* State Historical Society of Wisconsin, 1962.

15. Former General Richard V. Secord, commenting on the Iran-Contra hearings in the May 28, 1987 *Wall Street Journal,* said that our inability to keep a secret makes us a dangerous ally, and that we seek to purge ourselves of the knowledge about life in a dangerous and disorderly world, since this knowledge seems to "conflict with the American aspiration to some higher morality." Secord claimed that the basic rule of intelligence is that "if it is not necessary for a person to know something,then it is necessary for him not to know it."

16. Schloendorff v. Society of New York Hospitals, 211 N.Y. 125, 126, 105 N.E. 92, 93 1914.

17. Salgo v. Leland Stanford Jr. Board of Trustees, 317 F 2d 170, 1957.

18. Canterbury v. Spence 464 F2d at 780, 1972.

19. *The Final Epidemic, Physicians and Scientists on Nuclear War,* Eds. Ruth Adams

and Susan Cullen, The Educational Foundation for Nuclear Science, Chicago, IL 1981.

20. Docket Report, *op. cit.*
21. Faden and Beauchamp, *op. cit.*
22. For a discussion of the post war controversy about further development of nuclear weapons especially the super (hydrogen) bomb, see, *The Making of the Atomic Bomb, Part Three,* by Richard Rhodes, Simon and Schuster, N.Y. 1986.

CHAPTER 4

Essential parts of this chapter were published in Development Dialogue (1984:1-2), *a publication of the Dag Hammerskjold Foundation, Ovre Slottsgaten, Uppsala, Sweden.*

1. One megadeath means the death of one million people.
2. Exceptions are very small-scale use for medical purposes and as tracers, the purely scientific investigation of the structure of nuclei, etc.

CHAPTER 9

I wish to thank McGeorge Bundy for helpful suggestions

1. *Voter Options on Nuclear Arms Policy. Technical Appendix.* New York: Public Agenda Foundation, 1984, p. 24.
2. Ibid., p. 113.
3. Ibid., p. 118.
4. Rogers, Bernard, "For the Common Defense," *Harvard International Review,* Vol. IV, No. 7, May-June 1982, p. 8.
5. Von Weizsaecker, Carl Friedrich, *Ethical and Political Problems of the Nuclear Age,* London, 1958.
6. Schmidt, Helmut, *Defense or Retaliation,* London: Oliver and Boyd, 1962, p. 184.
7. Tucker, Robert C., Knorr, Klaus, Falk, Richard A. and Bull, Hedley, "Proposal for No First Use of Nuclear Weapons: Pros and Cons," Center of International Studies, Princeton University, Policy Memorandum No. 28, Sept. 15, 1963. Tucker and Falk argued for a policy of no first use, Knor and Bull against it. In a personal communication, Robert C. Tucker told me that he had become convinced already in 1951 of the necessity of no first use. His article was reprinted almost unchanged as "No First Use of Nuclear Weapons," *Praxis International,* Vol. 3, No. 1, April 1983, pp. 25-33.
8. Ullman, Richard H., "No First Use of Nuclear Weapons," *Foreign Affairs, Vol. 50, No. 4, July 1972, pp. 669-683.*
9. *Bundy, McGeorge, Kennan, George F., McNamara, Robert S. and Smith, Gerard, "Nuclear Weapons and the Atlantic Alliance," Foreign Affairs,* Vol. 60, No. 4, Spring 1982, pp. 753-68.
10. McNamara, Robert S., "The Military Role of Nuclear Weapons," *Foreign Affairs,* Fall 1983.
11. Such civilian-based defense methods are discussed, for example, in Sharp, Gene, *Making Europe Unconquerable: The Potential of Civilian-based Deterrence and Defense,* Cambridge, MA: Ballinger, 1985.
12. Bundy, McGeorge, "Maintaining Stable Deterrence," *International Security,* 3, No. 3, 1797, pp. 5-16.

13. *Voter Options on Nuclear Arms Policy: Technical Appendix,* op. cit., p. 129.

14. United States Arms Control and Disarmament Agency, *World Military Expenditures and Arms Transfers 1972-1982,* Washington, D.C.: ACDA Publication 117, April 1984. This publication states that for the Soviet Union "military expenditures and GNP were converted into dollars in differing ways." The Stockholm International Peace Research Institute (SIPRI Yearbook 1982) estimated Soviet military expenditures to be 8 percent of GNP.

15. Axelrod, Robert, *The Evolution of Cooperation,* New York: Basic Books, 1984.

16. Johansen, Robert C., "Building a New International Security Order: Policy Guidelines and Recommendations." In Stephenson, Carolyn M., *Alternative Methods for International Security,* Washington,D.C.: University Press of America, 1982, p. 62.

17. "Pentagon Draws Up First Strategy for Fighting a Long Nuclear War," *New York Times,* 30 May 1982.

18. A listing of about 6,000 peace organizations by zip code can be found in Forsberg, Randall et al., *Peace Resource Book,* Cambridge, MA: Ballinger, 1986.

CHAPTER 10

1. *The Random House Dictionary of the English Language,* College Edition, 1969.

2. Schlesinger, Arthur, Jr., "Foreign Policy and the American Character," *Foreign Affairs,* FALL 1983, p. 14.

3. See Dumas, Lloyd, "Human Fallibility and Weapons," *The Bulletin of Atomic Scientists,* November 1980.

4. Aldridge, Robert C., First Strike! *The Pentagon's Strategy for Nuclear War,* Boston: South End Press, 1983.

5. Crissey, Brian L. and Linn Sennot, "Analysis and Simulation of a Launch-On-Warning Policy," mimeographed paper: Illinois State University, April 1984.

6. See Coffey, Joseph, (Ed.), "Nuclear Proliferation: Prospects, Problems and Proposals," *The Annals of the American Academy of Political and Social Sciences, Vol. 430, March 1977 (whole issue).*

7. *See Norton, Augustus R. and Martin H. Greenberg (Eds.), Studies in Nuclear Terrorism,* Boston, G.K. Hall & Co., 1979.

8. —*Arms Control and Disarmament Agreements,* Washington, D.C.: United States Arms Control and Disarmament Agency, 1982, pp. 28-33.

9. *Ibid.,* pp. 113-119.

10. *Ibid.,* p. 115.

11. Mossberg, Walter S., "U.S. Seeks Better Hotline Links to Soviets to Curb Risk of Accidental Nuclear War," *Wall Street Journal,* April 13, 1983.

12. —*Arms Control and Disarmament Agreements,* pp. 109-112.

13. *Ibid.,* p. 111.

14. Cimons, Marlene, "U.S. and Soviets Will Modernize Their Hot Line," *Los Angeles Times,* July 18, 1984, p. 1.

15. Hart, Gary and Barry Goldwater, "Recent False Alerts From the Nation's Missile Attack Warning System," *Reports to the Committee on Armed Services,* Washington, D.C.: U.S. Government Printing Office, 1980.

16. See Mossberg, *Op. Cit.*

17. *Ibid.*
18. Cimons, *Op. Cit.*
19. *Ibid.*
20. Jackson, Henry, "U.S.-USSR Consultation: A New Peace Initiative," Fourth Annual President's Convocation, Washington State University, October 22, 1982.
21. See "A Risk Reduction Center" by the Nunn-Warner Working Group on Nuclear Risk Reduction, *The Bulletin of the Atomic Scientists*, June/July 1984, pp. 28-29.
22. *Ibid.*, p. 28.
23. *Associated Press*, June 16, 1984.
24. Nunn-Warner Working Group, *Op. Cit.*, p. 29.
25. Babst, Dean and Alex Dely, "Congressional Assessment Center for Accidental War," Department of Defense
    Authorization for 1984—Hearings," Washington, D.C.: U.S. Government Printing Office, 1983, pp. 590-594.

CHAPTER 11
1. Abrahamson, James A., "Statement On The Strategic Defense Initiative" before the Senate Armed Services Committee, 21 February 1985.
2. Crissey, Brian L., Sennott, Linn I., and Wallace, Michael D.; "A Model for Predicting the Time to Accidental Nuclear War During an International Crisis," Illinois State
    University and the University of British columbia, September 1984.
3. Morrison, David C., "Lost In Space: Satellites and Accidental Nuclear War," Chapter VI of Babst, Dean; Dely, Alex; Krieger, David; and Aldridge, Robert; *Accidental Nuclear War: The Growing Peril*, Peace Research Institute, Dundas, Canada, 1984.
4. Boushey, Homer A., Brigadier General (U.S. Air Force retired), suggested this accidental nuclear war scenario to the authors during a discussion on the subject.
5. Cited in Jacky, Jonathan, "The Star Wars Defense Won't Compute," *Atlantic Monthly*, June 1985.
6. *Strategic Defense and Anti-Satellite Weapons*, hearing before the Senate Foreign Relations Committee, 25 April 1984, pp. 69-74.
7. Hart, Senator Gary and Goldwater, Senator Barry, *Recent False Alerts from the Nation's Missile Attack Warning System*, a report to the Senate Armed Forces Committee, 9 October 1980, pp. 4-5.
8. Letter from Air Force Space Command headquarters at Peterson Air Force Base, Colorado, 16 February 1984.
9. "Nuclear Warning Plan Fails," *The Sacramento Bee*, 18 February 1984.
10. Rycroft, Al, "The Growing Danger of Unintentional Nuclear War," a paper prepared by Initiative For The Peaceful Use Of Technology, Ottawa, Canada, June 1985.
11. UPI dispatch, "SAC Commander Wants Proof of Attack Before Striking Back," *The Sacramento Bee*, 12 November 1984, p. A15.
12. Sandza, Richard, "Spying Through Computers," *Newsweek*, 10 June 1985.
13. Ibid.

14. Aldridge, Robert, *First Strike: The Pentagon's Strategy for Nuclear War*, (Boston, South End Press, 1983).
15. See *San Jose Mercury News*, 31 January 1985, p. 2A.
16. Article VI of the NPT states: "Each of the parties to the Treaty undertakes to pursue negotiations in good faith on effective measures relating to cessation of the nuclear arms race at an early date and to nuclear disarmament, and
    on a treaty on general and complete disarmament under strict and effective international control."

CHAPTER 13

1. *The Cold and the Dark: The World After Nuclear War.* A study by 200 scientists, including Carl Sagan and Paul Ehrlich, of the climatic and biological consequences of a nuclear war. W.W. Norton & Co, 1984.

CHAPTER 14

1. See Kravis, I.B., *et al. World Product and Income, International Comparisons of Real Gross Product,* published for the world Bank. Baltimore: Johns Hopkins University Press, 1982; and Kravis, I.B., *et al,* "Real G.D.P. Per Capita for More Than One Hundred Countries," *The Economic Journal,* 88 (1978), pp. 215-242.
2. United Nations General Assembly Sixth Special Session.
3. See, for example, the following publications of the Stanley Foundation: *The First Forty years,* Mascatine IA, 1985; and *The United Nations: Mission and Management,* Muscatine, IA, 1986.
4. J. Tinbergen and D. Fischer, *Warfare and Welfard,* Brighton: Wheatsheaf Books, 1987.

Suggested Reading

Aldridge, Robert C., *First Strike! The Pentagon's Strategy for Nuclear War*, Boston: South End Press, 1983.

Caldicott, Helen, *Missile Envy: The Arms Race and Nuclear War*, Toronto: Bantam Books, 1986.

Cousins, Norman, *The Pathology of Power*, New York: W.W. Norton & Co., 1987.

Erlich, Paul, Carl Sagan, et.al., *The Cold and the Dark: The World After Nuclear War* (a study by 200 scientists of the climatic and biological consequences of a nuclear war), New York: W.W. Norton & Co., 1984.

Fischer, Dietrich, *Preventing War in the Nuclear Age*, New Jersey: Rowman & Allenheld, 1984.

Galtung, Johan, *There Are Alternatives! Four Roads to Peace and Security*, Chester Springs, PA: Dufour Editions, 1984.

Gorbachev, Mikhail, *Perestroika: Our Hopes for Our Nation and the World*, New York: Harper & Row, 1987.

Gromyko, Anatoly and Martin Hellman (eds.), *Breathrough, Emerging New Thinking*, New York: Walker and Co., 1988.

Knelman, F. H., *America, God, and the Bomb*, Vancouver: New Star Books, Ltd., 1987.

Larson, Jeanne and Madge Micheels-Cyrus (eds.), Seeds of Peace: A Catalogue of Quotations, Philadelphia: New Society Publisher, 1986.

Lifton, Robert Jay and Nicholas Humphrey, *In a Dark Time: Images for Survival*, Boston: Harvard University Press, 1984.

Lifton, Robert Jay and Richard Falk, *Indefensible Weapons, The Political and Psychological Case Against Nuclearism*, New York: Basis Books, Inc., 1982.

Melman, Seymour, *Profits Without Production*, New York: Alfred A. Knopf, 1983.

Mische, Patricia M., *Star Wars and the State of Our Souls: Deciding the Future of the Planet Earth*, Minneapolis: Winston Press, 1985.

Smith, Charles Duryea, *The Hundred Percent Challenge: Building a National Institute of Peace*, Cabin John, Maryland: Seven Locks Press, 1985.

Walsh, Roger, *Staying Alive: The Psychology of Human Survival*, Boston: New Sciences Library, Shambhala, 1984.

Authors

Robert C. Aldridge is an aerospace engineer. He is author of *First Strike! The Pentagon's Strategy for Nuclear War*, and over a hundred magazine and newspaper articles on peace related issues. He is a member of the Nuclear Age Peace Foundation's Advisory Council.

Hannes Alfvén is a Nobel Laureate in Physics. He divides his time between the Royal Institute of Technology in Stockholm and the University of California at San Diego. He is author of *On the Origin of the Solar System; Cosmical Electrodynamics; Atom, Man and the Universe;* and *Living on the Third Planet.*

Dean Babst is coordinator of the Accidental Nuclear War Prevention Project at the Nuclear Age Peace Foundation. He is author of *Accidental Nuclear War: the Growing Peril,* and a co-editor with Robert Aldridge of *Nuclear Time Bomb.* Mr. Babst is the editor of the Foundation's International Accidental Nuclear War Prevention newsletter, *Nuclear Alert.*

Theodore Becker is chairman of the Political Science Department at the University of Hawaii. He is author or co-author of 8 books on comparative legal systems and on American Government. He co-founded and co-directed the first Neighborhood Justice Center in Hawaii, the Community Mediation Service.

Rodrigo Carazo is the founder and president of the United Nations University for Peace. He is a former president of the Republic of Costa Rica. He is a member of the Nuclear Age Peace Foundation's Advisory Council.

Dietrich Fischer is an Associate Professor of Computer Science at Pace University in White Plains, New York. He is currently on leave at the Center of International Studies at Princeton University on a MacArthur Foundation Fellowship on International Peace and Security Studies. He is the author of *Preventing War in the Nuclear Age.*

Gene Knudsen-Hoffman is a poet and peace activist. She is co-editor of the Nuclear Age Peace Foundation's booklet, *Reflections on the Sacred Gift of Life* and other books and articles.

Diana Hull, Ph.D. is a psychologist and former associate Professor of Psychology in the Department of Psychiatry at Baylor College of Medicine. She is the secretary of the Nuclear Age Peace Foundation, a founding

340

member of the Association of Media Psychology, and represents media psychologists on the Public Information Committee of the American Psychological Association.

Charles W. Jamison is an attorney (Harvard Law School, 1937). He is a founding director of the Nuclear Age Peace Foundation, and life-time Board Member. He has used his legal expertise to help establish several peace organizations.

Frank K. Kelly is Senior Vice President of the Nuclear Age Peace Foundation. He is a former Board Member of the National Peace Academy Campaign. Mr. Kelly served as a speech writer for President Truman and as staff director of the U.S. Senate's majority policy committee. For 17 years he was a vice president of the Center for the Study of Democratic Institutions. He is the author of *Court of Reason* and eight other books.

David Krieger is President of the Nuclear Age Peace Foundation. He is a political scientist and attorney. He is author of *Disarmament and Development, Countdown for Survival,* and co-editor of the *Tides of Change, Peace, Pollution and Potential of the Oceans.*

Gene R. La Rocque is a retired Rear Admiral in the U.S. Navy. He is the founder and director of the Center for Defense Information in Washington, D.C. He serves on the Advisory Council of the Nuclear Age Peace Foundation.

Seymour Melman is Professor Emeritus of Industrial Engineering at Columbia University. He is chairman of the newly formed National Commission for Economic Conversion and Disarmament. He has written numerous articles on economic conversion. Among his books are *Profits Without Production* and *The Permanent War Economy.*

Genevieve Nowlin is a former President of the Santa Barbara Chapter of the United Nations Association. She is an active member of the Nuclear Age Peace Foundation and many other groups working for international peace.

Jan Tinbergen is Professor Emeritus of Development Planning at Erasmus University in Rotterdam. He was the first recipient of the Nobel Prize for Economics. He serves as a member of the Nuclear Age Peace Foundation's Advisory Council.

Ted Turner is Chairman of Turner Broadcasting Systems. He conceived and initiated the Goodwill Games which were held in Moscow in 1986. He also founded and serves as Chairman of the Board of the Better World Society. He is a member of the Advisory Council of the Nuclear Age Peace Foundation.

George Wald is a Professor Emeritus of Biology at Harvard University.

He is a Nobel Laureate in Physiology/Medicine. He serves as a member of Nuclear Age Peace Foundation's Advisory Council.

Roger Walsh, M.D., Ph.D., is on the faculty of the Psychiatry Department at the University of California Medical School, and the School of Social Sciences at Irvine. His books and articles have received over a dozen national and international awards.

Sonia K. Weaver is the winner of the 1987 Swackhamer Prize Essay Contest. A graduate of Bluffton High School in Bluffton, Ohio, she is currently a student at Bethel College in Kansas.

Nuclear Age Peace Foundation